Corporate Governance in Emerging Markets

Corporate Governance in Emerging Markets

Editors
R.K Mishra
Shital Jhunjhunwala
J. Kiranmai

BLOOMSBURY
LONDON • NEW DELHI • NEW YORK • SYDNEY

First Published, 2013

BLOOMSBURY PUBLISHING INDIA PVT. LTD.
London New Delhi New York Sydney

ISBN: 978-93-82563-50-1

Published by Bloomsbury Publishing India Pvt. Ltd.
VISHRUT Building, DDA Complex, Building No. 3, Pocket C-6 & 7
Vasant Kunj, New Delhi 110 070

Laser Typeset by Script Makers
19, A1/B, DDA Market, Paschim Vihar, New Delhi 110063

Printed at Anvi Composers
1 DDA Market, Block A-1B, Pachim Vihar, New Delhi 110 063

Contents

Preface

The literature and research on corporate governance, at least in the English language has been lopsided towards the developed economies particularly the US and the UK. This is partly because they have been the pioneers of the modern concept of corporate governance, but an equally important reason is the fact that researchers and academicians in the developing countries of Asia, Eastern Europe and the Middle East find it difficult to express themselves in English. This is probably true of all social science research, and not just corporate governance.

The combined output of the emerging world is estimated to account for 38 percent of world GDP (at market exchange rates) in 2010, twice the share in 1990 and is expected to be more than the developed countries by 2020. Emerging economies consumption of commodities, world exports and inflows of foreign direct investments are believed to be already more than that of the developed economies. Almost a quarter of the *Fortune* Global 500 firms come from emerging markets.

Given the growing importance of the emerging economies, we have in this book looked at corporate governance issues in emerging markets. Most of these countries follow some form of the Anglo Saxon model and their governance concerns are similar to those of developed economies. Yet, some unique problems can also be found often seeded in their historical, cultural and political background. Besides BRICS nations a wide range of emerging markets such as, Colombia, Czech Republic, Egypt, Hungary, Mexico, Philippines, Poland, South Korea, Malaysia and Iran are covered.

Shital Jhunjhunwala
Editor

Does Better Corporate Governance and a Legal Framework Result in Ethical Behaviour of Firms in Emerging Markets?

Sreejesh S and Sanjay Mohapatra[1]
IBS IFHE University, Hyderabad
[1]*Xavier Institute of Management, Bhubaneswar*

ABSTRACT

Ethics is an all pervasive subject of business, but its presence is rarely observed and measured in matters of corporate governance. From the ethical point of view, the aim of corporate governance should be to ensure that certain moral standards are maintained and the legal system complied with, while dealing with both external and internal business decisions that impact stakeholders. However, the reality is that companies concentrate on efficient governance mechanisms at the cost of non-investor stakeholders, article with the objective of increasing shareholder profitability and the firm's short-term financial value. This phenomenon gets pronounced in emerging markets. In this context, this article provides a detailed framework and a model for analysing how the governance and legal framework have an effect on the ethical behaviour of firms in 21 emerging markets. The findings of the article suggest that the corporate governance and legal framework, does have an impact on the ethical behaviour of firms in emerging markets. The results also suggest that firms operating in these countries tend to have a direct relationship with the legal system and ethical behaviour, and a negative relationship with corporate governance and ethical behaviour.

Keywords: *Corporate Governance, Ethical Behaviour, Legal Framework, Emerging Markets*

INTRODUCTION

Promoted by the accounting and financial scandals in the developed and emerging markets, a number of researches have been conducted to identify and analyse the relationship between a firm's ethical practices and its operating and financial value maximization. At the same time, another stream of research centred on an analysis of how the differences in financial stuctures and legal systems have an effect on the firm level corporate governance practices (Klapper *et al.,* 2004). All these studies suggest that good governance would boost the market valuation of companies by improving their financial performance, reducing the risk that boards would take, resulting in ethical decisions. These decisions would help increase investor confidence. Indeed, the surveys conducted in emerging economies showed evidence that institutional investors will pay as much as 28 percent more for shares of well-governed companies in emerging markets[1]. This compelled companies in emerging markets, as also in developed markets, to adopt strict corporate-governance practices, and adhere to a legal framework while exhbiting ethical behaviour. This raised a fundamental question "is ethical behaviour influenced by corporate governance and the legal framework"? The question assumes significance particularly in emerging markets, where occurence of unethical behaviours is quite high.

Literature Review

In order to better understand the subject, the article will first review the major streams of literature that would illustrate the effect of 'corporate governance and legal framework' on ethical behaviour. The literature review consists of two parts (i) influence of corporate governance on ethical behaviour, and (ii) effect of legal framework on ethical behaviour.

Corporate Governance and Ethical Behaviour

Ethical behaviour of firms has been considered as an important aspect which has resulted in sustainable business success (Arjoon, 2005). However, for sustainability, displays of moral and ethical behaviour are not the purpose of showcasing good and sound governance practices, but are necessary enablers to accomplish strategic objectives. Many organizations have started initiatives for the implementation of sound ethical codes of conduct in business processes (Fleege and Adrian, 2004). This inclusion of sound ethical codes of conduct, as part of company initiatives, had been motivated to achieve strategic objectives. While complying with an ethical code of conduct, two main benefits accrued at the operational level – they are (a) refinement and improvement of internal processes, rules and regulations, and (b) improving economic and business policies for maximising returns for its stakeholders. Bondy *et al.,* (2004) stated that the adoption of sound ethical practices helps companies to increase their public image and prevent public criticism. According to Cleek *et al.,* (1998) and Fleege *et al.,* (2004), a well structured and designed code of conduct helps in preventing wrongdoings while promoting (a) honest and ethical behaviour within the firm which helps to handle actual or apparent conflicts of interest in personal and professional relationships;

[1] See Paul Coombes and Mark Watson, "Three surveys on corporate governance," (2000), *The McKinsey Quarterly*, No.4 special edition: Asia, revalued, pp. 74–78.

(b) compliance with applicable government laws, rules and regulations; (c) social responsibility, and (d) good and properly developed corporate culture.

There have been different theories in ethical and governance literature, which explain the reasons behind the creation and acceptance of ethical practices. The fundamental theories in this cateogory are: Stockholder theory, legitimacy theory, and stakeholder theory.

Stockholder Theory

According to this theory "Companies are only responsible to shareholders and all employee actions should be aimed at maximizing shareholder value without breaking the law" (Fleege *et al.,* 2004; Hasnas, 1998). Therefore, the crux of this theory is that the organizations, intention to follow ethics and ethical practices is to satisfy its stockholders.

Legitimacy Theory

Legitimacy theory is based on creating a generalized perception that the actions and activities of an organization are appropriate (legitimate) within a given social system. According to this theory, companies are continually attempting to ensure that their operations live up to the standards of societies where they do businesss. By making a code of ethics, corporates legimitize their behaviour(Luis Rodriguez, 2009).

Stakeholder Theory

Stakeholder theory attempts to describe, prescribe and derive alternatives for corporate governance, that include and balance a multitude of interests. According to this theory, an organization may adopt ethical practices to satisfy all its stakeholders. This theory argues that corporations are responsible not only to investors, but also to all its non-investor stakeholders. "Boards must understand that they are the representatives of all the stakeholders in the firm. All these stakeholders have invested either in physical assets or in human capital. The board members decisions will have an impact on these investments. Thus, individuals who can safeguard the interests of all the stakeholders explicitly, should be put on boards, to give those stakeholders some assurance that their interests will be taken into account"(Blair, 1995)[2]. This theory has become important and universal, especially in economies such as Japan, France and Germany (Vinteen, 2001)[3].

---

[2] Blair, M.M. (1995) *Ownership and control: Rethinking Corporate Governance for the Twenty-First Century.* Washington, DC: The Brookings Institution.

[3] Vinten, G. (2001) 'Shareholder versus stakeholder – is there a governance dilemma?' *Corporate Governance: An International Review*, Vol. 9, No. 1: 36–47.

Legal Framework and Corporate Governance

The extant literature has shown evidence of the relationship between the legal framework and corporate governance in emerging markets. A major destructive force affecting further development of emerging markets, is the lack of regulatory protection against minority shareholders and wealth misappropriation. This phenomenon gets pronounced during corporate takeovers (Parisi *et al.,* 2009). According to Dahya *et al.,* (2008) and La Porta *et al.,* (1998), the legal systems prevalent in a country can be categorized into two: (i) statutory provisions (*de jure* protection), and (ii) and the extent or degree to which the statutes are enforced (*de facto* protection). The authors state that the quality of legal systems would be a better predictor of the quality of corporate governance practices being followed in a firm. This is so because an effective legal system (and hence better corporate governance), will ensure protection of interests of minority stakeholders. While echoing the same result, Shlefer *et al.,* (1997) argue that the protection of minority shareholders would help to improve the performance and valuation of a firm's shares and market capitalization. Shlefer *et al.,* (1997) further contend that there are two most efficient approaches to improve, or instil good corporate governance practices. They are (i) through stringent legal protection of all stakeholders, in which better governance can be achieved through governmental regulation (ii) or/and through ownership of the company by minority investors who would have significant control rights. La Porta *et al.,* (1997, 2002) also support that a stronger form of a legal environment protects the stakeholders from exploitation by the board. This stringent legal environment tends to increase the effectiveness of corporate governance by adopting good auditing and accounting practices and strengthening the board structure. While illustrating similar results from his study, Pitelis (2004) feels that a vigilant legal system will induce good internal governance mechanisms, and reduce the chances of unfair treatment of minority stakeholders.

These findings get importance if we look at the scam created by Satyam Computer Services Ltd (Satyam). In 2008, Satyam surpassed US$ 2 billion in revenue and in the same year, it won many prestigious awards including the Goldon Peacock Award for corporate governance excellence. This was the second time that Satyam won this award from the World Council for Corporate Governance. In December, 2008 the company reported a scam of $1.4billion that shook its stakeholders and the global business community as a whole. This corporate failure taught a lesson that 'over motivated' financial value driven governance could lead to unethical practices. The scam raised several questions. Was the scam a result of lack of an effective legal framework; does corporate governance need to be practiced along with legal bindings. Further discussions on the subject brought out significant determinants that will influence ethical behaviour of a firm. The discussions led to a point where it was opined that a combination of a legal framework and corporate governance will influence ethical behaviour. However, no such literature was available that would illustrate, through empirical analysis, the combined effect of 'best practices in corporate governance and legal framework' on the ethical behaviour of firms. Therefore, this study examines whether, and how corporate governance and its legal systems impact a firm's ethical behaviour.

PROBLEM DEFINITION

The study does not formulate any hypothesis, instead we explore the following research question:

Research Question: Do the legal system frameworks and overall governance practices of a firm impact ethical behaviour? The question needs to be considered in the emerging markets context, and hence our scope of study was for firms in emerging markets only. The question tries to find solutions as to the mechanism that can be adopted in practice, which will ensure sustainable ethical practices. These ethical practices will look after the interests of all the stakeholders.

METHODOLOGY

The present study applies the PLS structural equation modeling (SEM) to estimate the theoretical model using the software program SmartPLS (Ringle, Wende and Will,2005). Many of the extant literatures suggested PLS (Wold, 1975) as the suitable method for estimating complex models. This suggestion was based on the well found, argument that other widely acceptable techniques that are used to estimate the relationship among latent variables, especially co-variance based SEM introduced by Joreskog (1973) as exemplified by many available software programs, including LISREAL (Joreskog and Sorbom, 1993), AMOS (Arbuckle, 1994), EQS (Bentler, 1995) and Mplus (Muthen and Muthen, 1994) make more strict assumptions on the data. At the same time, Fornell & Bookstein (1982) suggested that the two main problems associated with co-variance based SEM technique: *(1) improper solutions* (i.e. solutions outside the admissible parameter space).The term improper solution describes several possible problems with model estimation, ranging from model non-convergence to invalid values for parameter estimates. Non-convergence in estimation occurs when the maximum likelihood process cannot find a minimum fit function. Usually the estimated model does not converge because of very serious mistakes in how the model is specified. Hsu *et al.,* (2006) suggested several reasons for improper solutions (a) The theory is wrong; (b) the data are inaccurate; (c) the sample size is too small; or (d) covariance structure analysis is not appropriate for the analysis task (Fornell & Bookstein, 1982; Gerbing & Anderson ,1987); *(2) and factor indeterminacy*. Therefore, PLS was considered to be the suitable technique for general SEM purposes, and there are several reasons for the widespread use of PLS for measuring customer satisfaction, whith are; (i) PLS is not based on any strict assumptions about the data, especially the assumption of normality (Ferreira,

2010) (ii) PLS is best suited for predictive purposes (Chin, 1998; Ferreira, 2010); (iii) It will be more efficient in small sample size as well; (iv) it avoids the indeterminacy problem (Hulland,1999; Ferreira, 2010); and (v) working with both formative and reflective indicators (Ferreira, 2010).

Wold (1966) was the first person who introduced the idea of partial least squares in psychometric literature through his famous book *"Estimation of Principal Components and Related Models by Iterative Least Squares"*. However, the application of this in path models with latent variables has been published by Wold in 1979, and then the main references on the PLS algorithm are Wold 1982, 1985(Tenenhaus *et al.,* 2005).

DATA COLLECTION

The study used different data sources to create an unique and comprehensive data set to examine the relationship of corporate governance, legal system and ethical behaviour. First, the study used original and rich country level data of 21 emerging markets from the the global competitiveness report (http://www.weforum.org/issues/global-competitiveness) conducted by the World Economic Forum in FY 2011. The report featured a record number of 139 economies, and thus continues to be the most comprehensive assessment of its kind. The report contains a detailed profile of each of the economies featured in the study, as well as an extensive section of data tables with global rankings covering over 100 indicators. The constructs used in this study are from *"The Executive Opinion Survey:The Business Executives' Insight into their Operating Environment"* of the World Economic Forum. The report is based on responses received from a network of over 150 partner institutes. The respondents are recognized economics departments of national universities, independent research institutes, or business organizations. Most questions in the survey ask respondents to evaluate, on a scale of 1 to 7, where, 1 represents the 'perceived' worst possible situation; at the other end of the scale, 7 represents the best 'perceived' situation. For the second source of data collection, the study followed GMI International, which covers the corporate goverance rating of all the companies in the world. The questionnaire is shown in Table 1.

Table 1: Construct Measurement

Construct	*Scale*	*Source*
Efficiency of Legal Framework How efficient is the legal framework in your country for private businesses in challenging the legality of government actions and/or regulations?	1 = extremely inefficient; 7 = highly efficient	The Global Competitiveness Report 2010, World Economic Forum
Ethical Behaviour of Firms How would you compare the corporate		The Global Competitiveness Report

ethics (ethical behaviour in interactions with public officials, politicians, and other enterprises) of your firm?	1 = among the worst in the world; 7 = among the best in the world	2010, World Economic Forum
Strength of Auditing and Reporting Standards How would you assess financial auditing and reporting standards regarding company financial performance?	1 = extremely weak; 7 = extremely strong	The Global Competitiveness Report 2010, World Economic Forum
Efficacy of corporate boards How would you characterize corporate governance by investors and boards of directors in your firm?	1 = management has little accountability to investors and boards; 7 = investors and boards exert strong supervision of management decisions	The Global Competitiveness Report 2010, World Economic Forum
Protection of Minority Shareholders' Interests To what extent are the interests of minority shareholders protected by the legal system?	1 = not protected at all; 7 = fully protected	The Global Competitiveness Report 2010, World Economic Forum
Strength of Investor Protection Strength of Investor Protection Index	On a 0–10 (best) scale	The Global Competitiveness Report 2010, World Economic Forum
Overall Governance Rating Governance Rating Index	On a 0-10 (best) scale	GMI International, 2010

EMPIRICAL RESULTS AND DISCUSSION

The empirical tests (using PLS SmartPLS 2, http://www.smartpls.de/forum/) examine the association between corporate governance, legal framework and ethical behaviour of firms in emerging markets. Table 2 reports the results of the research question.

Question: *Does the legal system framework and overall governance practices of a firm impact ethical behaviour?*

In accordance with the research question, the coefficient of magnitude 0.002468, the path coefficient of auditing and reporting standards to governance is statistically insignificant (t value =0.048816). The other determinants such as efficacy of corporate boards (Beta Coefficient =0.355883, t value =7.068335), protection of minority shareholder's interest (Beta Coefficient =0.485070, t value=8.199997) and the strength of investor protection (Beta Coefficient =0.206833, t value=9.832842) is found to have significant effects, and indicates that these determinants are positively associated with the corporate governance of firms in these countries.

Table 2: Structural Parameter Estimates

Determinants Paths	*Path Coefficients*	*T-values*
Auditing & Reporting Standards Ethical Behaviour of Firms	0.273989***	8.965624
Efficacy Of Corporate Boards Ethical Behaviour of Firms	0.085268***	2.530100
Efficiency Of Legal Framework Ethical Behaviour of Firms	0.622658***	19.185348
Efficiency Of Legal Framework Auditing & Reporting Standards	0.599140***	25.198806
Efficiency Of Legal Framework Efficacy of Corporate Boards	0.648329***	36.822762
Governance Of Firms Ethical Behaviour of Firms	-0.202004***	7.202775
Shareholder's Interest(Minority) Ethical Behaviour of Firms	-0.133978***	3.273644
Strength Of Investor Protection Ethical Behaviour of Firms	0.050990***	3.362208
Auditing & Reporting Standards Governance of Firms	0.002468^{ns}	0.048816
Efficacy Of Corporate Boards Governance of Firms	0.355883***	7.068335
Efficiency of legal framework Governance of Firms	-0.658130***	10.945360
Efficiency of legal framework Shareholder's Interest	0.813633***	105.522550
Efficiency of legal framework Strength of Investor Protection	0.436072***	16.668897
Shareholder's interest(minority) Governance of Firms	0.485070***	8.199997
Strength of Investor Protection Governance of Firms	0.206833***	9.832842

*** Significant at the p<.01 level. ** Significant at the p <.05 level. ns: not significant

Here, the study considered the path coefficient from the overall corporate governance to the ethical behaviour of the firm (Figure 1). The result of the analysis shows that (Beta Coefficient= -0.202004, t value= 7.202775) is significant, and indicates that a country's firms corporate governance (exogenous variable) exerts a negative pressure on ethical behaviour (endogenous variable) of firms in that country. This means in emerging economies, as the rigidity of governance mechanism increases, the resultant impact, or the outcome on ethical practices, is minor or negative. In emerging economies, periodically, regulatory authorities have issued guidelines for improving governance practices, but these practices have produced negative repercussions in an ethical perspective. In summary, corporates in these emerging economies followed rule oriented governance practices, rather than 'intention orientated' practices. Given our SEM with the seven variables, the study has to analyse the other seven important path coefficients to test for significance, such as the legal framework on ethical behaviour, legal framework on overall governance and legal framework on governance determinants, and also other variables (Figure 1). These results indicate that the path coefficient of the legal framework on ethical behaviour (Beta coefficient=0.743418, t value=60.118263) is significant and positive, which explains the role of the legal framework on the restoration of ethical behaviour of firms in these economies. Even though the firm initiated governance mechanisms were not able to restore ethical behaviour (as seen from previous analysis), the legal framework succeeded in generating an atmosphere of 'intended ethical' behaviour. The legal framework on overall governance (Beta coefficient=0.058941, t value=1.316718) is insignificant, which shows that a failure of the legal system will impact negatively on the implementation of governance practices. This implies that in such a scenario, governance practices are skewed towards fulfilling interests of the majority stakeholders. The other path coefficients such as legal framework on auditing and reporting standards (Beta coefficient =0.599140, t value=25.198806) is significant, which means that the auditing and reporting standards of these firm have been strengthened due to the efficiency of the legal framework. This implies the presence of a vigilant regulatory body which will help in implementing good ethical practices in the firms.

The coefficient of legal system on the 'effectiveness' of corporate boards (Beta coefficient =0.648329, t value=36.822762) is found to be significant, which implies the fact that the legal systems have had a remarkable impact for the establishment of good and powerful corporate boards. The minority shareholder's interest (Beta coefficient = 0.813633, t value=105.522550) and strength of investor protection (Beta coefficient = 0.436072, t value=16.668897) found to have a significant impact, which proves the fact that the legal systems play an important role for the restoration and protection of investor and minority shareholder's interests.

Given these findings, the study further explores how these two (legal framework and governance) together influence the ethical behaviour of firms in emerging markets. For evaluating that objective, the study considered the total effect (total effect = significant direct+ indirect effects) of these dimensions on ethical behaviour of firms (Table 3). The results of the study shows that the joint impact of the legal and governance of firms in these countries on ethical behaviour of firms is significant and positive (Beta coefficient=0.743418, t value=60.118263).

Table 3: Total Effects*

	Total effect	T statistics
Auditing & reporting standards ⇒ Ethical behaviour of firms	0.273491***	8.860839
Auditing & reporting standards ⇒ Governance of firms	0.002468^{ns}	0.048816
Efficacy of corporate boards ⇒ Ethical behaviour of firms	0.013378^{ns}	0.443534
Efficacy of corporate boards ⇒ Governance of firms	0.355883***	7.068335
Efficiency of legal framework ⇒ Auditing & reporting standards	0.599140***	25.198806
Efficiency of legal framework ⇒ Efficacy of corporate boards	0.648329***	36.822762
Efficiency of legal framework ⇒ Ethical behaviour of firms	0.743418**	60.118263
Efficiency of legal framework ⇒ Governance of firms	0.058941^{ns}	1.316718
Efficiency of legal framework ⇒ Shareholder's interest(minority)	0.813633***	105.522550
Efficiency of legal framework ⇒ Strength of investor protection	0.436072***	16.668897
Governance of firms ⇒ Ethical behaviour of firms	-0.202004***	7.202775
Shareholder's interest(minority) ⇒ Ethical behaviour of firms	-0.231964***	5.040486
Shareholder's interest(minority) ⇒ Governance of firms	0.485070***	8.199997
Strength of investor protection ⇒ Ethical behaviour of firms	0.009209^{ns}	0.508691
Strength of investor protection ⇒ Governance of firms	0.206833***	9.832842

*Total effect = Significant direct+ indirect effects, *** Significant at the $p<.01$ level, ns: not significant

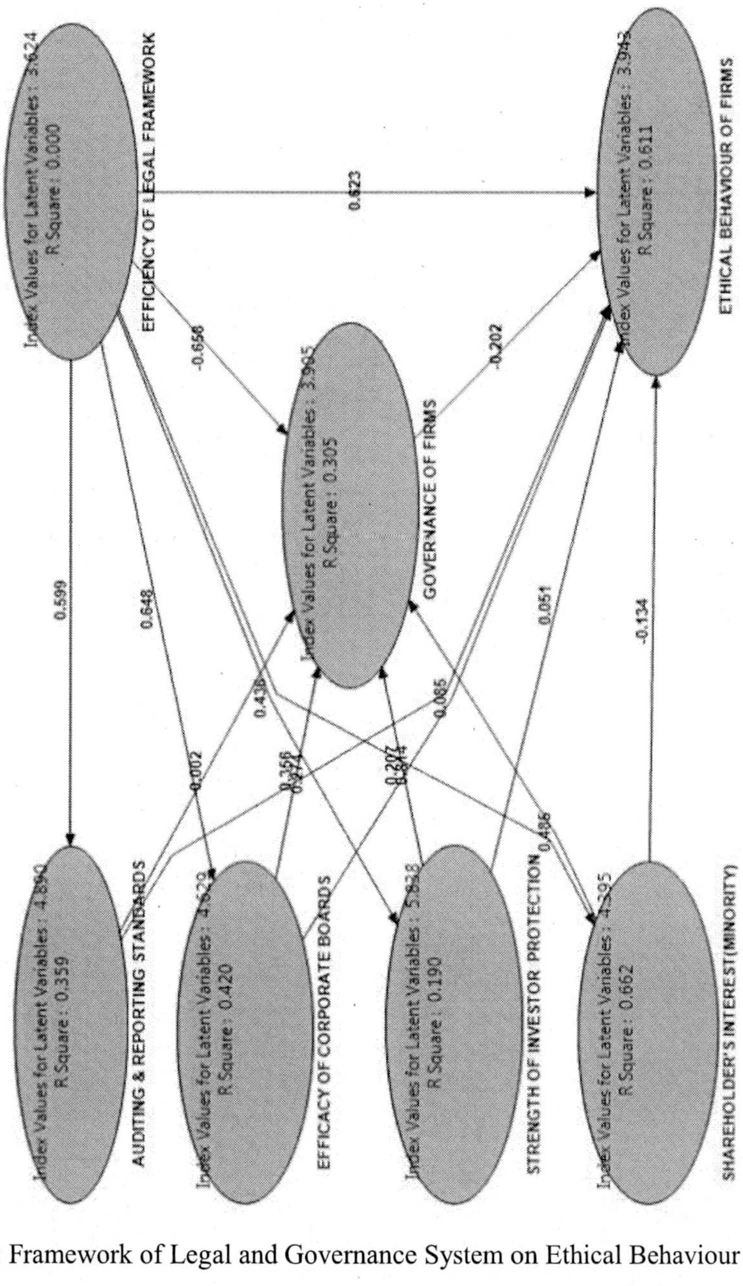

Figure 1: Framework of Legal and Governance System on Ethical Behaviour of Firms

IMPLICATIONS

The results of the study showed that rule based corporate governance systems will not be effective on the ethical behaviour of firms. This is evident from the fraud at Satyam Computer Services. For supporting this argument, Capelli *et al.,* (2010) stated that in the case of Satyam, as also in the case of Enron, it had a relatively strong set of independent nonexecutive directors, and followed SEBI standards for rule-based governance compliance. The Satyam board had the requisite composition of the board of directors, as was mandated by SEBI. However, a lack of a stringent legal system, which would impose severe penalties, did not result in 'intended implementation.' This meant that even though everything was fine on paper, still the performance of the board could not be measured. The moral story from this fraud is that a rule based corporate governance system, focused on only shareholder value maximization, does not guarantee ethical behaviour of firms, therefore focus should be on both rule and value based (stakeholder orientation) governance system, as in the case of Infosys Technologies Limited (Infosys)[4] in India.

Ethics in business relates to deciding 'what is right' and 'what is wrong' for the business. The constituents of such behaviours include adherence to truth, commitment to law and justice, and public integrity. 'Personal interests' (this refers to the perception that a group of stakeholders regards as desirable) has to be examined in the light of wider interests of the stakeholders. A binding, strong and effective legal system can help in deciding the KPIs of the board members. These KPIs will be measurable and transparent to all. The analysis in this study implies that each board should come up with KPIs for its board members that are to be aligned with the clauses in the legal system. This alignment will also help in arriving at a correct judgement of what is desirable, and will be in congruence with the stakeholders' morale. While creating this alignment, the organisations should focus on the following areas:

- Work with honesty, integrity and trustworthiness that helps to create ethical behaviour
- Propagation and maintenance of transparency and accountability in operations inside and outside the organisation, which include internal and external corporate governance mechanisms, especially duties, rules, processes and procedures related to work and services to members in the organization, or other stakeholders.
- Protection of the rights and interests of stakeholders, which include investor and non-investor stakeholders of the organization, which helps in creating confidence of the stakeholders over company actions.

[4] Infosys is one of India's largest and most famous software companies and provides a range of Information Technology (IT) consulting and software services to leading global organizations. Infosys is involved in customized software development, Internet consulting, application development and offshore software services.

CONCLUSION

The basic objective of corporate governance structuring is to motivate and control executives and employees in retaining fair business practices and effectively utilising various resources to maximise efficiency of a business for economic, moral and environmental benefits of the stakeholders. In this globalized environment, the tasks and duties and style of corporate governance must also change, but this change must have direction as well as a path, that will lead to best ethical practices and behaviour. However, without proper legal bindings, governance would lose direction and purpose of selecting the right path, and fail to create value for the company and its stakeholders. Therefore, a strong, measurable and effective legal system is essential for selecting the path and executing the right decisions. These actions will be applicable to, and would cover both external and internal corporate governance mechanisms.

In the modern globalised consumer driven market era, the definition and practice of governance has changed in a drastic way. Different from traditional concepts of corporate governance, in which good governance was considered to the interaction of three forces: the board, the management and the stakeholders. But with time, this has changed and today's practice of corporate governance is a multifaceted concept with focus on investor and non-investor stakeholders and centred on fair practices, moral responsibility towards actions and damages and welfare of society and the environment. The change of traditional corporate management to today's corporate governance, has given an ethical perspective of approaching long term gains, considering society, customers, stakeholders and the environment. Apply ethics of care in terms of protecting the environment and ensure the wellbeing of society and the nation.

SCOPE FOR FURTHER STUDIES

The present study has selected firms in some of the emerging markets only. It will be interesting to see the behaviour of firms in other emerging countries, and compare the behaviour of firms in emerging countries with that of developed countries. Such comparisons will help to understand, (i) if there is any effect of the legal system on ethical behaviour, and (ii) differences between legal systems in developed countries and emerging countries. The differences between the two legal systems (between developed and emerging countries) will help improve the legal systems in emerging countries.

References

Arjoon, Surendra. (2005). corporate governance: an ethical perspective. *Journal of Business Ethics, 61* (4), 343 – 352.

Arbuckle, James. (1994). AMOS: Analysis of Moment Structures. *Psychometrika*, 59 (1), 135–37.

Bentler, P. M. (1995). *EQS: Structural equations program manual.* Encino, CA: Multivariate Software, Inc.

Bondy, K., Matten, D. and Moon, J. (2004). The Adoption of Voluntary Codes of Conduct in MNCs: A Three-Country Comparative Study. *Business and Society Review*, 109 (4), 449-477.

Chin, W.W. (1998). The partial least squares approach for structural equation modelling in marcoulides, G.A (Ed.), *Modern Methods for Business Research (*pp. 295–336), London: Lawrence Erlbaum Associates.

Cleek, M.A., Leonard, S.L. (1998). Can corporate codes of ethics influence behaviour?. *Journal of Business Ethics*, 17 (6), 619-630.

Capelli, Peter., Harbir, Singh., Jitendra, Singh., & Useem, Michael. (2010). The India way: How India's top business leaders are revolutionizing management. *Harvard Business Press.* ISBN-13:978-1-4221-5824-1.

Dahya, J., Dimitrov, O., McConnell, J.J. (2008). Dominant shareholders, corporate boards, and corporate value: a cross-country analysis. *Journal of Financial Economics,* 87, 73–100.

Ferreiraa, I., Jose, C., & Pedro Saraivac. (2010). An integrated framework based on the ECSI approach to link mould customers' satisfaction and product design. *Total Quality Management,* 21(12), 1383-1401.

Fleege, Erin., and Adrian, Erin. (2004). The implementation of corporate ethics: a comparative study between Motorola and Ericsson. *Journal of Undergraduate Research,* VII, 1-9.

Fornell, C., & Bookstein, F.L. (1982). Two structural equation models: LISREL and PLS applied to consumer exit-voice theory, *Journal of Marketing*, 19, 440–452.

Gerbing, D. W., & Anderson, J. C. (1987). Improper solutions in the analysis of covariance structures: their interpretability and a comparison of alternate re-specifications. *Psychometrika,* 52, 99-111.

Hasnas, John., (1998). The normative theories of business ethics: a guide for the perplexed. *Business Ethics Quarterly,* 8(2), 19 - 42.

Hsu, Sheng-Hsun., Wun-Hwa, Chen., & Ming-Jyh, Hsieh. (2006). Robustness testing of PLS LISREL, EQS and ANN-based SEM for measuring customer satisfaction. *Total Quality Management,* 17(3), 355-371.

Hulland, J. (1999). Use of partial least squares (PLS) in strategic management research: a review of four recent studies. *Strategic Management Journal,* 20(2), 195-204.

Jöreskog, K. G. (1973). A general method for estimating a linear structural equation system, in Goldberger, A.S. and Duncan, O.D. (Eds.), *Structural Equation Models in the Social Sciences*(pp. 85-112), New York: Academic Press.

Klapper, L., & Love, I. (2004). Corporate governance, investor protection and performance in emerging markets. *Journal of Corporate Finance,* 10, 287–322.

Luis, Rodriguez-Dominguez., (2010). Corporate governance and codes of ethics. *Journal of Business Ethics,* 90(2), 187-202.

La Porta, R., Lopez-de-Silanes, F., Shleifer, A., Vishny, R. (1998). Law and finance. *Journal of Political Economy,*106, 1113-1155.

La Porta, R., Lopez-de-Silanes, F., Shleifer, A., Vishny, R. (1997). Legal determinants of external finance. *Journal of Finance,* 52, 1131-1150.

La Porta, Rafael, Florencio Lopez-de-Silanes, Andrei Shleifer, and Robert Vishny, (2002). Investor protection and corporate valuation, *Journal of Finance*, 57, 1147–1170.

Muthén, Bengt O. and Linda K. Muthén., (1994). Mplus User's Guide. Los Angeles: Muthén and Muthén.

Parisi, Franco, Ike Mathur and Lance Nail. (2009). Minority stockholders' protection in a new corporate control law: market implications in an emerging economy, *Emerging Markets Finance & Trade,* 45(6), pp.4-19.

Pitelis, C. N., (2004). Corporate governance, shareholder value and sustainable economic performance, *Corporate Governance: An International Review,* 12, 2, pp. 210-223.

Ringle, Christian M., Sven Wende, and Alexander Will. (2005). Smart PLS 2.0, www.smartpls.de.Accessessed on October 1, 2009.

Shleifer, A., Vishny, R., (1997). A survey of corporate governance. *Journal of Finance*, 52, 737-783.

Tenenhaus, Michel.,Vincenzo, Esposito. Vinzi., Yves-Marie, Chateline., and Carlo, Lauro. 2005. PLS Path Modeling, *Computational Statistics and Data Analysis,* 48 (1), 159–205.

Wold, H. O. A. (1966), Nonlinear estimation by iterative least squares procedures, in David, F. N. (ed.), *Research Papers in Statistics*, Festschrift for J. Neyman, Wiley, New York, 411-444.

Wold, H. (1975). Path models with latent variables, the NIPALS approach, in Blalock, H.M., Aganbegian, A., Borodkin, F.M., Boudon, R. and Cappecchi, V., (eds.).

Quantitative Sociology. *International Perspectives on Mathematical and Statistical Modeling,* New York, Academic Press, (pp. 307-353).

The Role of Corporate Governance: A Hurdle or Steroid in the Commercialization of Innovations?

P. John Ben and Neeraj Dwivedi
Indian Institute of Management, Lucknow

Abstract

Products such as the i-pod, i-pad and i-tunes have revolutionized the way we look at technology. Largely, the origins of such innovative products have always been in the developed countries. India however is well known for providing low cost services, especially in the area of information technology and business process outsourcing. Barring innovations such as the Nano, introduced by Tata Motors, there are only a few that really stand out. This study looks at two constructs a) efforts in innovation, and b) realized innovation and how they relate to the market value of firms. We also view some of the Corporate Governance (CG) mechanisms with skepticism and go on to suggest, with empirical support, that they could hamper or catalyze the critical stage of commercialization of innovations. In the process, our message to the principals is that they need to move beyond lip service and pay attention to the efficacy of processes within the ambit of the CG framework.

Keywords: *Corporate Governance, Innovation, R&D, Patents*

Introduction

Whilst firms have a plethora of choices when it comes to growth strategies, several seek to grow organically through the use of innovation, as seen through investments in Research and Development (R&D), signaling practices (as reflected by advertising), and capacity expansion as seen through capital expenditures. Our focus here is to look at innovation and competitiveness, and understand whether facilitating mechanisms such as corporate governance play a role in innovative practices to fructify, and be valued by the capital markets.

DEVELOPMENT OF THE RESEARCH THEME

It is well understood that the western world has more innovations to offer to society: examples range from the highly visible products of Apple such as the i-pad, i-pod and related technology products, to the more mundane products such as the 'post-it' notes from 3M. However, in the Indian scenario, we do not "see" very compelling innovative products and services, particularly receiving media attention and spotlight. Yet, sample this: we have practical innovations in packaging such as the shampoo, detergent and coffee sachets (Re. 1 to Rs. 10) which has enabled Fast Moving Consumer Goods (FMCG) companies to reach the bottom of the pyramid. In consumer durables, we have the Nano, arguably the world's cheapest car. In terms of services, we have clutter-breaking advertising by Hindustan Unilever through the "Daag achha hai" (translated as: 'stains are good'). Hence a potential issue influencing innovation could be to do with the mismatch between "realized innovation" and market value. In other words, there could be hidden problems in the commercialization of innovations. This could be analogous to one of the path breaking views evinced in Mintzberg & Waters (1985) where a "realized strategy" could turn out to be phenomenally different from an "intended strategy".

Hence, our research problem could be viewed in terms of understanding the possible hampering or facilitating factors between Realized Innovation (RI) and market value. A simple way is to model Innovation Efforts (IE) as the R&D expenditure, and the RI as the patents registered by the firm. Our question probes whether there are any factors facilitating or hampering the process, either during the R&D to patent stage, or the presence of patents resulting in appreciation by the capital markets in terms of higher price-to-book value. Effectively, we would like to explore whether any factors influence (positively or negatively) the commercialization process.

UNDERSTANDING INNOVATION AND COMPETITIVENESS

One important predictor of innovation in firms is R&D expenditure (Dalziel, Gentry & Bowerman, 2011). Innovation is central to the spirit of entrepreneurship and organic growth, and can give a fillip to organizational performance (Helfat, 1997). Also, it has been acknowledged that the relationship between R&D and innovation is often a complex one (Rothaermel & Hess, 2007). Hence, we can say that merely spending on R&D cannot effectively predict the firms' innovations. It also implies that competitiveness may not just stem from additional investments in R&D.

While the need for innovation is not vital for the viability of individual firms, innovation is a collective necessity for economic well-being (Clark & Guy, 1998). We also know from scholarly work (Francis, 1992; Chaudhuri & Ray, 1997, Roberts & Amit, 2003; Cho & Pucik, 2005; Lin 2011) that innovation could lead to more competitiveness, and firm value and can help a firm differentiate itself from others operating in the same industry. R&D expenditure is definitely an indicator of IE. However, most studies that look at R&D as a proxy for innovation, bypass the more fundamental assumption that all IE leads to RI and thereby to enhanced market share or market value.

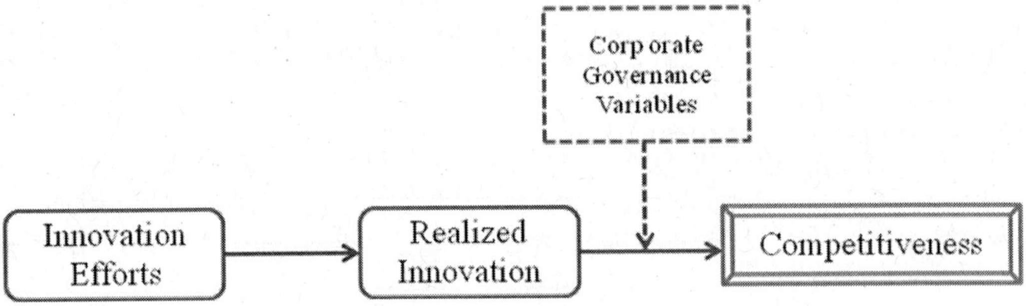

Figure 1: The Innovation-to-Competitiveness Process

Capital markets probably do not probe deeply into the organizations' innovation outputs or RI, in terms of products or services; they may pay lip service by merely ascribing the term 'an innovative company' by looking at relative R&D spends. An article studying the migration of technology sourcing to low cost, operationally efficient global locations observes that analytical tools cannot assess long term implications of R&D programs (Pisano & Shih, 2009). Patents are a fructified form of spends on R&D. They are looked upon as a tangible output of R&D spends. They are considered invaluable and intangible assets which are rewarded by capital markets (Sandner & Block, 2011). In our study, patents represent an advanced form of innovation and they are the first manifestation of the firms' efforts in R&D. Hence, we term patents as Realized Innovation (RI).

However, merely studying the effects of innovation on competitiveness could potentially blind us to the formalized organizational structures such as corporate governance which could play a powerful role in commercializing realized innovation. As we proceed to the subsequent sections, we look at the linkages of CG and competitiveness. In parallel, we also study, critical and interesting insights from literature which lead us into exploring the role of CG in innovation and competitiveness.

CORPORATE GOVERNANCE AND COMPETITIVENESS

Globally, it has been noted that Corporate Governance (CG) assures accountability and enhanced performance (Ho, 2005). However, empirical studies of the relationship between corporate governance and competitiveness have often thrown up mixed and inconclusive results. One reason could be that, CG has often been studied in discrete terms such as relating ownership structures to performance, or studying board characteristics and firm performance.

Hence, Ho (2005) notes that holistic studies could probably highlight this relationship better. From our perspective, we can say that the grey areas within this relationship could probably explain why certain cases of IE by firms do not yield RI.

In the last decade, there have been several papers studying the relationship between board characteristics and performance (Kiel & Nicholson, 2003; Dulewicz & Herbert, 2004; Finegold, Benson & Hecht, 2007; Jackling & Johl, 2009). In these research papers, the focus has been on the internal dynamics of the board, various demographics of the board members, and their impact on a firm's performance. In turn, firm performance is a measure that is tangible, and sensed by the marketplace. In studying boards, a wide variety of constructs have been used. The variables that make up the studies typically include the nature of ownership, the number of independent and dependent directors (Jackling & Johl, 2009), the education profile and the industry experience of the top management teams, and a few process variables such as the methods of decision making processes (Ingley & Walt, 2005) undertaken by the top management teams.

Capital markets pay enormous attention to CG as seen through higher market valuations for firms such as Infosys or Tata Motors, which have been known for better transparency in their annual reports and media communication. Literature has also strongly noted that more transparency in CG practices leads to higher market valuations (Durnev & Kim, 2005; Garay & Gonzalez, 2008; Khanchel El Mehdi, 2007). This implies that better CG mechanisms could lead to higher market valuations.

The moot point is that industry practices in terms of better CG have definitely been rewarded by the markets. Academic literature has also supported this to some extent. However, this relationship comes with certain exceptions. Our attempt is to understand the strength of this relationship, especially in the light of innovation efforts (IE) and RI.

Corporate Governance and Innovation

In this section, we attempt to provide a backdrop to the role of CG in innovation. Porter (1990) suggests that four interdependent, yet mutually reinforcing characteristics of a nation, determine whether it can provide a conducive environment for firms in a particular industry to compete successfully. These are a) factor conditions, b) demand conditions, c) related and supporting industries, and d) firm strategy, structure and rivalry. The last point is of interest to us. In understanding, the structure of firms, CG comes into play. To some extent, CG determines the structure of firms. Therefore, we have some hints indicating the role of CG in innovation.

Second, we look at this linkage from the perspective of organizational control theory developed by Lazonick & O'Sullivan (1996) who define CG as an organizational issue; they argue that CG determines the allocation of resources and is aimed at developmental, organizational and strategic outcomes of the firm. Drawing from their work, we can argue that developmental work also involves innovation as one of its core components. Hence, there could be a subtle impact of CG on innovation.

Third, patents are a form of Intellectual Property (IP) and are specific, high value assets in a firm's arsenal, as it seeks organic growth. Hence, the question of property rights and protection of IP becomes critical here. The criticality is so evident that firms seeking alliance partners decide on an equity joint venture or contractual partnership, based on the perceived levels of patent protection (Hagedoorn, Cloodt & Kranenburg 2005). The other important point is that governments have differing views on IP protection which are driven by various political and economic factors (Lewin 2007). In emerging markets, regulators and legal bodies are unable to enforce stringent measures in the event of IP rights violations. From the agency perspective, we are clear that while principals - founders and shareholders seek to further firm growth, agents (CEOs, managers and boards) may have different views on account of selfish motives. Hence, it becomes even more imperative for us to study CG effects on IP protection and on the commercialization of patents.

Therefore, while we enlarge the potential role of CG in strategic decision making, it also implies that the actors involved in these processes are complex and heterogeneous, and often step outside the boundaries of the firm (Lacetera 2001). Innovation and investment in innovation falls within the purview of strategic decision processes. Hence, it reinforces our motivation to study the linkages of innovation with competitiveness in the context of CG.

Development of Hypothesis

Firms that decide to invest in Research & Development (R&D) are keen on reaping rewards through innovative products or services that will help them grow. In this process, patents are an intermediate step; once patents are registered and approved, then the commercialization process is the last pending stage. Hence, we hypothesize that patents are influenced by the spends on R&D by the firm, hence:

H1: *R&D intensity is positively related to the number of patents for a firm.*

Unless patents are registered and approved, the firm cannot go ahead with its new product. In other words, the Realized Innovation (RI) is still an intermediate step. The firm now needs to commercialize the product or service, and hope to see better market appreciation. Market value can be taken as one measure of competitiveness. It follows that:

H2: *Patents are positively related to the market value of the firm*

While we attempt to define the CG structures or behavior that could explain firm value, we look at suitable proxies that can substitute for board processes or characteristics. There are a few studies that look at understanding the role of CG in the context of the relationship between innovation and firm value. Among these, Hoskisson, Hitt, Johnson & Grossman (2002) explore the effects of institutional holding on corporate innovation strategies. The variables under study here are institutional ownership and board independence. Their study is in the American context, where ownership concentration is low and institutional shareholders are active. Outside directors have been found wanting when it comes to investing in R&D (Kor, 2006); the paper also examines the interaction effect of the top management team on R&D intensity. A third paper by Lee & O'Neill (2003) notes that differing country contexts are associated with different ownership patterns, and accordingly results in totally different approaches towards R&D management. From these studies, the only CG variables of interest to us are a) board independence, and b) ownership stake or concentration.

In the Indian context, however, Clause 49 of the Securities and Exchange Board of India (SEBI) mandates 33 percent board independence in the case of a non-executive chairman and 50 percent if the chairman is an executive member / promoter. Under these circumstances, we arrive at the points of interest in CG which are relevant for our study in the Indian context: a) board independence, b) CEO duality and c) promoter stake – ownership stake held by the founder-owner and his kin. Predominantly, earlier studies have looked at the direct relationship of boards with firm performance, discussed earlier in our study. Hence, our interest lies in understanding if there is any interaction of CG with the commercialization of innovations – we would like to study the interaction of patents with the CG variables. This leads us to the following three hypotheses:

H3: *Board independence negatively moderates the relationship between realized innovations and firm value*

H4: *The promoter stake positively moderates the relationship between realized innovations and firm value.*

H5: *CEO duality negatively moderates the relationship between realized innovations and firm value.*

METHODOLOGY

We used the database PROWESS which is maintained by the Centre for Monitoring the Indian Economy (CMIE). First, we eliminated all firms which reported negative profits for fiscal year 2011. Then, we removed all firms which were less than Rs 500 crores in turnover. Post this, we set two criteria, both of which need to be satisfied: a) R&D as a proportion of sales for fiscal year 2011 >= 0.5%, and b) magnitude of R&D spends >= Rs.1 crore. This yielded us 274 companies. Out of this sample, we eliminated firms that had not filed a single patent as of calendar year 2011. This resulted in 83 firms which have been taken up for study.

Stage 1: R&D Intensity and its Relationship with the Number of Patents

Here, our dependent variable is the number of patents. Since the number of patents ranges from 0 to 101, we make it a continuous variable by using the natural logarithm. The independent variable is the mean R&D intensity across the last six years (from the year 2005-2011).

Stage 2: Patents' Relationship with the Market Value of the Firm

Here, the dependent variable is the price-to-book value of the firm as of March 31, 2011. The data is taken from PROWESS. Since the number of patents varies from 1 to 101, we normalize the variable by taking the natural logarithm of the number of patents filed by the firm.

Stage 3: Identifying the Moderating Influence of Corporate Governance Variables on the Market Value of Firms

Here we use three corporate governance variables: (a) board Independence, (b) promoter stake, and (c) Chief Executive Officer (CEO) duality.

Corporate Governance Variables

A brief on the three main corporate governance variables in this study: 1) board independence is measured by the percentage of independent board members serving on the board of a firm, 2) CEO duality is present if the CEO handles the role of both the Chairman of the board (a monitoring role) and as CEO of the firm (executive role, full time), and 3) promoter stake: measured as a percentage shareholding of the owner(s) and his family members.

ANALYSIS & RESULTS

Regression 1

Patents are regressed against R&D intensity. We observe an R^2 of 0.115 and an adjusted R^2 of 0.104. The F value is 10.534 and significant at 99 percent confidence level (0.002). The regression output is shown in Table 1.

Table 1: LN_PATENT Regressed against R&D Intensity

	Model	*Unstandardized Coefficients*		*Standardized Coefficients*	*t*	*Sig.*
		B	*Std. Error*	*Beta*		
1	(Constant)	1.092	.149		7.305	.000
	RD_INTENSITY	20.591	6.344	.339	3.246	**.002**

We note that R&D intensity (RD_INTENSITY) is positively influencing the patents (LN_PATENT). The relationship is significant at the 1 percent level.

Regression 2

Price-to-book value (P_BV) is regressed against the patents. We observe an R^2 of 0.224 and an adjusted R^2 of 0.214. The F value is 23.314 and significant at 99 percent confidence level (0.000). The regression output is as follows:

Table 2: P_BV Regressed Against Patents

	Model	*Unstandardized Coefficients*		*Standardized Coefficients*	*t*	*Sig.*
		B	*Std. Error*	*Beta*		
1	(Constant)	1.593	.650		2.450	.016
	LN_PATENT	1.725	.357	.473	4.828	**.000**

We observe that the patents positively influence the market valuation of the firm. The relationship is significant at the 1 percent level.

On regressing the price-to-book value against the R&D intensity, we find the relationship is not significant. The standardized coefficient, Beta is observed to be -0.054 and the *t* statistic is – 0.0485. The F value is 0.235 and is not significant even at the 10 percent level.

We can therefore infer that patents are influenced by the R&D intensity, and in turn impact the market valuation of firms. In practice also, this makes sense because patents are a concrete product of the efforts and spends on R&D. In other words, patents form the Realized Innovation, (RI) which could possibly further influence the capital markets to place a premium on the firm.

Regression 3

Here we include the three corporate governance variables and the regression is carried out with the price-to-book value as the dependent variable. The independent variables are LN_PATENT (natural logarithm of the number of patents), SIZE_DUMMY (a nominal variable with three classes- small, medium and large firms on the basis of turnover), RD_INTENSITY (a continuous variable denoting the mean ratio of R&D expenditure to the total income for the previous six years), BRD_IND indicating board independence measured as the ratio of the independent directors to the total number of directors as on 31 March 2011, CEO_DUAL indicating the CEO duality (0 if it is not present and 1 if the CEO holds a dual role) and PROM_STAKE denoting the promoters owner(s) and his family members) shareholding percentage. P_BV denotes the price-to-book value for the firm for the year ended 31 March 2011.

The F value was found to be significant at the 1 percent level with a value of 7.146. The regression table is as follows:

Table 3: Regression of P_BV Against CG Variables, R&D Intensity & Patents

Model	*Unstandardized Coefficients*		*Standardized Coefficients*	*t*	*Sig.*
	B	*Std. Error*	*Beta*		
(Constant)	-.311	3.300		-.094	.925
LN_PATENT	1.911	.384	.524	4.970	**.000**
SIZE_DUMMY	.905	.643	.139	1.407	.164
RD_INTENSITY	-57.489	22.611	-.260	-2.543	**.013**
BRD_IND	-.853	4.187	-.020	-.204	.839
CEO_DUAL	-2.238	.872	-.240	-2.568	**.012**
PROM_STAKE	3.065	2.435	.124	1.259	.212

We note that while patents are positively related to the market value of the firm, the R&D intensity shows a negative relationship. Among the corporate governance variables, we note that only the CEO duality is negatively related to the market value.

Hence, we proceed to test if the corporate governance (CG) variables are moderating the relationship between patents and market value. We use three interaction terms which are: (1) interaction of board independence with patents, (2) interaction of promoter stake with patents, and (3) interaction of CEO duality with patents. With price-to book value as the dependent variable, three different regressions are carried out; in each, one CG variable, the interaction term and the patent variable (three independent variables) are present. The regression outputs are as follows:

Table 4: Regression of P_BV Against Patents (LN_PATENT), Board Independence (BRD_IND) and Interaction Term (Patents with Board Independence)

Model		*Unstandardized Coefficients*		*Standardized Coefficients*	*t*	*Sig.*
		B	*Std. Error*	*Beta*		
1	(Constant)	-.170	2.841		-.060	.952
	LN_PATENT	2.299	.425	.630	5.414	.000
	BRD_IND	3.128	4.997	.072	.626	.533
	IntP_BRD_IND	-1.338	.579	-.312	-2.311	**.023**

The F statistic pertaining to Table 4 is noted as 10.155, significant at the 99 percent level of confidence; the R^2 is 28 percent. The interaction term is significant at $p < 0.05$.

Table 5: Regression of P_BV Against Patents (LN_PATENT), Promoter Stake (PROM_STAKE) and Interaction Term (IntP_PRSTK - Patents with Promoter Stake)

	Model	*Unstandardized Coefficients*		*Standardized Coefficients*	*t*	*Sig.*
		B	*Std. Error*	*Beta*		
1	(Constant)	4.279	1.793		2.386	.019
	LN_PATENT	.521	.514	.143	1.014	.314
	PROM_STAKE	-5.316	3.244	-.215	-1.639	.105
	IntP_PRSTK	2.092	.652	.519	3.208	**.002**

For Table 5, the F statistic is 12.314, significant at the 99 percent level of confidence, the R^2 is 32 percent. The interaction term is significant at $p < 0.01$.

Table 6: Regression of P_BV Against Patents (LN_PATENT), CEO Duality (CEO_DUAL) and Interaction Term (IntP_CEODUAL - Patents with CEO Duality)

	Model	*Unstandardized Coefficients*		*Standardized Coefficients*	*t*	*Sig.*
		B	*Std. Error*	*Beta*		
1	(Constant)	1.575	.797		1.977	.052
	LN_PATENT	2.248	.428	.616	5.250	.000
	CEO_DUAL	.126	1.277	.013	.098	.922
	IntP_CEODUAL	-1.547	.713	-.329	-2.171	**.033**

For Table 6, the F statistic is 11.59, significant at the 99 percent level of confidence, the R^2 is 31 percent. The interaction term is significant at $p <0.05$.

INTERPRETATION & DISCUSSION

We note that all the three interaction terms are significant. Besides, the sign of the coefficients tell us about the direction of the relationship: the promoter stake positively moderates the relationship between patents and the market value of the firm. In other words, if the firm is largely family owned with the promoter stakes being high, it is possible that the promoter is keen to focus more on organic growth than inorganic. This could result in higher R&D spends and therefore more patents, leading to better market value. Seen in the context of the agency theory, this merely confirms that the principals (owners) would work in the interests of the firm, and are more liable to focus on a good mix of organic and inorganic growth.

In the case of board independence, we note that the coefficient has a negative sign, implying that a larger proportion of independent directors could probably weaken the linkage between patents and market value. To put it in a different way, perhaps it hints at the possibility of problems in the commercialization of patents. However, in most firms, the role of independent directors is not a powerful one, they could be influential, but we feel that they may not be able to really facilitate or hamper any kind of positive development that the firms would undertake. Hence, this finding needs to be taken with a pinch of salt.

In the case of CEO duality, we note a negative relationship with market value. This sign also conforms to the earlier regression when CG variables were taken along with the IE, RI variables. (Refer Table 3). If CEOs handle dual roles, then it is possible that they are more driven towards an internal focus: they tend to spend their time and efforts on transactional issues, and may not be focused on commercialization of innovations. According to agency theory, if they play an executive role, then, in an effort to garner greater compensation, they may focus more on inorganic growth, since their salaries could be directly linked to the business size. Hence, our interpretation supports the findings that CEOs handling dual responsibility could weaken the commercialization process of patents, thereby negatively influence market valuation of the firms. All our hypotheses have been supported and found to be significant. The revised model suggested by our findings is shown thus:

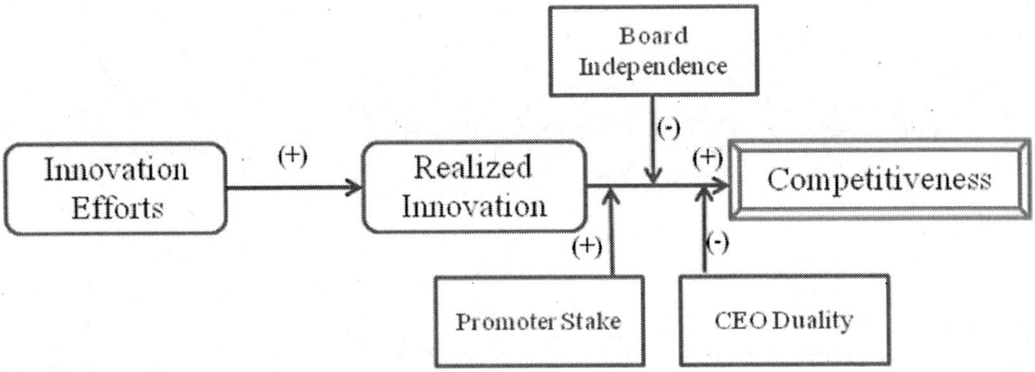

Figure 2: CG Variables and Their Impact on the Innovation-Market Value Process

MANAGERIAL IMPLICATIONS: LIMITATIONS

Whilst paeans of praise have been sung honouring the merits of corporate governance, there are faint indicators that certain characteristics or processes within the CG framework could hamper the commercialization of innovations. Our study clearly brings out the point that while some variables of CG could facilitate commercialization of innovations, or lead to higher market value, there are some variables that could undermine the fructification of patents.

The message to the firm founders is twofold: 1) a blind conformance to CG norms may not be the solution to the ills of a slow-growth firm, or firms that have become stagnant. It is important to conform to SEBI guidelines, nevertheless owners need to keep an eye on encouraging innovation. Any efforts that result in stifled innovation need to be addressed. 2) Owners and founders need to introspectively look at the quality of the people and the processes within the CG framework. This is more important than mere conformance to numbers. For example, if SEBI mandates a minimum of three board meetings in a year, are they resulting in useful, growth-oriented actions? Similarly if a board has four independent directors, are they articulating useful ideas? Can they be taken up for progressive action? More of such provocative questions need to be posed and answers demanded. Only then realized innovations would result in innovative products and services that can be seen and subsequently appreciated by the capital markets.

This study does have some limitations. First, we have estimated those proxies for CG that are easily accessible from the annual reports of firms. In reality, CG processes and practices could be very different. Second, we have used a single measure for innovation: patents. There could be other measures that signify innovation. Moreover, we have taken only R&D intensity as a measure of innovation efforts. Again, there could be several antecedents to the registration of patents. Third, many of the firms in our sample may not have brought out a single visible innovative product into the market; yet they feature in our sample solely because they have at least one registered patent.

FUTURE RESEARCH DIRECTIONS

Our study has identified some potential chinks in the CG armour which has several large and listed companies. However, it must be noted that we use convenient proxies for CG, and there is a desperate need to study the actual board processes, interactions and strategic decisions. This calls for a reasonable amount of field work. It is expected that such studies would complement and enhance the rather sketchy and layered nature of our findings.

A second area could be the study of more process or action oriented proxies, such as board meetings, the presence and the number of committees of the board. These would ensure that we move beyond static characteristics and attempt to look at some action-level parameters also. Additionally, this would also ensure that researchers look into the real events that transpire in board meetings, and come up with more illustrative findings.

A third area of study is to take up cases of innovative firms and understand how they managed to commercialize innovations. A look at their leadership teams and boards would throw more light on board processes and efficacies. This is also in line with Filatotchev (2008:174) who, while writing on future directions in corporate governance research states: "there is a need to extend our understanding of governance issues beyond economic and financial perspectives to embrace strategy and knowledge dimensions as well as contextual issues." It succinctly sums up our thought for the future: more contextual studies of CG and possible repercussions on firms seeking innovative products and services.

REFERENCES

Chaudhuri, S & Ray, Saugata 1997, 'The Competitiveness Conundrum: Literature Review and Reflections', *Economic and Political Weekly*, Vol. 32, No. 48 pp. 83-91.

Cho, H & Pucik, V 2005, 'Relationship between Innovativeness, Quality, Growth, Profitability and Market Value', Strategic Management Journal, Vol. 26, No. 6, pp. 555-575.

Clark, J & Guy, K. 1998, 'Innovation and competitiveness: a review', *Technology Analysis & Strategic Management*, Vol. 10, No.3, pp. 363-395.

Dalziel, T, Gentry, RJ., & Bowerman, M. 2011, 'An integrated Agency-Resource Dependence View of the Influence of Directors' Human and Relational Capital on Firms' R&D spending', *Journal of Management Studies*, Vol. 48, No.6, pp.1217-1242.

Dulewicz, V & Herbert, P 2004, 'Does the composition and practice of Boards of Directors bear any relationship to the performance of their companies?', *Corporate Governance: An International Review*, Vol. 12, No. 3, pp. 263-280.

Durnev, A. & Kim, E 2005, 'To steal or not to steal: Firm attributes, legal environment, and valuation', *Journal of Finance*, Vol. 60, pp. 1461–1493.

Filatotchev, I 2008, 'Developing an Organizational Theory of Corporate Governance: comments on Henri L. Tosi, Jr. (2008) "Quo Vadis? Suggestions for future Corporate Governance Research" *Journal of Management & Governance*, Vol. 12, pp. 171-178.

Finegold, D, Benson, GS. & Hecht, D 2007, 'Corporate Boards and Company Performance: review of research in light of recent reforms', *Corporate Governance: An International Review*, Vol. 17, No. 6, pp. 744-761.

Francis, A 1992, 'The Process of National Industrial Regeneration and Competitiveness', *Strategic Management Journal*, Vol. 13, Special Issue: Fundamental Themes in Strategy Process Research (Winter, 1992), pp. 61-78.

Garay, U. & Gonzalez, M 2008, 'Corporate governance and firm value: The case of Venezuela', *Corporate Governance: An International Review*, Vol. 16, pp. 194–209.

Hagedoorn, J, Cloodt, D & Van Kranenburg, H 2005, 'Intellectual property rights and the governance of international R&D partnerships', *Journal of International Business Studies*, Vol. 36, No. 2, pp. 175-186.

Helfat, CE. 1997, 'Know-how and asset complementarity and dynamic capability accumulation: the case of R&D', *Strategic Management Journal*, Vol. 18, pp. 339–60.

Ho, C. 2005, 'Corporate Governance and Corporate Competitiveness: An international analysis', *Corporate Governance: an international review*, Vol. 13, No.2, pp. 211-253.

Hoskisson, RE, Hitt, MA, Johnson RA & Grossman, W 2002, 'Conflicting Voices: The Effects of Institutional Ownership Heterogeneity and Internal Governance on Corporate Innovation Strategies', *The Academy of Management Journal*, Vol. 45, No. 4, pp. 697-716.

Ingley, C & Walt, N. 2005, 'Do Board Processes Influence Director and Board Performance? Statutory and performance implications', *Corporate Governance: An International Review*, Vol. 13, No. 5, pp. 632-653.

Jackling, B & Johl, S 2009, 'Board Structure and Firm Performance: Evidence from India's Top Companies', *Corporate Governance: An International Review*, Vol. 17, No. 4, pp. 492-509.

Khanchel El Mehdi, I 2007, 'Empirical evidence on corporate governance and corporate performance in Tunisia', *Corporate Governance: An International Review*, Vol. 15, pp. 1429–1441.

Kiel, GC. & Nicholson, GJ 2003, 'Board Composition and Corporate performance: how the Australian experience informs contrasting theories of corporate governance', *Corporate Governance: An International Review*, Vol. 11, No. 3, pp. 189-205

Kor, YY 2006, 'Direct and Interaction Effects of Top Management Team and Board Compositions on R&D Investment Strategy', Strategic Management Journal, Vol. 27, No. 11, pp. 1081-1099.

Lacetera, N 2001, 'Corporate Governance and the Governance of Innovation: The case of Pharmaceutical Industry', *Journal of Management and Governance*, Vol. 5, pp. 29-59.

Lazonick, W. and O'Sullivan, M 1996, 'Organization, Finance and International Competition', *Industrial and Corporate Change* Vol 5, No.1, pp. 1–49.

Lee, PM & O'Neill, HM 2003, 'Ownership Structures and R&D Investments of U.S. and Japanese Firms: Agency and Stewardship Perspectives', *The Academy of Management Journal*, Vol. 46, No. 2, pp. 212-225.

Lewin, P 2007, 'Creativity or Coercion: Alternative Perspectives on Rights to Intellectual Property', *Journal of Business Ethics*, Vol. 71, No. 4, pp. 441-455.

Lin, F 2011, 'Innovation and firm performance: an application of determinants in Taiwan', *International Journal of Technology Management*, Vol. 54, No.1, pp. 12-28.

Mintzberg, H & Waters, JA 1985, 'Of strategies, deliberate and emergent', *Strategic Management Journal*, Vol. 6, No. 3, pp. 257-272.

Pisano, GP & Shih, WC 2009, 'Restoring American competitiveness' *Harvard Business Review*, July-August issue.

Roberts, PW & Amit, R 2003, 'The Dynamics of Innovative Activity and Competitive Advantage: The Case of Australian Retail Banking, 1981 to 1995', *Organization Science*, Vol. 14, No. 2, pp. 107-122.

Rothaermel, FT and Hess, AM 2007, 'Building dynamic capabilities: innovation driven by individual-,firm-, and network-level effects' *Organization Science*, Vol. 18, pp. 898–923.

Sandner, PG & Block, J 2011, 'The market value of R&D, patents and trademarks' *Research Policy*, Vol. 40, No. 7, pp. 969-985.

The Association Between Board Composition and Extent of Disclosure in Non Profit Organisations

Roshayani Arshad, Norliza Omar and Normah Omar
Accounting Research Institute and Universiti Teknologi MARA, Malaysia

ABSTRACT

This study examines the relationships between board composition and the extent of disclosures in the annual reports of NPOs. Board composition and the extent of disclosures are obtained from the content analysis of annual reports of 224 societies registered with the Registrar of Societies in Malaysia for the financial period 2010. The extent of disclosures is based on the overall disclosure and subsets of disclosures in annual reports while board composition consists of board size, board professionalism and board members with political connections. Significant positive relationships between some board compositions and the overall extent of disclosures as well as subsets of disclosures indicate that some characteristics of board members are important resources for the NPOs. The findings in this study also indicate that some of these directors are using disclosures in annual reports in managing their inter-organizational relationships for ensuring continuous flow of financial and other resources for their organisations. Of the board composition, only board members with political connections are significantly positively related with the overall extent of disclosures and subsets of disclosures. The significant positive relationships between board size and board professionalism with some subsets of disclosure in the annual reports suggest that a more comprehensive regulatory requirements or at the very least, the existence of best practices with regards to reporting practices can be useful mechanisms in enhancing transparency in the non-profit sector in Malaysia. Overall, these results infer that an optimum mix of board members is paramount in ensuring efficient resource strategy, and consequently enhance the level of transparency in the non-profit sector.

Keywords: *Board Composition, Disclosures, Non-Profit Organizations*

INTRODUCTION

Non-profit organisations(NPOs) are generally defined as associations, charities, and other voluntary organizations formed to further cultural, religious or public service objectives (Bottiglieri et al., 2011). While their goals are not focused on profit maximisation as for-profit organisations, efficiency issues do exist in NPOs (Behn et al., 2010). For example, donors want to know that the NPO is trustworthy in handling the funds they receive, and also in the use of these funds. Failure to communicate sufficient information can lead to negative perceptions regarding the organization's effectiveness in managing their resources, and consequently lead to withdrawals of support by the donors and other stakeholders. In this respect, NPOs are also competing for resources, in the form of fundings, volunteers or other resources, as for-profit organisations in pursuing their goals. A rich body of literature on corporate disclosures suggests that disclosure in annual reports is associated with reduction in information asymmetry, efficiency of resource allocation and economic growth (e.g. Healy & Palepu, 2001; Hossain & Hammami, 2009). Drawing on similarities with regard to efficiency issues in the NPOs and for-profit organisations, this study argues that provision of information in annual reports of NPOs is important in meeting the information needs of donors and other stakeholders.

Provision of comprehensive information in the annual reports of NPOs is an important mechanism in enhancing the credibility of the organization and trusts of the various stakeholders. However, NPOs are generally subjected to less stringent reporting requirements, and the information reported can be insufficient as these organizations are less pressured to provide transparent information. In addition, the information disclosed is also subject to considerable discretion of the non-profit managers. For example, non-profit managers' disclosure incentives can be influenced by various motivations: to attract greater donations, market differentiation, public trusts and accountability. Such incentives can lead to varying levels of comprehensiveness in the information disclosed. Consistent with this argument, Burger & Owen (2010) find that many NPOs that claimed to be transparent, either failed to provide information, or provide inaccurate information.

According to the Resource Dependence Theory (RDT), organizations characterised by dependence on external resources will survive if they can manage the flow of resources and reduce the uncertainty in their environment (Pfeffer & Salancik, 1978). In this respect, RDT contends that the board of directors can be a useful mechanism in minimising dependence on resources or gain resources. Prior empirical studies provide evidence that the board of directors is associated with successful resource dependence strategy (e.g. Pfeffer, 1973 and Sanders & Carpenter, 1998). More recent studies suggest that the type of directors on the board is associated with different benefits for the organizations. For example, board members from financial institutions are more likely to affect financing obtained by the organizations (Luoma and Goodstein, 1999) and stakeholder directors are more likely to improve corporate social performance (Johnson and Greening, 1999). These studies suggest potential association between the board of directors and the provision of information in the annual reports of NPOs, as part of managing resource dependence strategy by the directors. Hence, it is important to examine whether there are any associations between the composition of board members and the extent of disclosures in the annual reports of the NPOs.

The objective of this study is to examine the association between board composition and the extent of disclosures in the annual reports of NPOs in Malaysia. Specifically, the extent of disclosures will be examined based on the total extent of information disclosed and subsets of information disclosed in the balance sheets, income statements and notes to accounts. Such examination is expected to provide some insight into the role of the board composition specifically and enhancement of transparency by NPOs generally.

This paper will proceed by outlining the financial reporting requirements of NPOs in Malaysia. It will then review the literature on the relationships between board composition, and respectively, resource dependence theory and extent of disclosures, from which hypotheses will be developed. Finally, this paper will proceed to the empirical stage of variable measurement, sampling, data analysis, discussion of results, limitations and suggestions for future research.

Financial Reporting Requirements of NPOs in Malaysia

In Malaysia, NPOs comprised of organizations that are either charitable organizations, or societies. NPOs with revenue of more than RM1 million can be registered as companies limited by guarantee, and must be registered with the Companies Commission of Malaysia (CCM) and is held accountable by the *Companies Act* of 1965. For NPOs with revenue less than RM1 million, they must be registered with the Registry of Societies Malaysia (ROS), within the Ministry of Home Affairs, and are held accountable by the Societies Act of 1966.

In relation to disclosure and reporting requirements, there is no specific accounting standard for the NPOs. Nevertheless, NPOs are encouraged to comply with the international financial reporting standards issued by the International Accounting Standard Board and adopted by the Malaysian Accounting Standard Board, or reporting standards applicable for private entities in the preparation and presentation of their financial statements. In summary, the overall disclosure and reporting requirements of NPOs in Malaysia reflect a minimum regulatory requirement environment. In the absence of any efforts towards more formal reporting requirements or recommended best practices, significant variations in the reporting practices of the NPOs in Malaysia are expected. This in turn can result in difficulties for stakeholders to understand the reported information.

LITERATURE REVIEW AND GENERATION OF HYPOTHESES

Resource Dependence Theory, Board Composition and Disclosures

NPOs are characterized by their dependence on donations and other resources. According to the Resource Dependence Theory (RDT), organizations operating in this environment will survive if they can manage the flow of resources and reduce the uncertainty in their environment (Pfeffer & Salancik, 1978). RDT literature contends that the board of directors enable organizations to minimize dependence on resources or gain resources through successful resource dependence strategy (e.g. Pfeffer, 1973 and Sanders & Carpenter, 1998). For example, Aggarwal et al., (2011) find that board size is positively related to the performance of NPOs. They argue that individual directors on the board bring assets that are valuable to the NPO. In another study, Luoma & Goodstein (1999) argue that board members from financial institutions are more likely to affect the financing obtained by organizations (Luoma & Goodstein, 1999). These studies suggest that board composition matters in ensuring successful resource strategies. This study focuses on three types of board composition: board size, board professionalism and board members with political connections.

In managing successful resource strategies, an organization must establish some relationships with other organizations or institutions, because they need to acquire resources that are currently scarce within their own organization (Oliver, 1990; Thibault & Harvey, 1997). A wide body of empirical research on disclosures about for-profit organizations highlights that disclosures in annual reports is an important mechanism for managers to communicate the activities and performance of their organizations to other organizations (Healy & Palepu, 2001; Hossain & Hammami, 2009) and stakeholders. Drawing on this literature, this study proposes that disclosures in annual reports of NPOs can be a useful mechanism in establishing inter-organizational relationships with other organizations or insitutions. The ability of an NPO to establish these relationships is expected to result in the flow of resources to the organization. This study proposes that there is an association between board composition and the provision of information in the annual reports of NPOs, as part of managing resource dependence strategy by the directors.

Board Size and Extent of Disclosures

RDT literature suggests that board size in NPOs is likely to vary with the amount of complexity and uncertainty in the external environment (Boyd, 1990; Dess & Beard, 1984; Pfeffer, 1972, 1973; Pfeffer & Salancik, 1978). For example, more board members with links to important resources in the external environment will be recruited on the boards of NPOs.

NPOs are dependent on public donations, government fundings, other types of funds and resources reflect that NPOs are accountable to multiple stakeholders. This in turn, suggests that NPOs are required to communicate adequate information about their organizations and operations for potential resource providers to make informed decisions. Adequate information provides assurance to the resource providers and other stakeholders that the organizations are legitimate and reputable NPOs. The increasing number of NPOs indicates that the competition for funds and other resources is constantly growing. Hence, it is paramount that an NPO communicates sufficient information in order to maintain the trust of the various stakeholders. Loss of trust can potentially reduce an organisation's ability to attract or maintain donors and other resource providers, communicate with other organizations and the reputation as a legitimate NPO. This infers that boards of NPOs need to be concerned with the issue of reporting sufficient information to their various stakeholders. The likelihood of meeting the information needs of these stakeholders is only possible if there are sufficient members on the board. This is based on the argument that a larger board size is more likely to be comprised of members with varied experience, expertise, knowledge and experience (Aggarwal et al., 2011). Based on this reasoning, the following hypothesis is developed:

H1: *The size of the board is significantly positively related to the extent of disclosures.*

Board Professionalism and Extent of Disclosures

The previous discussion highlights that boards function as a resource for the NPOs, as each director on the board bring assets to the organisation. Brown (2005) suggests that board capital consists of experience, expertise and reputation. The human capital of the board members can facilitate them in guiding the strategic direction of the NPOs. Mwenja & Lewis (2009) argue that board members are an important resource for the NPOs as effective strategic direction taken is a significant contribution to the long term survival of the NPOs. Hence, it is expected that board members with professional backgrounds are more capable in assisting the NPOs in analyzing and understanding the complex environment in which the NPOs operate. One aspect of such complexity is related to managing organizational responsiveness to the information needs of multiple stakeholders. In order to ensure long term survival of the organization, board members need to manage the relationships with the various stakeholders (Rehli & Jager, 2011). Based on this argument, it is expected that board members with professional backgrounds are more capable of influencing management disclosure practices that are perceived to be useful to a wide range of stakeholders. Hence, the following hypothesis is developed:

H2: *The percentage of board members with professional affiliations is significantly positively related to the extent of disclosures.*

Political Connections and Extent of Disclosures

In ensuring continuous flow of resources to an organization, it is important that the organization develops and maintains a healthy relationships with the various stakeholders.

Mwenja & Lewis (2009) argue that through these relationships or external social networks, the organization will be able to expand the organization's donor base, and consequently bring in resources for the organization. In line with this argument, past studies provide evidence that board members with political connections are associated with preferential access to funds (e.g. Claessons et al., 2008 and Faccio & Masulis, 2006). It is possible that through their existing and wide external social networks and reputations, they can exert more influence in attracting new donors, as well as other resource providers from a wide range of stakeholders. Concurrently, their external network ties, including various governmental agencies and regulatory authorities also increases these board members involvement in strategic decisions of the NPOs (Carpenter & Westphal, 2001). They are expected to be more supportive of calls for transparency, a subset of accountability issues in NPOs promoted by these bodies. This infers that such board members will be able to make more meaningful contributions in enhancing the transparency of NPOs. Consequently, this is expected to result in more comprehensive disclosures of information in the annual reports of NPOs. Following this argument, the following hypothesis is developed:

H3: *The percentage of board members with political connections is significantly positively related to the extent of disclosures.*

METHODS

Sample and Data Collection

The sample consists of 224 societies registered with the Registrar of Societies (ROS) for the financial year 2010. The research approach involves content analysis of the societies' annual reports. Content analysis has been widely employed in prior studies to measure voluntary and mandatory disclosures in annual reports (Hackston & Milne, 1996; O'Donovan, 2002; Clemens & Douglas, 2006).

Extent of Disclosure

The extent of disclosures in annual reports of societies in this study is measured, based on a self-constructed index. The identification of items to be included in the index is guided by the review of prior studies relevant to disclosures in annual reports of NPOs (Beck, Campbell & Shrives, 2010; Molina-Azorin et al., 2009), mandatory disclosures as required by the Societies Act 1966, and recommended practices in other countries. In Malaysia, there are no particular regulatory requirements in relation to financial reporting practices for NPOs registered with ROS, except for brief requirements on the need to prepare and submit balance sheets and statements for revenue and expenditure by the Society Act 1966. As such, the identification of such practices is also guided by a review of best practices adopted by others.

Of relevance to this study, best practices in Singapore, New Zealand and United Kingdom are reviewed. Based on the review of relevant literatures and recommended practices, a list of items to be included under financial reporting practices disclosures is identified. This is followed by discussions with several officials from the ROS, in order to get insights into the types of information required by ROS for effective monitoring of societies.

Finally, once the disclosure items have been identified, a pilot study of content analysis of annual reports of societies for the year ending 31 December 2010 was carried out. A sample of 20 societies was selected at random for the pilot study. A list of disclosure items disclosed in the annual reports of these societies are extracted and compared against the categories and disclosure items included in the developed disclosure index. Based on this preliminary content analysis, a review of the categories and disclosure items was made and minor modifications were made to the items of disclosure. The final disclosure index contains 60 disclosure items. A summary of the items listed in the Disclosure Index (DI) is shown in Table 1.

Table 1: Summary of Items Listed in DI

Extent of Disclosures	*Number of Items*
Balance Sheets (18 items)	
Non-Current Assets	2
Current Assets	6
Current Liabilities	3
Non-Current Liabilities	4
Society's Funds	3
Statement of Financial Activities (19 items)	
Funds Generated from Activities	4
Funds from Donations	4
Other Income	2
Operating Expenses	9
Notes to Accounts (23 items)	
Balance Sheets Items	7
Statement of Financial Activities Items	7
Others	9
Total	60

For each society, the extent of disclosures are assessed using an equal-weighted index, where a point is awarded for each item of information disclosed. Disclosure scores for each society is totalled and not given any specific percentage, as it is considered that each item of disclosure is equally important. This scoring approach is also consistent with prior studies on disclosures in for-profit organisations (Chau & Gray, 2002; Haniffa & Cooke, 2002). The extent of DI for each society j is constructed as follows:

$$DI = \sum_{i=1}^{m_j} \frac{d_j}{N}$$

Where N = number if items expected for j[th] society, $N \leq 60$
d_j = 0 to 3 as per rating in Table 2.

Table 2: Rating Points for Items Listed in DI

Scores	Descriptions
0	Not Disclosed
1	Disclosed with qualitative information only
2	Disclosed with qualitative and/or quantitative information
3	Disclosed with detailed information, contains both qualitative and quantitative information

The index indicates the extent of disclosures for a society j, where N is the maximum number of relevant items a society may disclose and d_i is equal to 0 to 3 points as indicated in Table 2, where the minimum score is zero and the maximum score is 3. The total maximum scores for a company *mj* is 180 (60 items × 3 points) while the minimum score can be zero.

Measurement of Variables

There are three independent variables in this study, board size, board members with professional affiliations, and board members with political connections. In addition to the identified independent variables, this study also includes one organisational characteristic identified in prior research as determinants of management disclosure decisions (e.g. Gray et al., 1995; Haniffa & Cooke, 2005) as a control variable. This variable is size. The definition and measurement of variables used in this study are listed in Table 3.

Table 3: Definition and Measurement of Variables

Variable Acronym	*Definition*	*Measurement*
DI	Extent of disclosures	Self constructed disclosure index.
BS	Extent of disclosures in the balance sheets	Self constructed disclosure index.
SA	Extent of disclosures in the	Self constructed disclosure index.

	statement of activities	
NOTES	Extent of disclosures in the notes to accounts	Self constructed disclosure index.
B_SIZE	Board size	Total number of board members.
B_PROF	Board members with professional affiliations	Percentage of board members with professional affilitations to total number of board members. Professional affiliation refers to members with professions in areas such as accounting, management, engineering, architecture and medical.
B_POL	Board members with political connections	Percentage of board members with political connections to total number of board members. Political connections refer to members being conferred awards by the government of Malaysia. For example, board members with Dato', Tan Sri and Datuk Paduka.
SIZE	Size of NPO	Total revenues

RESULTS AND DISCUSSION

Descriptive Statistics

Table 4 presents descriptive statistics on the dependent variable, DI. The results of descriptive statistics for continuous independent variables and control variables are presented in Table 5.

Table 4: Descriptive Statistics for Dependent Variables

	Label	*Minimum*	*Maximum*	*Mean*
Total extent of disclosure	DI (%)	0.00	49.00	12.00
Extent of disclosure – balance sheets	BS (%)	0.00	47.00	11.00
Extent of disclosure – statement of activities	SA (%)	0.00	57.00	16.00
Extent of disclosure – notes to accounts	NOTES (%)	0.00	61.00	10.00

Table 4 reported that the overall DI is very low. The mean value for DI 12 percent. Further analyses also reveal that the mean values for BS, SA and NOTES are 11 percent, 16 percent and 10 percent respectively. It is interesting to note that the minimum values for the extent of disclosures in each of these statements are zero. This indicates that some NPOs in the sample of study did not provide any information with regard to either one of these statements. The maximum values for all the statements are moderately high, with the highest maximum value of 61 percent reported for NOTES.

Table 5: Descriptive Statistics for Independent Variables

	Label	*Minimum*	*Maximum*	*Mean*
Board size	B_SIZE	4	33	13.52
Board members with professional affiliations	B_PROF(%)	0.00	1.00	0.12
Board members with political connections	B_POL(%)	0.00	1.00	0.04
Size of NPO	SIZE (RM)	0.00	9,057,225.00	290,817.35

Table 5 reported that board size of NPOs ranges from a minimum of 4 members to 33 members. Consistent with prior studies (Boyd, 1990; Dess & Beard, 1984; Pfeffer, 1972, 1973; Pfeffer & Salancik, 1978) this result indicates that some NPOs are fairly large in size. In relation to board composition, Table 5 reported that some NPOs have 100 percent members with professional affiliations while others have 100 percent board members with political connections. Finally, Table 5 reported that some NPOs are very small with no revenue to a fairly large size with maximum revenue of RM9.057million. However, the mean value for size of NPO is only RM290,817.35.

Multivariate Analysis

In this study, linear multiple regression is used as the basis of analysis for testing H1 to H3. The hypothesized relationships are odeled as follows:

Model 1: $DI = \beta_0 + \beta_1 BOD\_SIZE + \beta_2 B\_PROF + \beta_3 B\_POL + \beta_4 SIZE + \varepsilon_t$

The association between board composition and the subsets of extent of disclosures in the balance sheets, statement of activities and notes to accounts are based on the following models:

Model 2: $BS = \beta_0 + \beta_1 B\_SIZE + \beta_2 B\_PROF + \beta_3 B\_POL + \beta_4 SIZE + \varepsilon_t$
Model 3: $SA = \beta_0 + \beta_1 B\_SIZE + \beta_2 B\_PROF + \beta_3 B\_POL + \beta_4 SIZE + \varepsilon_t$
Model 4: $NOTES = \beta_0 + \beta_1 B\_SIZE + \beta_2 B\_PROF + \beta_3 B\_POL + \beta_4 SIZE + \varepsilon_t$

where variable definitions are given in Table 1.

In these regression models, multicollinearity was tested using the variance inflation factor and tolerance levels, and found to be well within the satisfactory range. The results of the regression analysis are presented in Table 6 and Table 7 and are now discussed in terms of tests of each of the hypotheses.

Table 6: Multiple Regression Results for Factors Affecting the Extent of Disclosures

DV	DI		
R^2	0.562		
Adjusted R^2	0.554		
F-Statistic	70.279		
Sig	0.000[a]		
	Beta	t	Sig
(Constant)		-0.270	0.788
IV			
B_SIZE	0.007	0.150	0.881
B_PROF	0.078	1.633	0.104
B_POL	0.093	2.023	0.044*
SIZE	0.700	14.672	0.000***

Results of the multiple regression analysis in Table 6 report that the adjusted R^2 is 0.554. H1 predicts that B_SIZE is significantly positively related to DI. The results in Table 6 reveal an insignificant relationship. However, further analyses as reported in Table 7 reveals that B_SIZE is significantly positively related to SA. Hence, HI is partially accepted. These results highlight that the type of directors on the board, matters in ensuring successful resource strategy. This is consistent with prior studies where type of directors on the board is associated with different benefits for the organizations (Luoma and Goodstein, 1999; Johnson and Greening, 1999). It is important that the combination of directors on the boards recognises the importance of reporting information in annual reports of NPOs as a mechanism in managing inter-organizational relationships with other organizations or insitutions. Hence, an optimum board composition, instead of board size that matters in facilitating the enhancement of accountability in NPOs.

With regard to board members with professional affiliation, the results in Table 6 reveal that B_PROF is not significantly related to DI. Nevertheless, the results in Table 7 reveal that B_PROF is significantly positively related with BS and NOTES. Hence, H2 is partly accepted. These results highlight that B_PROF are more concerned with information reported in these two sections of the annual reports. While it is expected that B_PROF are more capable in influencing management disclosure practices that are perceived to be useful to a wide range of stakeholders, the minimum regulatory reporting requirements and lack of recommended best practices for reporting purposes of NPOs in Malaysia are likely to reduce B_PROF motivations in enhancing the overall extent of disclosures in annual reports of NPOs.

Table 7: Multiple Regression Results for Factors Affecting the Extent of Disclosures (Subsets)

DV	*BS*			*SA*			*NOTES*		
R^2	0.388			0.554			0.323		
Adjusted R^2	0.376			0.546			0.311		
F-Statistic	34.649			68.008			26.115		
Sig	0.000[a]			0.000[a]			0.000[a]		
	Beta	*t*	*Sig*	*Beta*	*t*	*Sig*	*Beta*	*t*	*Sig*
(Constant)		0.276	0.783		-0.115	0.909		1.209	0.228
IV									
B_SIZE	-0.004	-0.076	0.939	0.087	1.886	0.061*	-0.061	-1.081	0.281
B_PROF	0.161	2.855	0.005**	-0.013	-0.262	0.793	0.175	2.952	0.004**
B_POL	0.132	2.422	0.016*	0.087	1.865	0.063*	1.118	2.063	0.040*
SIZE	0.515	9.123	0.000***	0.719	14.928	0.000***	0.455	7.664	0.000***

Coefficient for each variable is shown with t values in parentheses. * Significant at 10 per cent level (1-tailed test); * * Significant at 5 per cent level (1-tailed test); * * * Significant at 1 per cent level (1-tailed test)

Coefficient for each variable is shown with t values in parentheses. * Significant at 10 per cent level (1-tailed test); * * Significant at 5 per cent level (1-tailed test); * * * Significant at 1 per cent level (1-tailed test)

Of the board composition, results in Table 6 and Table 7 reveal that B_POL is significantly related with DI as well as BS, SA and NOTES. Hence, H3 is accepted. These results suggest that B_POL is a valuable resource for NPOs in ensuring continuous flow of resources to organisations. These results also infer that these board members acknowledge the importance of disclosures in annual reports as a mechanism to develop and maintain a healthy relationships with the various stakeholders that is paramount in managing succesful resource strategies. In addition, as these board members are associated with external social networks that could include various governmental agencies and regulatory authorities that are involved in promoting transparency, B_POL is expected to be more supportive of calls for transparency. Concurrently, they are also expected to be more actively involved in the strategic decisions with regard to the enhancement of transparency by NPOs.

CONCLUSIONS AND LIMITATIONS

This study examines the relationships between various board compositions and the extent of disclosures in annual reports of NPOs. The significant positive relationships between some board compositions and DI as well as subsets of DI indicate that some characteristics of board members are important resources for the NPOs. In addition, the findings in this study also indicate that some of these directors are using disclosures in annual reports in managing their inter-organizational relationships in ensuring continuous flow of financial and other resources for their organisations.

Of the board composition, only B_POL is significantly positively related with DI, BS, SA and NOTES. These results suggest that B_POL are actively involved in influencing the disclosure of information in annual reports of NPOs. The significant positive relationships between B_SIZE and B_PROF with some subsets of disclosure in the annual reports suggest that a more comprehensive regulatory requirements or at the very least, the existence of best practices with regard to reporting practices can be useful mechanisms in enhancing transparency in the non-profit sector in Malaysia. In addition, these results also infer that an optimum mix of board members is paramount for ensuring efficient resource strategies and consequently enhance the levels of transparency. The overall findings in this study have practical implications for various regulatory authorities in their continuous efforts on improving the governance and transparency of the non-profit sector.

Finally, there are some limitations in this study. First, this study examined the influence of various board compositions on the extent of disclosures based on board members identified in the annual reports. Second, this study focuses only on three types of board members. Future research may also consider the use of questionnaires or interviews with the broader types of board members in gauging their influence on the extent of disclosures in the annual reports of NPOs. Nevertheless, this study provides useful insights in understanding the relationships between various board compositions and the extent of disclosures by NPOs in a developing country environment.

REFERENCES

Aggarwal, R.K., Evans, M. E., & Nanda, D. (2011). Nonprofit boards: Size, performance and managerial incentives. Journal of Accounting and Economics, doi: 10.1016/jacceco. 2011.08.001.

Beck, A. C., Campbell, D., and Shrives, P. J. (2010). Content Analysis in Environmental Reporting Research: Enrichment and Rehearsal of the Method in a British-German Context. *The British Accounting Review, 42,* 207-222.

Behn, B. K., DeVries, D. D., & Lin, J. (2010). The determinants of transparency in nonprofit organizations: An exploratory study. *Advances in Accounting, incorporating Advances in International Accounting, 26*, 6-12. doi: 10.1016/j.adiac.2009.12.001.

Bottiglieri, W. A., Kroleski, S. L., & Conway, K. (2011). The Regulation of Non-Profit Organizations. *Journal of Business & Economics Research, 9*(9), 51-60.

Boyd, B. (1990). Corporate linkages and organizational environment: A test of the resource dependence model. *Strategic Management Journal, 11*(6), 419-430.

Brown, W. A. (2005). Exploring the association between board and organizational performance in nonprofit organizations. *Nonprofit Management and Leadership, 15*(3), 317-339. doi: 10.1002/nml.71.

Burger, R., & Owens, T. (2010). Promoting Transparency in the NGO Sector: Examining the Availability and Reliability of Self-Reported Data. *World Development, 38*(9), 1263-1277. doi: 10.1016/j.worlddev.2009.12.018.

Carpenter, M. A., & Westphal, J. D. (2001). The Strategic Context of External Network ties: Examining the impact of director appointments on board involvement in strategic decision making. *Academy of Management, 44*(4), 639-660.

Chau, G. K., & Gray, S. J. (2002) Ownership Structure and Corporate Voluntary Disclosure in Hong Kong and Singapore. *The International Journal of Accounting, 37*(2), 247-265.

Claessens, S., Feijen, E., & Laeven, L. (2008). Politicalconnections and preferential access to finance: The role of campaign contributions. *Journal of Financial Economics, 88*(3), 554-580.

Clemens, B., & Douglas, T. J. (2006). Does coercion drive firms to adopt 'voluntary' green initiatives? Relationships among coercion, superior firm resources, and voluntary green initiatives. *Journal of Business Research 59*, 483-491.

Dess, G. G., & Beard, D. W. (1894). Dimension of Organizational Task Environments. *Administrative Science Quarterly, 29*(1), 52-73.

Faccio, M., & Masulis, R. W. (2006). Political Connections and Corporate Bailouts. *The Journal of Finance, 61*(6), 2597-2635.

Gray, R., Kouhy, R., & Lavers, S. (1995). Corporate social and environmental reporting: a review of the literature and a longitudinal study of UK disclosure. *Accounting, Auditing & Accountability Journal, 8*(2), 47-77. doi: 10.1108/09513579510146996.

Hackston, D., & Milne, M. J. (1996). Some Determinant of Social and Environment in New Zealand Companies. *Accounting, Auditing & Accountability Journal, 9*(1), 77-108.

Haniffa, R. M., & Cooke, T. E. (2002). Culture, Corporate Governance and Disclosure in Malaysia Corporations. *Abacus, 38*(3), 317-349.

Haniffa, R. M., & Cooke, T. E. (2005). The impact of culture and governance on corporate social reporting. *Journal of Accounting and Public Policy, 24*(5), 391-430.

Healy, P. M., & Palepu, K. G. (2001). Information Asymmetry, Corporate Disclosure, and the Capital Markets: A Review of the Empirical Disclosure Literature. *Journal of Accounting and Economics, 31*, 405-440.

Hossain, M., & Hammami, H. (2009). Voluntary Disclosure in the Annual Reports of an Emerging Country: The Case of Qatar. *Advances in Accounting, Incorporating Advances in International Accounting, 25*, 255-265.

Johnson, R. A., & Greening, D. W. (1999). The Effects of Corporate Governance and Instittutional Ownership Types on Corporate Social Performance. *Academy of Management Journal, 42*(5), 564-576.

Luoma, P., & Goodstein, J. (1999). Stakeholders and Corporate Boards: Institutional Influences on Board Composition and Structure. *Academy of Management Journal 42*, 553-563.

Molina-Azorin, J. F., Claver-Cortes, E., Lopez-Gamero, M. D., & Tari, J. J. (2009). Green Management and Financial Performance: A Literature Review. *Management Decision, 47*(7), 1080-1100.

Mwenja, D., & Lewis, A. (2009). Exploring the impact of the board of directors on the performance of not-for-profit organizations. *Business Strategy Series, 10*(6), 359-365. doi: 0.1108/17515630911005646.

O'Donovan, G. (2002). Environmental Disclosures in the Annual Report: Extending the Applicability and Predictive Power of Legitimacy Theory. *Accounting, Auditing & Accountability Journal, 15*(3), 344-372.

Oliver, C. (1990). Determinants of Inter-Organizational Relationships: Integration and Figure Directions. *The Academy of Management Review, 15*(2), 241-265.

Parsons, L. M. (2007). The Impact of Financial Information and Voluntary Disclosure on Contributions to Not-For-Profit Organizations. *Behavioral Research in Accounting, 19*, 179-196.

Pfeffer, J. (1972). Size and composition of corporate boards of directors: The organisation and its environment. *Administrative Science Quarterly, 17*, 219-228.

Pfeffer, J., & Salancik, G. (1978). *The External Control of Organisations, A Resource Dependence Perspective*. New York: Harper and Row.

Rehli, F., & Jager, U. P. (2011). The Governance of International Nongovernmental Organisations: How Funding and Volunteer Involvement Affect Board Nomination Modes and Stakeholder Representation in International Nongovernmental Organisations. *Voluntas, 22*, 587-612. doi: 10.1007/s11266-011-9197-1.

Sanders, W. M. G., & Carpenter, M. A. (1998). Internationalization and Firm Governance: The Roles of CEO Compensation, Top Team Composition, and Board Structure. *The Academy of Management Journal, 41*(2), 158-178.

Thibault, L., & Harvey, J. (1997). Fostering Interorganizational Linakges in the Canadian Sport Delivery System. *Journal of Sport Management 11*, 45-68.

Trussel, J. M., & Parsons, L. M. (2008). Financial Reporting Factors Affecting Donations to Charitable Organizations. *Advances in Accounting, 23*, 263-285.

Corporate Governance in Malaysia: A Glass Half Full?

Sin Huei, Ng and Ken Kyid, Yeoh[1]
INTI International University Malaysia
[1]Taylor's Business School, Malaysia

ABSTRACT

It is believed that extensive political involvement in business fundamentally impacts the overall quality of both firm- and country-level corporate governance in a particular country. Using the corporate and institutional environment in Malaysia as our chosen example, we aim to show the profound influence that national government policies and approaches in the running of their respective capital markets has on the corporate governance practices and norms in a particular country. Specifically, we show that political conflicts of interest can and have caused controlling shareholders of publicly-listed corporations to have greater inclination to engage in the expropriation of their minority shareholders. This tendency is particularly prevalent amongst large business groups where the link between politics and the business groups is most clearly shown. We conclude that a culture of good corporate governance is extremely difficult to cultivate without good public/political governance.

Keywords: *Principal-Principal Problems, Expropriation of Minority Shareholders, Rent-Seeking, Corporate Governance Reform*

AIM OF THE STUDY

Principal-principal conflicts of agency (i.e. conflicts between majority/controlling shareholders and their respective outside minority shareholders) that exist amongst publicly-listed firms in Malaysia are exacerbated by a corporate environment with generally low corporate transparency, rampant rent-seeking activities, and a business culture that is relationship-based. Such an environment creates many opportunities for controlling shareholders of Malaysian listed entities to expropriate firm resources, through underhand corporate activities such as tunnelling. In fact, expropriation is prevalent as most publicly-listed corporations in Malaysia have highly concentrated ownership structures[1]. Since, it is obvious that major corporate governance characteristics at the country-level fundamentally give rise to distinctive types of governance concerns, in-depth understanding of the historical development of a particular country's institutional and corporate environment is vital. Such an understanding (within the context of Malaysia) is the primary aim of our paper.

Corporate culture in Malaysia and many other East Asian countries is one that is relationship-based (Rajan and Zingales, 1998). This is opposed to the arm's length corporate culture in Anglo-Saxon countries. According to the path dependence view of governance, publicly-listed companies in Malaysia are located in an unique institutional setting as its governance environment differs from that of other countries. In addition, apart from South Africa, Malaysia is the only country in the world that has an affirmative action policy for its main ethnic group (Adam, 1997) (i.e. Malays) that forms the majority of the country's population. Specifically, this policy aims to improve the relatively backward economic status of the Malays, as compared to other major ethnic groups in the country. As the government, as well as the ruling political parties have been the main machinery used to disseminate unearned incentives in the name of making the affirmative policy a success, publicly-listed companies in Malaysia (especially those that are majority owned and those who are very well-connected politically) typically embrace the culture of cronyism and rent seeking.

Indeed, the close link between business and politics in Malaysia is well documented (e.g. Gomez and Jomo, 1999; Faccio, 2006; Gomez, 2006). According to Gomez and Jomo (1999), two forms of political favouritism exist in corporate Malaysia today. They are where (i) official status is awarded to firms that are managed by ethnic Malays, and (ii) informal ties exist between senior politicians and firms that are controlled by either the Chinese or Malay individuals/families. Firms with official status are also known as government-linked corporations (GLCs) in which the government itself is the largest shareholder, and has absolute control over the firms.

Having described the general corporate and institutional environment in Malaysia, we present a detailed account of the historical development of government policy towards the corporate sector in the following sections of our paper. As mentioned earlier, our main intention is to show how such policies fundamentally altered the nature of corporate governance practices and have caused new, distinctive governance problems in the Malaysian capital market.

---

[1] Ownership is 'concentrated' in Malaysia as opposed to the 'dispersed' ownership structure in the US and the UK. The largest shareholder of a typical listed company in Malaysia (with the majority of them family shareholders) on average holds about one-third or more of the company's shares, and the top five shareholders own around 60 percent of the company's shares (Fazilah *et al.*, 2002).

The Laissez-Faire Era after Independence (1957-1969)

Political favouritism in corporate Malaysia can be traced back to 1957 when the then Malaya gained independence from the British. As is the case with many other British colonies during the British colonial period, the people of Malaya were subjected to the 'divide and rule' policy (Verma, 2004). The Malays, being the indigenous people of the country, and forming over half of the population, were mostly confined to the villages and lived as peasants, working as fishermen and civil servants. Chinese and Indian people have migrated to Malaya since the nineteenth century, and have therefore been part of the Malayan society for over a century. Naturally entrepreneurial, the Chinese mainly settled in urban areas were involved in businesses; trading and tin mining, and the Indians mainly worked and lived in the rubber estates controlled by the British (Verma, 2004).

Among the three main ethnic groups (Malays, Chinese and Indians), the Chinese were the most economically dominant, as many of them were actively involved in productive economic activities. Income inequality among the races started to become a cause for concern. The Malays were mindful of and insecure about the economic dominance of the Chinese. For example, in 1957/58, the average monthly household income for the Chinese was, in Malaysian Ringgit (RM), 300 followed by Indians RM237 and Malays RM139 (Snodgrass, 1980). The Malays (particularly the pre-colonial Malay ruling class), were more interested in political power and colonial administrative services and occupied positions immediately subordinate to those held by the British administrators.

As a separate development, the United Malays National Organisation (UMNO) was founded in 1946 as a political party to protect the Malays' interest, and many of those who led UMNO actually began their careers in colonial administration (Jomo, 1988). Due to the weaker socio-economic position of the Malays compared to other ethnic groups, especially the Chinese, when Malaya gained independence from the British in 1957, the Special Rights status for the Malays was incorporated as Article 153 in the Federal Constitution of Malaya to safeguard Malays' interests by reserving quotas for Malays in certain areas as stipulated in the article. On independence, the Malays had gained political power from the British, but economic power resided with the Chinese. As stated by Jomo (1988), political power without an economic base was essentially fragile and untenable in the long run.

To promote Malay capitalism, UMNO, the dominant ruling party since independence, carried out some 'economic development' programmes and activities for the Malays under the Malay Special Rights. For instance, in 1965, the First National Bumiputera[2] Economic Congress was held and Bank Bumiputera was established, both aiming to improve the Malays' economic status and accumulation of Malay capital (Jomo, 1988). Despite these efforts, actual progress did not bring satisfactory results. Moreover, due to the practice of the

[2] *Bumiputera* is a term used to refer to the indigenous people of Malaysia which consist mainly of ethnic Malays.

laissez-faire system after independence from 1957-1970, Chinese economic dominance continued to grow and expand, whereas the majority of Malays continued to be economically subordinate. The income inequality between the Chinese and the Malays became even more serious.

By 1970, the average household monthly income for the Chinese had increased to RM399 while the Malays remained lowest at RM177 (Heng, 1997). Chinese ownership in the corporate sector in 1970 was 34.4 percent, while the Malay ownership was negligible at a mere 2.4 percent (Heng, 1997). After over a decade's accumulation of discontent and frustration over uneven economic development among different ethnic groups, inter-racial antagonism finally resulted in post-election race riots of 1969. The government was convinced that the economic deprivation of the Malays was one of the main causes of the riots.

THE TWO-PRONGED AFFIRMATIVE ECONOMIC POLICY

Fundamental changes to the Malaysian socio-economic, political and corporate landscape took place after the riots with the implementation of the ambitious 20-year New Economic Policy (NEP) (1970-1990), which aims to rectify the socio-economic imbalance among races (Horii, 1991). The two-pronged objective of the NEP was to eradicate poverty and restructure Malaysian society, so that race dictating status within the economic function could eventually be eliminated. UMNO's hegemony in the government gave the Malay party leverage to pursue a series of ethnic affirmative actions under the NEP involving subsidies, licenses, credit schemes, ethnic employment quotas, tertiary education opportunities and federal scholarships etc.

More importantly, in the corporate and commercial sectors, various steps and measures were taken with the aim of rectifying inter-ethnic imbalances in the equity ownership and control of ownership in the country so that by 1990 *"at least 30 percent of the total commercial and industrial activities in all categories and scales of operation should have participation by Malays and other indigenous people in terms of ownership (*including the corporate equity ownership*) and management"* (Malaysia, 1971, p.158). It is said that the NEP had led to *"partial abandonment of the previously more laissez-faire (economy)...in favour of greater state intervention, primarily for ethnic affirmative actions, including the accelerated expansion of the Bumiputera middle class...and the creation of Bumiputera capitalists"* (Gomez, 1999, p.37).

From the perspective of the Chinese businessmen, the implementation of the NEP forced them to realize that in order to continue to have access to the means to accumulate wealth, they needed to cultivate ties with the influential Malays in UMNO. The Chinese capitalists began to recruit Malay politicians, politically influential Malays, and Malay ex-civil servants as company directors; some businessmen even began funding UMNO and its leaders (Gomez,

1999). Crony capitalism is believed to have flourished during the NEP era. Both Chinese businessmen and the Malays' political elite found the informal ties mutually lucrative. Some Chinese capitalists have been known to finance ambitious politicians as a means of gaining access to government patronage.

The 'New Rich'

In 1981, the appointment of Mahathir Mohamad as the President of UMNO and Prime Minister of Malaysia further strengthened the promotion of Malay capitalism (Gomez and Jomo, 1999). Though Mahathir was disappointed at the mentality of some Malay businessmen and their overdependence on the government for contracts/concessions and subsidies as well as their 'Ali Baba'[3] way of doing business, he still relied on the 'internal way' of addressing the problem. Fearing that the Malays would pass their new-found wealth to the Chinese, Mahathir mentioned that *"the best way to keep shares between the Bumiputera hands is to hand them over to the Bumiputera most capable of retaining them..."* [Far Eastern Economic Review (13 April 1979)]. Due to Mahathir's efforts to explicitly promote Malay capitalism, many Malay corporations (including publicly-listed corporations) that were set up to implement government projects during the 1980s and 1990s developed close links to the Malay political elite, including Mahathir himself.[4] In other words, such continuous efforts have led to the emergence of numerous crony capitalists and the proliferation of 'money politics'[5] (Gomez and Jomo, 1999). Political patronage has created avenues for politicians to gain access to large sums of money for party and general election campaigns.

A group of politically influential 'new rich' emerged in the mid-1980s, many of whom were UMNO members (Malay businessmen-cum-party members) and some Chinese businessmen.[6] The emergence of this 'new rich' has led to a concentration of corporate wealth. Selective distribution of state-controlled concessions resulted in corruption, business scandals and conflict of interests, involving senior government leaders. Business groups and firms controlled by well-connected business owners have been involved in corporate insider

---

[3] Ali Baba is the practice of using companies owned by Malays (Ali represents a Malay) to secure tenders for government projects/contracts and later on pass on the contracts/projects to the Chinese (Baba represents a Chinese) to actually run the projects. In return, Ali will get a mutually agreed amount in payment or a certain percentage of the profits for the deal (Heng, 1997). 'Ali Baba' is commonly known as the way to 'get rich quick.'

[4] Gomez and Jomo (1997) provide a list of publicly-listed corporations that are closely associated with the top three most powerful politicians in the 1990s; Mahathir himself, Anwar Ibrahim (the then Deputy Prime Minister), and Daim Zainuddin (the then Finance Minister).

[5] According to Gomez and Jomo (1999), money politics refers to a number of related issues, including political party involvement in business, abuses of power for corrupt purposes, and political patronage.

[6] Mahathir believed that it is also imperative to channel some of the state concessions to Chinese businessmen. He also recognized the importance of Chinese capital for sustaining growth and industrialization (Gomez, 1999).

trading and manipulation of stock prices, as well as in obtaining large amounts of questionable loans on favourable terms from the banks or financial institutions controlled by the government[7] (Gomez, 1999).

In summary, the way in which the NEP had been implemented (especially during Mahathir's era) resulted in an intimate relationship being forged between the state, the political party (UMNO) and business (Searle, 1999). It is contended that this growing intimacy resulted in the enmeshing and blurring of boundaries between business, politics and the state. Gomez and Jomo (1999) also opined that the spheres of government, party or private interests are no longer considered as distinct entities. National, political and private interests may be pursued in tandem, an arrangement described as 'commonness' rather than 'conflict of interest'.

THE STATE OF CORPORATE GOVERNANCE: HALF FULL OR HALF EMPTY?

The political business environment discussed earlier has implications for the development of corporate governance in Malaysia. The very existence of money politics and the complexity of political patronage networks mean that it will be very challenging for regulators to reform corporate governance and promote good governance systems in corporations, whilst at the same time penalizing those errant corporations who do not abide by the law. Very often, law enforcement and reforms of corporate governance, cannot be fully carried out due to political interference and politically influential businessmen as La Porta *et al.* (2000) comment *"what the reformers see as protection of investors, the founding families (controlling shareholders) call "expropriation of entrepreneurs." No wonder, then, that in all countries – the families have opposed legal reform"* (p. 21).

In Malaysia, though regulatory bodies such as the Securities Commission (SC) are given sufficient power vested in the Malaysian Securities Acts 1993 to act against errant companies or directors, as mentioned earlier, law enforcement is still lacking[8] as put forward by Low (2004) in his comments on the performance of corporate governance practices among East Asian nations[9]:

> *"...given the perception of a dichotomy between the "rules on the books" and the extent of enforcement by regulators of capital markets... While Malaysia scored the highest amongst the ten countries surveyed in both 2002 and 2003 for the rules and*

[7] The extent to which banks had been abused by politicians became evident when two state-controlled banks, Bank Bumiputera and SIME Bank, incurred huge losses in 1998, believed to be associated with questionable loans.

[8] See the Appendix for statistic relating to the enforcement scores of Malaysia according to the Asian Corporate Governance Association (ACGA).

[9] The country's performances was measured based on scores obtained from the annual surveys carried out by the Asian Corporate Governance Association, an independent non-profit organisation, and CLSA Emerging Markets, a leader in brokerage and investment banking.

regulations it has implemented, the perception of its enforcement of the same was abysmal." (p. 193-194)

Low's comments are shared by Gunasegaram (2007b) who opines that law enforcement is critical if laws are to be implemented effectively, and in this area Malaysian regulatory bodies fail miserably, the cause of the failure being significantly related to political interference. The Malaysian regulatory environment is found to be the 'weakest factor' in the overall corporate government framework in Malaysia, according to a report released by the Institute of International Finance (IIF) in August 2007 (Tat, 2007).

Gomez (2006) also shares the same view with Gunasegaram (2007a) that the low achievement of enforcement in Malaysia is to a certain significant extent associated with the 'selective imposition of rules and regulations' by the political executives in power when he says:

"These politicians can determine if regulatory institutions should act against businessmen, even when there is evidence of corruption. By ostensibly enforcing corporate governance provisions, politicians in control of the executive have transferred corporate assets into the hands of their allies…" (p. 132)

In essence, the controlling shareholders who have close political connections may have a greater tendency to expropriate minority shareholders because political protection can shield them from the risk of any serious legal punishment from the regulators (Berkman *et al.*, 2010). Moreover, controlling shareholders also want to seize the benefits that their connections bring to the firms, to at least cover the costs of building such connections (Qian *et al.*, 2010; Morck *et al.*, 2004). Some may argue that the value of the ownership that controlling shareholders hold would increase if protection for minority shareholders is improved. So why would they want to lobby against legal reforms? The answer provided by La Porta *et al.* (1999) is straight forward – if the potential to expropriate the minority shareholders diminishes, so does the value of control, which may be a significantly larger part of the controlling shareholders' total wealth.

The Genting's Case

Cases of acts of expropriation by controlling shareholders are not unheard of in Malaysia. One of the relatively recent, questionable transactions highlighted, involved one of the large family-controlled business groups in Malaysia, the Genting Group. The transaction involved the acquisition of the 25-storey office building for RM259 million, and lands for RM24.5 million, by one of the affiliated firms, Genting Malaysia (formerly Genting Resorts) from its parent company, Genting Berhad in September, 2009. The Genting group operates under the pyramidal ownership structure in which Genting Malaysia's ownership is controlled by Genting Berhad whose ownership is controlled by the founding family. Several issues of concern have been raised by the investors in the particular related party transaction (RPT) (Business Times, 16 December 2009): (i) Genting was criticized for not portraying the spirit of good corporate governance in the RPT, as it did not seek the approval of its minority shareholders for the RPT, (ii) since both companies are publicly-listed (Genting Malaysia and Genting Berhad), they should appoint their own 'independent' property valuer/advisor instead of sharing the same independent advisor as they did, (iii) the fact that several directors were serving as independent directors in both companies at the same time, raises the question of the independence of these directors, (iv) the fact that Genting Malaysia is a cash cow causes the investors to link the RPT as an act of cash extraction by Genting Berhad, the parent company.

The World Bank (2001), in its report on the Malaysian capital market, comments that *"there has been criticism about lack of autonomy and transparency of the regulatory authorities in Malaysia"* (p. 6). The relevance of considering the political structure and norms in Malaysia and their impact on the governance of listed firms is substantiated by the fact that *"the very strength of resistance to many of the changes needed significantly to enhance the protection of minority shareholders' rights and to improve corporate governance often exerts itself most strongly through clientelistic relationship-based systems of political governance"* (Yeoh, 2010, p. 112). Thus, political preconditions must be suitable, in the first place, in order for effective corporate governance reforms to take root. Reform that sounds impressive on paper but not in spirit, is a key concern in Malaysia. As Park (2005) notes, although there is no major distinction in the rules and regulations of corporate governance in many Asian countries, there are significant differences in relation to the market perception of their governance practices.

CRONYISM, RENT-SEEKING, AND 'REFORM'?

Cronyism has been criticized for the misallocation of resources in the Malaysian economy, causing overall waste and inefficiency in the corporate sector. As mentioned earlier, Malaysia, as with many other East Asian countries, is considered as having a relationship-based corporate system as opposed to the arm's length based system in Anglo-Saxon countries (Rajan-Zingales, 1998).[10] Rent-seeking, which is expenditure of resources to procure government-endowed rents (Khan, 2000) is considered inefficient from an economic perspective, but provides the main income in an relationship-based system. Politically-connected business groups or firms are often labelled as rent-seekers, who attempt to gain as much unearned rewards as possible through their connection with politics and the state

[10] The relationship-based system is also known as relationship-based capitalism and the arm's length-based system is also known as market-based capitalism.

(Khanna and Yafeh, 2007).[11] It is claimed that politically-connected business groups or firms have many privileges which are otherwise unavailable, such as preferential access to state-controlled concessions, subsidies, preferential or 'soft' loans, preferential bailouts and barriers to foreign competition. Rent-seeking behaviour is, however, regarded as leading towards inefficient use of a firm's resources[12], low transparency, over-reliance on the government, and having an adverse impact on the market performance of firms. Such inherent problems in the relationship-based system make the privileged firms unprepared and unable to withstand any external shock in the environment. Johnson and Mitton (2003) find that politically-connected firms in Malaysia were more seriously affected compared to non-politically connected firms during the Asian Financial Crisis of 1997-1998.

Shleifer and Vishny (1998) assert that political relationships are potentially harmful for shareholder value. The authors opine that the politician's 'helping hand' may also be a 'grabbing hand' which causes minority shareholders to be expropriated.[13] Specifically, empirical evidence (for instance, Bertrand *et al.*, 2002; Friedman *et al.*, 2003; Cheung *et al.*, 2006) shows that business groups are particularly conducive to expropriation such as 'tunnelling'[14] and related party transactions (RPTs)[15] at the expense of the minority shareholders of the affiliated firms in the group. This is particularly true for large business groups with close political connections in Malaysia, in which the elite controlling shareholders often control a substantial portion of the country's wealth. It is reported by Claessens *et al.* (2000) that, in Malaysia, the top 15 families control corporate assets worth 76.2 percent of the country's GDP compared to only 2.1 percent in Japan and 2.9 percent in the US. This percentage is one of the highest in Asia and suggests that controlling shareholders of large business groups could be highly influential and 'lobby' the government into implementing policies that are in their favour and 'interfere' in policies that are 'unfriendly' to them.

Authors such as Searle (1999) and Yeoh (2010) suggest that political connections are more prevalent in large publicly-listed businesses when it is commented that *"it is in big publicly-listed businesses that the nexus between business, politics and state is most clearly displayed"* (Yeoh, 2010, p.97). The consequences of letting a small number of large business groups control a large portion of a country's wealth are explained by Morck *et al.* (2005, p. 657):

[11] Corruption is conduct that is sometimes associated with rent-seeking.

[12] As substantial company resources are being used to seek and secure rents.

[13] See Yeoh (2010) for a compilation of some of the examples of political involvement in Malaysian publicly-listed firms and mistreatment of minority shareholders.

[14] Tunnelling is the term introduced by Johnson *et al.* (2000) to describe the activity of transferring assets and resources out of firms by controlling shareholders.

[15] A related-party transaction takes place when a transaction is entered into by at least two entities—where one has control over the other, or where the parties come under the same control of another (CFA, 2009)

"...entrusting the governance of huge slices of a country's corporate sector to a tiny elite can bias capital allocation, retard capital market development, obstruct entry by outsider entrepreneurs, and retard growth. Furthermore, to preserve their privileged positions under the status quo, such elites might invest in political connections to stymie the institutional development of capital markets and to erect a variety of entry barriers."

In short, due to the close link between politics and business, the proliferation of money politics and cronyism[16] has adversely impacted corporate governance because as put forward by Yeoh (2010, p. 102):

"...they culminated in a culture where the ruling elite and their corporate patrons/clients/proxies (most being major shareholders/owners of public-listed firms) as well as captive market regulators are involved in numerous blatant scandalous, manipulative and even fraudulent activities in the capital markets, often to the detriment of minority shareholders."

CONCLUSION

Corporate governance practices of a country are closely associated with the standard of *public* governance of the country. From this discussion, it can be concluded that rent-seeking activities which create and protect corporate profits can be rampant in countries with unsatisfactory public governance. Thus, it is doubtful that the quality of corporate governance can be improved if the public governance level is still at an unsatisfactory level, whereby businesses collude with politics 'in search of rents' and 'in protection of rents' for their businesses. Regulators must be fully empowered in enforcing rules and regulations pertaining to corporate governance, despite expected resistance from certain groups such as political elites or government officials who are allies of the controlling shareholders of the business groups. For that to happen, political will is important to first reform public governance, in order to effectively control problems such as cronyism, corruption and money politics and to reduce political interference in businesses.

[16] The latest development in the political scenario in this country shows that money politics, corruption and cronyism in UMNO have become rampant over the years. As an illustration, the number of cases of complaints regarding money politics/corruption during the UMNO party election year has increased over the years, and in the most recent UMNO party election which was held in 2009, a staggering 900 cases of complaints regarding money politics were reported to the party disciplinary committee (The Star, 9 November 2008, 17 March 2009).

REFERENCES

Adam, K. (1997) The Politics of Redress: South African Style Affirmative Action, *The Journal of Modern African Studies*, 35(2), 231-249.

Berkman, H., Cole, R. A. and Fu, L. J. (2010) Political Connection and Minority Shareholder Protection: Evidence from Security-Market Regulation in China, *Journal of Financial and Quantitative Analysis*, 6(45), 1392-1427.

Bertrand, M., Mehta, P. and Mullainathan, S. (2002) Ferreting Out Tunneling: An Application to Indian Business Groups, *Quarterly Journal of Economics*, 117, 121-148.

CFA Institute (2009) *Related-Party Transactions – A Cautionary Tale for Investors in Asia*, Centre for Financial Market Integrity, CFA Institute, Charlottesville.

Cheung, Y. L., Rau, P. R. and Stouraitis, A. (2006) Tunneling, Propping, and Expropriation: Evidence from Connected Party Transactions in Hong Kong, *Journal of Financial Economics*, 82, 343-386.

Claessens, S., Djankov, S. and Lang, L. H. P. (2000) The Separation of Ownership and Control in East Asian Corporations, *Journal of Financial Economics*, 58, 81-112.

Faccio, M. (2006) Politically Connected Firms, *American Economic Review*, 96(1), 369-386.

Fazilah, A. S. (2002) Ownership Structure in the Malaysian Corporation Sector: Its Impact on Corporate Governance, Performance, Financing and Investment Patterns, *Working Paper Series*, 23, Centre on Regulation and Competition, University of Manchester, Manchester.

Friedman, E., Johnson, S. and Mitton, T. (2003) Propping and Tunneling, *Journal of Comparative Economics*, 31, 732-750.

Gomez, E. T. (1999) *Chinese Business in Malaysia: Accumulation, Accommodation and Ascendance*, Curzon, Surrey.

Gomez, E. T. (2006) Malaysian Business Groups: The State and Capital Development in the Post-currency Crisis Period, in *Business Groups in East Asia: Financial Crisis, Restructuring, and New Growth*, Chang S. (Ed.), Oxford University Press, Oxford.

Gomez, E. T. and Jomo, K. S. (1997) *Malaysia's Political Economy: Politics, Patronage, and Profits*, Cambridge University Press, Cambridge.

Gomez, E. T. and Jomo, K. S. (1999) *Malaysia's Political Economy: Politics, Patronage, and Profits*, revised edition, Cambridge University Press, Cambridge.

Gunasegaram, P. (2007a) Taking Miscreants to Task, *The Edge*, 11th June.

Gunasegaram, P. (2007b) Question Time: High-profile Cases Still Waiting to be Resolved, *The Edge*, 12th May.

Heng, P. K. (1997) The New Economic Policy and The Chinese Community In Peninsular Malaysia, *The Developing Economies*, 35(3), 262-292.

Horii, K. (1991) Disintegration of the Colonial Economic Legacies and Social Restructuring in Malaysia, *The Developing Economies*, 29(4), 281-313.

Johnson, S, La Porta, R, Lopez-de-Silanes, F. and Shleifer, A. (2000) Tunneling, *American Economic Review*, 90, 22-27.

Johnson, S. and Mitton, T. (2003) Cronyism and Capital Controls: Evidence from Malaysia, *Journal of Financial Economics*, 67(2), 351-382.

Jomo, K. S. (1988) *A Question of Class: Capital, the State and Uneven Development in Malaya*, Oxford University Press, Singapore.

Khan, M. H. (2000) Rent-seeking as Process, in Khan, M. H. and Jomo, K. S. (Eds.), *Rents, Rent-seeking and Economic Development: Theory and Evidence in Asia*, Cambridge University Press, Cambridge.

Khanna, T. and Yafeh, Y. (2007) Business Groups in Emerging Markets: Paragons or Parasites? *Journal of Economic Literature*, 45, 331-372.

La Porta, R., Lopez-De-Silanes, F. and Shleifer, A. (1999) Corporate Ownership around the World, *Journal of Finance*, 54(2), 471-517.

La Porta, R., Lopez-de-Silanes, F., Shleifer, A. and Vishny, R. (2000) Investor Protection and Corporate Governance, *Journal of Financial Economics*, *58*(1-2), 3-27.

Low, C. K. (2004) A Road Map for Corporate Governance in East Asia, *Northwestern Journal of International Law & Business*, 25, 165-203.

Malaysia (1971) *Second Malaysia Plan, 1971-1975*, Kuala Lumpur: Government Printers.

Morck, R. (2005) How to Eliminate Pyramidal Business Groups: The Double Taxation of Intercorporate Dividends and Other Incisive Uses of Tax Policy, *NBER/Tax Policy & the Economy*, 19(1), 135-179.

Morck, R., Stangeland, D. A. and Yeung, B. (2004) Inherited Wealth, Corporate Control, and Economic Growth: The Canadian Disease, in Morck R. (Ed.), *Concentrated Corporate Ownership*, University of Chicago Press, Chicago.

Morck, R., Wolfenzon, D. and Yeung, B. (2005) Corporate Governance, Economic Entrenchment, and Growth, *Journal of Economic Literature*, 43(3), 655-720.

Park, K. S. (2005) Stock-take of Developments in Corporate Governance in Asia, *Paper Presented at the 2005 Asian Roundtable on Corporate Governance*, Bali, Indonesia.

Qian, M., Pan, H. and Yeung, B. Y. (2010) Expropriation of Minority Shareholders in Politically Connected Firms, *Finance and Corporate Governance Conference 2011 Paper*, Social Science Research Network.

Rajan, R. and Zingales, L. (1998) Financial Dependence and Growth, *American Economic Review*, 58, 559-586.

Searle, P. (1999) The Riddle of Malaysian Capitalism: Rent-Seekers or Real Capitalists? *ASAA Southeast Asia Publications Series*, Allen & Unwin, Australia.

Shleifer, A. and Vishny, R. (1998) *The Grabbing Hand: Government Pathologies and Their Cures*, Harvard University Press, Cambridge, Mass.

Snodgrass, D. R. (1980) *Inequality and Economic Development in Malaysia*, Oxford University Press, Kuala Lumpur.

Tat, H. K. (2007) Enforcement the Key, *The Edge*, 19th November.

Verma, V. (2004) *Malaysia: State and Civil Society in Transition*, Malaysia. Lynne Rienner Publishers Inc.

World Bank (2001) Report on the Observance of Standards and Codes (ROSC): Corporate Governance Country Assessment: Malaysia, available at: http://www.worldbank.org/ifa/rosc_cg_malaysia.html, accessed 17th November, 2009.

Yeoh, K. (2010) *The Behaviour of Individual Investors in Malaysia: A Governance Perspective*, Unpublished PhD Thesis, Newcastle Business School, University of Northumbria at Newcastle, United Kingdom.

APPENDIX

The following Tables below show comparisons between Malaysia, Singapore and Hong Kong in terms of the scores (over a scale of 10) of their corporate governance practices:

Country	*Score on Regulations (2002)*	*Score on Regulations (2003)*	*Score on Regulations (2004)*	*Score on Regulations (2005)*	*Score on Regulations (2007)*	*Score on Regulations (2010)*
Hong Kong	8	8	6.6	6.4	6.0	5.9
Malaysia	9	9	7.1	5.9	4.4	4.9
Singapore	8	8.5	7.9	7.4	7.0	6.5

Country	*Score on Enforcemen t (2002)*	*Score on Enforcemen t (2003)*	*Score on Enforcemen t (2004)*	*Score on Enforcemen t (2005)*	*Score on Enforcemen t (2007)*	*Score on Enforcemen t (2010)*
Hong Kong	6	6.5	5.8	5.8	5.6	6.3
Malaysia	2.5	3.5	5.0	4.9	3.5	3.8
Singapore	7	7.5	6.5	5.6	5.0	6.0

Sources: Low (2004) for 2002 to 2004 data and 2005 to 2010 data are extracted from 'CG Watch 2005', 'CG Watch 2007' and 'CG Watch 2010' reports which are downloadable from the Asian Corporate Governance Association (ACGA) website: http://www.acga-asia.org, accessed 24th January, 2011.

Malaysia's 'scores on enforcement' remained low and behind those of Singapore and Hong Kong and its 'scores on regulations' have declined more than that of Singapore and Hong Kong since 2005.

Islamic Work Ethics (IWE) as A Mechanism for Good Governance Among Employees of Banking Institutions In Malaysia

Siti Khadijah Ab. Manan, Ahmad Saiful Azlin Puteh Salin and Norlela Kamaluddin

Accounting Research Institute, Malaysia

ABSTRACT

Current literature in the field of management shows that the study on work ethics is gaining popularity among researchers for a very obvious reason, namely due to the threat of moral hazards. Cases of corporate scandals and collapses provide evidence that moral misconducts among employees have contributed to the financial disaster of many companies. Hence, it is believed that practicing Islamic work ethics is one way to ensure that an organization is well governed. This study would therefore attempt to investigate the practices of Islamic Work Ethics (IWE) among employees of banking institutions in Malaysia. As banking institutions are important and considered as the backbone of the country's economy, it is important to ensure that the work ethics of the employees remain genuine and sound. A survey method is employed to assess the IWE of the the employees. The findings of this study indicate that the bank employees exhibited good IWE practice.

Keywords: *Accountability, Effort, Honesty, Islamic Work Ethics, Shari'ah, Teamwork*

INTRODUCTION

A good governance structure is necessary for safety and soundness of an institution. This is so as the institution has many different layers of stakeholders to be pleased, in terms of interest and objectives. Since the major financial crisis in 1997-1998 that hit the Malaysian economy, the government has taken robust actions to build strong and solid fundamentals of financial and banking institutions. A lot of policies and actions have been implemented, such as benchmarking to the Basel Accord, improvising the code of corporate governance, executing capital and financial markets master plan, gradual liberalization, and leveraging the strength by encouraging banks to merge. These actions have been taken to make the banking system vigilant and competitive, for contributing to the growth and development of the country.

Nevertheless, this growth and improvement is in a risky position, if the ethics of the actors and players in this industry are at stake. As banking institutions are important and considered as the backbone of the country's economy, it is important to ensure that the work ethics of the staff remain genuine and sound. This is substantial, so that fraud and unethical practices are not committed in the banking sectors. Players in the financial sectors are not safe from financial fraud and scandals. The case of Lehmann Brothers, Anglo Irish Bank, Bernard Madoff Investment, AIG and Meryll Lynch are examples of scandals that caused the US to suffer the sub-prime crisis that also adversely affected the economy of many countries around the world.

Knowing this, it is crucial to understand the level of ethical practices of the employees of the banking institutions in Malaysia, thereby indicating the soundness of the governance of the institutions. Therefore, the main objective of this study is to explore the level of IWE practices among bank employees in Malaysia.

The article is organized in the following order. Section two provides an in-depth discussion on the concept of work and work ethics from an Islamic perspective. Section three presents the review of literature on the IWE dimensions. Section four elaborates on the method and data of the study. Section five presents the results and discussions of the findings. The final section presents the conclusion and directions for future research.

Islamic Perspective on Work and Work Ethics

Workers play an important role in ensuring the smooth functioning of an organization. Having morally and ethically behaved workers in an organization, will have a favourable impact on the organization itself. There is a genuine belief that Islam emphasizes on the creative and productive efforts as a source of happiness and accomplishment. This is in line with what Allah promises us in the Quran: "*...Allah promised you His forgiveness and bounties*" (2:268). The verse implies that forgiveness and bounties are promised to those who put strenuous efforts in fulfilling their work responsibly in accordance with Allah's will. Instead, begging and living as a parasite on the labours of others are condemned by Islamic teaching. In this regard, the Prophet Muhammed (P.B.U.H) has preached that: *"No one eats better food than that which he eats out of his own labour"* (Bukhari,no. 1979). Islam perceives work as an *ibadah* (a religious duty) and *jihad* (cause of Allah). Prophet (P.B.U.H) has preached: "The honest, trustworthy merchant will be with the Prophets, siddeeqs and martyrs." (At-Tirmidhi, no. 1209).

Work is a dedicative effort in striving to further self interest economically, socially and psychologically, to sustain social prestige, to advance societal welfare and reaffirm faith. In other words, work is a means to safeguard the five essential human needs, namely their *din* (faith), their *nafs* (human self), *`aql* (intellect), their *nasl* (posterity) and their *mal* (wealth). Hence, it is important for human beings to pursue whatever work is available, whenever it is available, subject to the will of Allah SWT as Allah SWT has decreed in the Quran: "... *disperse through the land and seek of the bounty of Allah*" (62:10).

The concept of work as an *ibadah* (religious duties) and *jihad* (striving for something), ascertains that the involvement and participation in economic activities (work) is not merely a means to sustain a thriving and healthy society, but also a divine call. According to Ali (1988), the value of work in IWE is derived from the accompanying intentions, rather than from the results of work. Thus, the most essential feature of work as an *ibadah* and *jihad* is *niyyah* (intention). In Islam, intention (*niyyah*) of every man's action must be ultimately for Allah's SWT alone. Hence, work must be conducted sincerely (*ikhlas*) for the sake of Allah's pleasures. This has been explained in the Qur'an: *"Say; verily I am commanded to serve Allah with sincere devotion"* (39:14). Sincere intention will ensure that the work effectively and efficiently follows the revealed guidance, which in turn contributes to *al falah* (successful in this world and hereafter). In addition, Ali (1988, p.577) has described work as :

"... *an obligatory activity and a virtue in light of the needs of man and the necessity to establish equilibrium in one's individual and social life. Work enables man to be independent and is a source of self-respect, satisfaction and fulfillment. Success and progress on the job depend on hard work and commitment to one's job. Commitment to works also involves a desire to improve community and societal welfare. Society would have fewer problems if each person were committed to his work and avoided unethical methods of wealth accumulation. Creative work and cooperation are not only a source of happiness but considered noble deeds too."*

The Islamic view on work is futher elucidated in the concept of work ethics. Basically, the Islamic system comprises of three main fundamental teachings, in which the first is *aqidah* or a strong belief in the Oneness of Allah; the second is *ibadah* or one's submission and obedience to Allah; while the third is *akhlaq*. This is indeed the Islamic ethical system that work ethics fall under (Beekun, 2004). Basically, *akhlaq* refers to one's good behaviour, manner, attitude or values guided by the *Qur'an* and *Sunnah*. Hence, it is subjected to the evaluation of Allah SWT: *"... verily the most honoured of you in the sight of Allah is the most righteous of you."*(49:13). *Akhlaq* differs from the conventional view of "do no harm," because Islam argues that this can also imply that not to harm others may be neutral, in the sense that one may not do any good either. Therefore, Imam Al- Ghazali had refined the view by recommending three ways of doing good, so as to imply the true meaning of *akhlaq*. First and foremost, one has to show beneficence (*ihsan*) to others. Second, one has to refrain from harming others. Lastly, one who harms others is considered irreligious and immoral. The three attributes are in conformity with Allah's revelation in the Qur'an: *"We sent yee not, but as a mercy for all creatures."* (21:107). Islam uses several other terms to describe the concept of *akhlaq* such as *khayr* (goodness), *birr* (righteousness), *qist* (equity), *'adl* (justice), *haqiqah* (truth), *ma'ruf* (known and approved), and *taqwa* (piety). Pious actions are described as *salihat,* and impious actions are described as *sayyiat* Abuznaid (2009). Islam also provides mankind with the most influential model to uphold *akhlaq* in every activity as stated in the Qur'an: "*We have indeed in the Apostle of Allah a beautiful pattern of (conduct) for anyone whose hope is in Allah and the Final Day, and who engages much in the praise of Allah*"(33:21).

While the term IWE refers to a set of moral principles that distinguishes what is right from what is wrong in the Islamic context (Beekun, 2004), and is originally based on the *Qur'an* and the *Sunnah* of the Prophet Muhammad (P.B.U.H) (Ali, 2005; Rizk, 2008). Hence, in this study, it is suggested that IWE may be defined as a set of values and principles that guide individuals' rights and responsibilities at work based on Islamic teachings that follow doctrines in the *Qur*'an and *Sunnah.* In other words, the teachings of Islam emphasizes that it is Islamic values that dominate behaviour (work ethics) of an individual, and not the other way around. The following are examples of the *Quranic* verses and the *Sunnah* regarding IWE:

a. Allah says: "*O ye who believe! Fear Allah and be with those who are true (in word and deed)*" (9:119).
b. Allah says: "*Allah commands justice, the doing of good …*"(16:90).
c. Allah says: "*Say; verily I am commanded to serve Allah with sincere devotion*" (39:14).
d. Prophet (P.B.U.H) has preached: "The honest, trustworthy merchant will be with the Prophets, siddeeqs and martyrs." (At-Tirmidhi, no. 1209)
e. Prophet (P.B.U.H) advised: "*Allah loves that when anyone does a job, he does it perfectly.*" (Al-Bayhaqi, no. 4915)

The following section discusses in specific detail the Islamic work ethics, particularly the variables of this study.

ISLAMIC WORK ETHICS (IWE)

Discussions on IWE will be based on the four primary dimensions of IWE set by Ali & Falcon (1995) and Ali & al-Owaihan (2008). The four dimensions are: effort, competition, transparency, and morally responsible conduct. In this study however, the dimensions are refined into a broader perspectives, as suggested by Norlela and Siti Khadijah (2010), namely effort, teamwork, accountability, and honesty.

Effort

Effort in Islam is held in the highest regard. Islam encourages humans to acquire skills and technology, and highly praises those who strive, in order to earn a living as stated in the Quran: *"Whoever works righteousness, man or woman and has faith verily to him will We give a new life, a life that is good and pure and We will bestow on such their reward according to the best of his action"* (16:97). Islam also demands its adherents to be efficient and proficient that is to do more than what is minimally required as mentioned by Allah: *"Verily Allah commands that you establish justice and be efficient and proficient"* (16:90). Therefore, a good individual should always feel obliged to put in extra effort, time (not over time), and interest so that he would provide more than what is minimally required.

Islam emphasizes that the exerted effort of an individual should be linked to *itqan*, *istiqamah* and *tawakkal*. *Itqan* means knowledgeable and conscientiousness in all endeavours (Syed Othman et.al., 1998). Islam encourages all its adherents to acquire the necessary *'ilm* (knowledge of things) before executing any action (work). The Prophet (P.B.U.H) advised: *"Whoever wish for the world need to have knowledge, whoever wish for the hereafter need to have knowledge, whoever wish for both need to have knowledge*" (Nik Mohamed Affandi, 2002) and narrated by Abu Hurairah, the Messenger of Allah said: "...when the power or authority comes in the hand of unfit persons, then wait for the Hour (Doomsday)." (Bukhari, no. 56)

Knowledge is not simply a case of "the what," but is also the skill required to perform the task. *Itqan* also requires man's effort to discover (*tadabbur*) Allah's bounties. In this regard, the Prophet (P.B.U.H) propagated that: The Prophet Muhammad (peace be upon him) said: "Acquiring knowledge in (the) company (of others) for an hour in the night is better than spending the whole night in prayer." (At-Tirmidhi, no.91).

Application of the acquired knowledge must be implemented with conscientiousness. Conscientiousness requires the presence of perseverance, passion and commitment in individual performance. Conscientiousness must be followed with continuous self evaluation (*muhasabah*), in order to correct the wrongs and to improve on the good actions as Allah has mentioned in the Quran: *"You are the best of peoples, evolved for mankind enjoining what is right and forbidding what is wrong"* (3:110). *Istiqamah* means consistency and passion for excellence. Islam admits excellence as a virtue and encourages its adherents to excel in everything that they do. Prophet (P.B.U.H) advised: *"Allah loves that when anyone does a job, he does it perfectly."* (Al-Bayhaqi, no. 4915).

Islam also demands its adherents to be efficient and proficient, that is to do more than what is minimally required. Allah has decreed: *"Verily Allah command that you establish justice and be efficient and proficient"* (16:90). Therefore, a good Muslim will always feel obliged to put in extra effort, time (not over time), and interest, so that he would provide more than what is minimally required. Furthermore, *istiqamah* also requires the Muslims to be patient (*sabr*) while undertaking any task or job entrusted to them. Allah has decreed: *"O ye who believe! Persevere in patience and constancy; vie in such perseverance; strengthen each other; and fear Allah that ye may prosper"* (3:200). Patience has two aspects (Syed Othman et. al. 1998). *First,* mental patience that resists the hunger of desires and anger. Mental patience is required in controlling anger and greed for wealth. *Second,* bodily patience which is endurance of physical pain felt in performing devotional or non devotional acts. Hence, patience can be divided into three; *first,* patience in carrying commandments; *second,* patience in avoiding *maksiat*; and *last,* patience in facing difficulties and hardships. Consequently, patience is importantly required in work to face any disagreement, temptation of taking bribery and laziness.

Tawakkal means surrendering oneself to Allah the Almighty solely. This is indeed one's ultimate effort after *itqan* and *istiqamah*. Allah commands us: *"But on Allah put your trust if you have faith"*(5:23). However, the concept of *tawakkal* must be incorporated with *itqan* and *istiqamah* as well as supplication (*du'a*). Allah has decreed: *"When My servants ask thee concerning Me, I am indeed close to them. I listen to the prayer of every suppliant when he calleth on Me. Let them also with a will listen to my call and believe in Me that they may walk in the right way"* (2:186). Therefore, *tawakkal* is the essential final step of an effort. *Tawakkal* will guide man to accept virtuous or deficient and consequences positively result from his endeavour. Hence, the concept of *tawakkal* infuses the spirit of perseverance in all work which in turn ensures the excellent quality of one's effort. Furthermore, Allah promises to provide adequate bounties to he who surrenders himself to Allah: *"... and if anyone puts his trust in Allah, sufficient is Allah for him. For Allah will surely accomplish His purpose. Verily for all things has Allah appointed a due portion"* (65:3).

Teamwork

Islam promotes teamwork, thus employees can help each other to fulfill their needs in this world and the hereafter as stated in the Quran: *"... and we raise some of them above others in ranks, so that some may command work from others ..."* (43:32) and *"And those in whose wealth is a recognized right for the (needy) who asks and him who is prevented (for some reason)"* (70:24-25). Competition in team work must be executed fairly, justly and honestly, and can be realized through the implementation of the concept of *mu'awanah, 'adl* and *syura*. *Mu'awanah* refers to cooperation among individuals to promote good and forbid evil as Allah has stated in the Quran: *"... help ye one another in righteousness and piety, but help ye one another in sin and rancor. Fear Allah for Allah is strict in punishment"* (5:2). Thus, Islam encourages competition among man in preventing immoral action, as well as inciting virtuous action in his work place. This task can be effectively and efficiently performed by imposing the spirit of *ukhuwwah* (brotherhood) as decreed by Allah in the Quran: *"The believers are but a single brotherhood. So make peace and reconciliation between your two contending brothers. And fear Allah that ye may receive mercy"* (49:10) and also notified by the Prophet (P.B.U.H): Narrated by Ma'rur, I saw Abu Dhar wearing a Burd (garment) and his slave too was wearing a Burd, so I said (to Abu Dhar), "If you take this (Burda of your slave) and wear it (along with yours), you will have a nice suit (costume) and you may give him another garment." Abu Dhar said, "There was a quarrel between me and another man whose mother was a non-Arab and I called her bad names. The man mentioned (complained about) me to the Prophet. The Prophet said, "Did you abuse so-and-so?" I said, "Yes" He said, "Did you call his mother bad names?" I said, "Yes". He said, "You still have the traits of (the Pre-Islamic period of) ignorance." I said. "(Do I still have ignorance) even now in my old age?" He said, "Yes, they (slaves or servants) are your brothers, and Allah has put them under your command. So the one under whose hand Allah has put his brother, should feed him of what he eats, and give him dresses of what he wears, and should not ask him to do a thing beyond his capacity. And if at all he asks him to do a hard task, he should help him therein." (Bukhari, no.76). Thus in Islam, competition among man is carried out without oppression, and injustice, and instead it employs the value of cooperation; while *'Adl* (justice) means the rendering of trust where it is due. Islam demands human beings to uphold justice in every action as decreed by Allah: *"Allah commands justice and the doing of good"* (16:90). In Islam, justice is prevailed in promoting positive virtues like honesty, moderation and generosity, as well as prohibiting evils like eliminating *risywah* (bribery), greed and extravagance. Thus, Islam prohibits *zulm* that is the opposite of *'adl*. The Prophet (P.B.U.H) warned about doing *zulm*: *"Beware of injustice for injustice will be equivalent to darkness on the Day of judgment"* (Bukhari, no. 2447). *'Adl* is also significantly related to *ihsan* which refers to right action, goodness, charity and proficiency. Other meanings of *ihsan* can be extracted from the Sunnah whereby the Prophet (P.B.U.H) was asked: "… What al-Ihsan is? Upon this he (the Holy Prophet) said: (Al-Ihsan implies) that you fear Allah as if you are seeing Him, and though you see Him not, verily He is seeing you. He (the inquirer) said: You (have) told the truth." (Muslim, no. 6). *Ihsan* will educate man to voluntarily sacrifice extra effort, time, and wealth, as an addition to the compulsory requirement in rendering the rights or trust. In turn it will enhance productivity. *Syura* (mutual consultation) refers to collective mutual consultation and empowerment. Allah has mentioned in the Quran: "*Those who hearken to their Lord, and establish regular prayer, who conduct their affairs by mutual consultation, who spend out of what We bestow on them for sustenance…"* (42:38). Hence *syura* in team building refers to the participative work force moulded in the spirit of oneness. For example, by sharing power such as power in decision making, people basically respect and trust one's competency, strength and reliability. This in turn enhances creativity, innovation and passion for improved quality and productivity (Syed Othman et. al. 2008). Furthermore, it will strengthen and intensify the efforts and relationship among human beings in the team building.

Honesty

Honesty could mean telling the truth even though it is difficult to do so (Norlela et al. , 2010). In other words, the person does not conceal anything that should be disclosed. If he is an accountant, he has to report all the transactions accurately according to the accounting steps and procedures in place (Atiyah, 1993). The Almighty Allah had instructed us to be honest in any sort of dealings. Allah says: "*O ye who believe! Fear Allah and be with those who are true (in word and deed)*" (9:119). In the same context, the Prophet (P.B.U.H) stated: Abdullah reported, the Messenger of Allah (P.B.U.H) said: "Truthfulness leads to righteousness and righteousness leads to Paradise. A man may speak the truth until he is recorded with Allah as truthful. Lying leads to wickedness and wickedness leads to the Fire. A man may tell lies until he is recorded with Allah as a liar." (Muslim, no. 6308).

The Prophet (P.B.U.H) strongly warned that: "It is narrated on the authority of Abu Hurairah that the Messenger of Allah (may peace be upon him) happened to pass by a heap of eatables (corn). He thrust his hand in that (heap) and his fingers were moistened. He said to the owner of that heap of eatables (corn): What is this? He replied: Messenger of Allah, these have been drenched by rainfall. He (the Holy Prophet) remarked: Why did you not place this (the drenched part of the heap) over other eatables so that the people could see it ? He who deceives is not of me (is not my follower). (Muslim, no. 183). Hence, whoever knows a defect in something is obliged to disclose it. At the same time, the Prophet (P.B.U.H) motivates the honest person by saying that: "The honest, trustworthy merchant will be with the Prophets, siddeeqs and martyrs." (At-Tirmidhi, no. 1209).

Honesty and the ability to act with integrity lie not in the act of "never speaking a false word, " rather in humans choosing to "always speak words and perform acts that create safe, caring, and healthy spaces for human development" (Howatt, 2002). Honesty also is the belief that one stands by his word as well as the belief that one is interested in the company's welfare, and will not take unexpected actions that will negatively impact the company (Wetzels, Ruyter & Birgele, 1998). Without honesty and integrity, an administrator cannot build trust. Without trust, a co-operative and collaborative relationship with the others cannot be attained (Scarnati, 1997). Trust is the catalyst that makes it possible for organizations to function. It is the bonding agent that holds personal and business relationships together. It manifests itself in the form of concrete deeds and actions. Trust breeds credibility, thereby generating credible, believable and trusted people..

Accountability

Allah wants man to know whether his acts and deeds might be good or evil. Man ought to know himself and learn about his points of strength and points of weakness, so as to reach a balanced physical, emotional and spiritual quotient, and not become conceited by his success, or become desperate if he encounters a certain loss or failure. As Allah mentioned in the Holy Qur'an: *"O you who believe! Be careful of (your duty to) Allah, and let every soul consider what it has sent on for the morrow, and be careful of (your duty to) Allah; surely Allah is Aware of what you do. And be not like those who forsook Allah, so He made them forsake their own souls: these it is that are the transgressors. Not alike are the inmates of the fire and the dwellers of the garden: the dwellers of the garden are they that are the achievers"* (59: 18-20).

Accountability is frequently described as the means by which individuals and organizations report to a recognized authority (or authorities), and are held responsible for their actions (Ebrahim, 2005). Accountability exists when there is a bonding between one party with another. Hence, individuals or organizations have certain rights over the conduct of another, as well as seek reasons for actions taken and the individual or organization is answerable to a higher authority for the action taken, and for handling the resources received (Hasan & Siti Nabiha, 2010). This internal dimension of accountability is motivated by a "felt responsibility" as expressed through individual action and organizational mission. In other words, accountability is trustworthiness. People are considered to be trustworthy when they behave in ways expected of them in the absence of surveillance. They do not merely comply with external forces such as surveillance pressures, but also internalized the behaviours (Brockner, Siegel, Phyllis, Daly, Joseph, Martin, & Tyler, 1997). A trustworthy person is a person who will keep the trust entrusted to him responsibly and faithfully. Allah says in the Qur'an: *"Allah does command you to render back your trust to those to whom they are due; and when ye judge between man and man that ye judge with justice; verily how excellent is the teaching which He gives you for Allah is He who hearth and sees all things"* (4:58). In this regard, every Muslim has an 'account' with *Allah*, in which all good and all bad deeds are 'recorded'; an account which will continue until death, for *Allah* discloses to the people their accounts on the day of judgment (4:62). The Messenger of Allah (P.B.U.H.) has mentioned self-accountability as: "The wise person is one who holds himself accountable and works for what comes after death. And the weak, impotent person is one whose self follows its vain desires and he (simply) puts his hope in Allah" (At-Tirmidhi, no. 2459).

Fulfilling one's trust could mean fulfilling the rights of the person who gives the trust to you (Abdurrahman, 2005). In other words, as a trustee you should render the trust that had been given to you back to the owner. As far as trustworthiness in work is concerned, an individual worker should fulfil his obligations at the workplace to his best. If he is given a task to complete, he has to perform the task responsibly and accountably. He will exert his effort to the best, as he believes that laziness and absenteeism are vice. He will always try to ensure that the task given is not overdue (Rice, 1999). In other words, he will meet the deadlines of the task given to him. He will emphasize on excellence and good quality of work, as he realizes that such attitudes are promoted. The Prophet (P.B.U.H) says: *"Allah likes that when someone does anything, it must be done perfectly well"* (Al-Bayhaqi, no. 4915).

Method and Data Collection

This study employs the survey method, whereby primary data are collected via the distribution of questionnaires. The population of this study comprises of bank employees who work in a commercial area in Klang Valley in Malaysia. In this study, simple random sampling was used to draw a total of 500 samples, in order to have a precise and unbiased sample.

A set of questionnaires were distributed to each of the selected samples via personally-administered survey. Several sets of Likert-scale statements were posed to the samples to get their perspectives on IWE practice. Statements relating to IWE dimensions namely effort, teamwork, honesty and accountability are expected to be responded by indicating the chosen scale of 1 = Strongly Disagree up to 10 = Strongly Agree. The internal consistency and reliability of the instrument used in this study can be considered good as Cronbach Alpha values (effort=0.676, teamwork=0.833, honesty=0.881, accountability=0.946) are good, and therefore acceptable for the study.

Out of the total 500 distributed questionnaires, 383 (or 76.6 percent response rate) questionnaires were returned and used for analysis of this study. This favourable response could mainly be due to the direct approach by the researchers in collecting the data.

Findings and Analysis

The following sub-sections present the demographic profile of the respondents and discusses the analysis of the study's findings which comprised the practice of IWE among employees of the banks.

Demographic Profile of the Respondents

A total of 383 questionnaires were usable and processed for the study. Of this total, 62 percent are female and the majority (80.7) percent of the respondents are Malay. Only a handful of them are Chinese and Indian (11.7 percent and 7.3 percent respectively). This could imply that many of the subordinate employees approached are Malays, who are not involved in top management of the banks.

Generally, the respondents are considered young as 62.1 percent of them were aged below 35 years. As for the respondents' marital status, 68.2 percent of them were married, while the other 29.7 percent are still single. As far as the respondents' religious background is concerned, most that responded were Muslims (80.7 percent) and very few are Christians (6.8 percent) and Hindus (8.9 percent).

With regard to educational levels, many of the respondents had either diplomas (39 percent) or bachelor's degree (24.1 percent), and quite a significant number of them (28.3 percent) had completed secondary school and the rest of them had a professional certificate (6.3 percent) or post-graduate degrees (2.4 percent).

IWE Practice Among Employees

The respondents were assessed on their IWE practice by asking them to indicate their level of agreement on the statements relating to each of IWE dimensions namely effort, teamwork, honesty and accountability. The following sub-sections elaborate the employees' IWE practice.

Employees Effort

Effort may comprise of perseverance, passion and commitment in individual performance, thereby a good ethical employee would do more than what is minimally required, and he has consistency and passion for excellence [9]. In this study, employees are given the following statements to capture the attributes of effort.

Table 1: Employees' Effort at Work

Items	*Criteria*	*Mean*	*Std. Dev.*
1.	I will always try to finish my work within office hours every day.	8.43	1.769
2.	I rarely take extra hours to finish the job given to me.	6.75	2.563
3.	I took coffee break only if necessary.	7.18	2.624
4.	Most often, I take my coffee while working.	8.21	1.900
5.	I always complete my personal duties e.g. prayer within the specified lunch hour.	8.41	1.561
6.	I constantly strive at work to achieve better results.	8.68	1.423

The mean outputs shown in Table 1 indicates that generally the employees of the bank showed good commitment at work, and have passion for excellence. Nevertheless, the employees could hardly go home on time as they have to take extra hours (item 2; mean 6.75) to finish their work, although they tried hard to complete their task within the specified time given (item 1; mean 8.43).

Employees Honesty

An honest person does not conceal anything that should be disclosed. In other words, he will tell the truth even though it is hard to do. In his work, an honest person will stand by his word, and he has the ability to act with integrity. The following table shows the list of statements that capture honesty. The mean scores of each attribute for honesty in this study are greater than 8. This could imply that the employees are honest in their work.

Table 2: Employees Honesty at Work

Items	*Criteria*	*Mean*	*Std. Dev.*
1.	I will not call sick deliberately.	8.71	1.738
2.	I rarely take leave during office hours to do my personal matter.	8.48	1.689
3.	I will not deliberately utilize office equipment for personal use.	8.32	1.918
4.	I always meet my deadlines.	8.81	1.615
5.	I always do my best at work.	8.87	1.419
6.	I always try to adhere to work values in order to guarantee success.	8.90	1.342

The mean scores of each attribute for honesty in this study are greater than 8. This could imply that the employees are honest in their work.

Employees Teamwork

Working in a team would allow an individual to participate in a work force which was moulded in the spirit of oneness. This could strengthen and intensify the efforts and relationship among individuals in the team.

Table 3: Employees Teamwork Practice

Items	*Criteria*	*Mean*	*Std. Dev.*
1.	Employees in my division are divided into several working teams.	8.21	1.867
2.	Each working team is assigned with a specific group project.	8.19	1.833
3.	I always give my contribution in accomplishing the group project.	8.43	1.587
4.	I often consult my team members to overcome obstacles and to avoid mistakes.	8.50	1.656
5.	I give my full cooperation to my team.	8.87	1.342
6.	I am often awarded for my full commitment in my team work.	7.12	2.252

The table shows the mean outcomes of the employees' teamwork practice. Overall, the employees had shown good participation in their teamwork where cooperation was almost given in full (item 5; mean 8.87).

Employees Accountability

Accountable individuals are self-reliant individuals who constantly work hard to meet responsibility, and they are responsible for their actions. They also behave in ways expected from them in the absence of surveillance.

The following table displayed the attributes of accountability within this study's framework. The mean scores of all the attributes are close to 9. These findings could indicate that the employees are accountable and are willing to be held responsible if they did something wrong.

Table 4: Employees Accountability Practice

Items	*Criteria*	*Mean*	*Std. Dev.*
1.	I constantly work hard to meet responsibilities	8.94	1.343
2.	I always take responsibilities if I did something wrong.	8.90	1.315
3.	I often work hard to get ahead in life.	8.95	1.257
4.	I do my jobs as it is my responsibility, not because I am instructed to do.	8.98	1.312
5.	I emphasize on quality and excellence at work.	8.92	1.289

The table displayed the attributes of accountability within this study's framework. The mean scores of all the attributes are close to 9. These findings could indicate that the employees are accountable and are willing to be held responsible if they did something wrong.

Overall IWE Practices Among Employees

The respondents were assessed on their overall IWE practices in terms of effort, teamwork, honesty and accountability. Table 5 shows the employees' mean scores on the IWE variables.

Table 5: Overall Employees' Mean Scores on IWE Variables

Variable	*Mean*	*Std Dev*
Effort	7.94	1.25
Teamwork	8.22	1.31
Honesty	8.68	1.29
Accountability	8.93	1.18

The mean analysis for each of the IWE variables indicates that the employees scored the highest in accountability (mean 8.93; SD 1.18), followed by honesty (mean 8.68; SD 1.29) and teamwork (mean 8.22; SD 1.31). They scored a bit low in effort (mean 7.94; 1.25). The highest mean on accountability could indicate that the employees behaved in ways as expected of them, even in the absence of surveillance. The lowest mean on employees' effort on the other hand, might imply their reluctance to do more than what they were minimally required to do. The overall scores nevertheless seemed favourable. Hence, it can be concluded that the bank employees exhibited good IWE practices.

CONCLUSION

Good governance of an institution, among others, is reflected by the work ethics of employees in the institution. The findings of this study indicated that employees of banking institutions in Malaysia exhibited favourable practice of IWE, thereby implying the soundness of governance of the institutions. However, there are some limitations that can be considered for future research. This study was only limited to banks in the Klang Valley, thus a larger sample can be used with more industries (non-financial institutions) for the future study. This study also did not intend to compare the levels of the IWE between the employees of the Islamic and conventional banking systems. Thus, it would be interesting to examine if the IWE of bank employees in Islamic banks is higher than those in the conventional banking sector. Apart from that, a comparative study of the IWE between Muslim and non-Muslim employees who work in Islamic banks can be conducted, to gather information on whether the environment and surroundings of working in an Islamic bank influence non-Muslims to adopt IWE. Finally, a comparison between IWE and Protestant Work Ethics (PWE) practices can also be carried out.

REFERENCES

Abdurrahman, S.A. (2005), *Fiqh Pekerja* (translated by Achmad Sunarto), Indonesia: Pustaka Anisah.

Abuznaid, S.A. (2009). Business ethics in Islam: The glaring gap in practice, *International Journal of Islamic and Middle Eastern Finance and Management,* 2(4), 278-288.

Accounting in Islamic religious organisations. *World Academy of Science, Engineering and Technology*, 66, 1133-1139.

Ali, A. J. & Falcone, T. (1995). Work ethic in the USA and Canada, *Journal of Management Development,* 14 (6), 26-34.

Ali, A.J (1988). Scaling an Islamic work ethic. *The Journal of Social Psychology*, 128 (5), 575-583.

Ali, A.J. & al Owaihan, A. (2008). Islamic work ethic: a critical review. *Cross Cultural Management: An International Journal,* 15 (1), 5-19.

Ali, A.J. (1992). Islamic work ethic in Arabia. *Journal of Psychology*, 126 (5), 507-520.

Al-Imam Al-Bayhaqi (n.d). Syu'b al-Iman. Bab 35. No. 4915 www.islamweb.net.

Al-Imam Al-Bukhari (1994). Sahih al-Bukhari. Translated by Muhammad Muhsin Khan 1994. Riyadh: Maktaba Dar-us-Salam.

Al-Imam al-Tirmidhi (2007). Jami' al-Tirmidhi. Translated by Abu Khaliyl 2007. Riyadh: Maktaba Dar us-Salam.

Al-Imam Muslim (1972). Sahih Muslim. Translated by Abdul Hamid Siddique Pakistan: Sh. Muhammad Ashraf.

Atiyah, M. K. (1993). *Sistem Perakaunan Dalam Islam (terj).* Kuala Lumpur: Dewan Bahasa dan Pustaka.

Beekun, R.I. (2004). *Islamic Business Ethics*, Good word Books Pvt., New Delhi.

Brockner, J., Siegel, Phyllis A., Daly, Joseph P., Martin, C. & Tyler, T. (1997). When Trust Matters: The Moderating Effect of Outcome Favorability. *Administrative Science Quarterly,* 42, 558-583.

Ebrahim, A. (2005). Accountability Myopia: Losing Sight of Organizational Learning. *Non-Profit and Voluntary Sector Quarterly*, 34 (1), 56-87.

Green. F. (2004). Why has work effort become more intense? *Industrial Relations: A Journal of Economy and Society*, 43(4), 709-741.

Hasan, B.A. & Siti-Nabiha, A.K. (2010). Towards good accountability: The role of Accoucting in lstamic religious Organisations. World Academy of Science, Engineering and Technology, 66, 1133-1139.

Howatt, B. (2002). Quality Workplace Discussion Brief. Howatt HR Consulting Inc. www.howatthrconsulting.com. Retrieved on 25 March 2011.

Nik Mohamed Affandi Nik Yusoff (2002), *Islam & Business*, Subang Jaya: Pelanduk Publications (M) Sdn. Bhd.

Norlela, K. & Siti Khadijah A.M. (2010). The conceptual framework of Islamic work ethic, *Malaysian Accounting Review (MAR)*, Special Issue, 9 (2), 57-70.

Rice, G. (1999). Islamic ethics and the implications for business, *Journal of Business Ethics*, 18(4), 345-358.

Scarnati, J.T. (1997). Beyond technical competence: honesty and integrity. *Career Development International*. 2(1), 24–27.

Syed Othman, A. H., Syed, O. S. A., Nik, M. N. H., & Aidit, G. (1998). *Islamic Management for Excellence*. Kuala Lumpur: Institute Perkembangan Minda.

Wetzels, M., K. De Ruyter & M. Van Birgele. (1998). Marketing service relationships: the role of commitment. *Journal of Business & Industrial Marketing*. 13 (4/5), 406-423.

The Human Person As the Anchor for Ethical Corporate Governance

Claret P.E.D'Souza
Mangalore University, Mangalore

ABSTRACT

Ethics is the science of moral values. Business ethics is a science of moral values in business exchanges. Corporate ethics is a science of executive moral values relative to strategic corporate decisions, choices, and their consequences [Webster Dictionary's definitions (1985/2000)]. In all of these, the human person is the anchor, or the focal point. Our common ground, regardless of our religion and religious beliefs, ethnic and national composition, is our recognition of the importance of the human person and human personhood. Corporate ethics and morals deal not only with executive decisions and actions, but even raise more fundamental questions: What I ought to be? What I ought to do? What kind of executive person do I want to become?
In the wake of a series of scams the world over, a recapture of a strong sense of business, corporate and personal ethics is urgently imperative in business, corporation and human conduct.

Keywords: *The Human Person, Ethics, Corporate Governance*

INTRODUCTION

Recent advances in the physical, biological and social sciences have not only spawned radical technological and market breakthroughs, but have, more importantly, unearthed tremendous human potentiality for design, creativity and innovation, for invention, discovery, venture and entrepreneurship, for capital accumulation and wealth creation, for individual self-actualization and collective common good. We are experiencing a growing consciousness of the increased power that human beings have over nature, and over the future development of the human race. This power can be both a blessing and a curse: it is a blessing if harnessed to do good, to preserve and respect human dignity, to bring about justice, and to promote peace and human solidarity; it can be a curse, if the same power is abused to do evil, destroy human worth, generate unjust structures, and provoke war and terrorism, global destruction and disintegration. We can make or mar our destiny.

More than at any other period in human history, humankind is currently at the crossroads of war or peace, growth or decline, progress or regression, life or death, hell or heaven. We cannot leave these opposite polarities and possibilities to chance. We must design and invent, plan and predict, monitor and control our future and that of our posterity. In this regard, the concept of human personhood cum human responsibility is a fundamental part of this new self understanding and undertaking. Ethics and morality are a critical component on this creative journey to destiny. Corporate ethics, in particular, requires the development of a clear understanding of the relationship between executive autonomy and freedom, between human creativity and market innovation, and between human culture and corporate social responsibility.

Regardless of our religion and religious beliefs, ethnic and national composition or persuasion, is our recognition of the value of the human person and human personhood. The centrality of the question of human personhood is common to theology and philosophy, morals and ethics, and even laws and values. Corporate ethics and morals deal not only with executive decisions and actions, but even raise the more fundamental questions: What ought I to do? What ought I to be? What kind of executive person do I want to become? Even those who consider basing ethics on a set of universal and absolute values, presuppose the necessity of the human personhood. We can never predicate moral goodness, or moral badness of beings that are not human persons (Häring1978: 85; Hildebrand 1953: 167). We are human persons every moment of our being (this is the fixed nature of human personhood); yet, human personhood means that we go beyond or transcend what we are at a given moment (this is the dynamic nature of human personhood). Both aspects of human personhood are necessary; they make us what we are – human, personal, ethical, moral, accountable and responsible personalities.

THE HUMAN PERSON

Aristotle's balanced formula for man was: man is a rational animal. Within ancient Greek philosophical thought and categorization, this definition meant that the human being is endowed with the highest of three types of souls: as a vegetative soul, the human is capable of nutrition, growth, and reproduction; as an animal soul, the human is capable of movement and experiences; as a rational soul that unites the other two, the human is capable of knowledge and choice. That is, this rational soul expresses itself in the twofold activity of thinking and willing. We are even more: our knowledge is reflective and our choices are informed and reflective. Our skills and potential for knowledge and choice empower us to be "causes" or "authors" of our own action, and hence, accountable and responsible for the effects of our actions. Thus, being and action are intrinsically linked in the rational and voluntary nature of our being. In the Aristotelian vision of human nature, corporeal matter is informed by the spiritual principle of the rational soul (Rehrauer 1996: 23-25).

On the surface, human behaviour is basically a set of actions that are governed by one's feelings, emotions, attitudes and beliefs regarding proposed ends, ideals, goals and objectives. In general, most actions stem from, and are affected by one's personality or character. To the extent that these actions are human, they are usually assessed by several dyadic qualifications such as right or wrong, good or bad, ethical or unethical, moral or immoral, just or unjust, and fair or unfair. In general, actions are praiseworthy if good, and blameworthy, if bad. If good, one should be credited for them; if bad, one must accept blame and responsibility for the intended and unintended consequences.

Ethics is concerned with responsible human behaviour. Corporate ethics is concerned with responsible human behaviour in relation to executive decisions, actions and their outcomes. Good business executives execute good decisions and actions that generate good outcomes, and avoid bad decisions and actions that result in bad consequences.

Human behaviour, however, cannot be reduced to a set of decisions and actions. There is a profound unity and interrelatedness that affects four basic characteristics of what it means to be human:

- We are uniquely *sensitive* fed by our five senses
- We are *affective* and feeling human beings
- We are *cognitive* or knowing human beings, and
- We are *volitive* (voluntary and intentional) human beings

In the scholastic tradition, this human personhood is represented by the "soul" that unifies the body and spirit, the physical and the mental, the understanding and the will, the voluntary and the involuntary, and human instincts and human drives (Harré and Shorter 1983; Strawson 1959). Whether one holds with Socrates that all knowledge is innate, ready to be drawn out through education (e-ducere in Latin), or with Plato that all knowledge is fundamentally remembering, or with Aristotle that all knowledge begins with sensation, in any case, the raw data for our reasoning is given through our sensory organs of the body working in harmony with the soul (Thomas Aquinas: Summa Theologiae, Ia: 77-78, 84-85). The unifying principle and power is the human person.

While on the one hand, our human personhood is fed and moulded by the internal stimuli of our sensitive, cognitive, affective, and volitive lives, on the other, it is also influenced by external stimuli whether they come from:

- Our family and school stimuli
- Our ergonomic stimuli

- Our market stimuli
- Our ideological stimuli

Our human personhood receives, internalizes, filters, sorts, unifies, blends, lives and relives all the internal and external stimuli in a mysterious, transcending synthesis and unity that really defines us. Given the internal and external stimuli, that is, our physical, spatial and temporal world, our human personhood develops certain personality characteristics, behaviour patterns, cultivates certain virtues (or vices), capacities or limitations, needs and wants, desires and dreams, habits and passions of heart, ethics and morals, and transforms us into responsible (or irresponsible) persons.

The human person is not a simple or random by-product of the internal and external stimuli. Our human personhood is a unique combination of four internal-external forces that unify, interpret, internalize and respond to the internal-external stimuli: *our immanence, our individuality, our sociality, and our transcendence* (Mascarenhas, 2012).

Our Unique Immanence

Etymologically, immanence (in + manere in Latin) means to remain in, or to be operating and living within something. We are living within our state, that is within our country that is within this earth, which is within the solar system that is within the universe. We dwell in the universe that is in time, space, motion and gravitation. Because of our immanence, we have needs, wants and desires; we have also thereby capacities and limitations. We are bound by physical laws of the universe, and we are limited by the physical capabilities of our muscular and skeletal structure. Needs and limitations change and differ depending upon our age, gender, education, occupation, culture, religion, and where we are at any given moment. The body is the foundation for feeling, and is the home of the intelligence. There is unity between the human person and the body. The soul when joined to the body becomes the unifying principle of all activities. Because of this soul or spirit, we are immanent in the world in an unique way: we can sense the world, feel the world, explore, study and know the world, change and manipulate the world, and control. Ethics must see the human person not only in our universal aspects, but in our unique combination of mind and matter, body and soul, time and eternity, and unique immanence. For example, in the case of Ramalinga Raju of Satyam, we need to analyze the crimes, taking into consideration his unique immanence.

Our Unique Individuality

We are an unique combination of body and soul, mind and matter, faculties and powers, the conscious and the unconscious, the physical and the emotional, the intellectual and the spiritual, the individual and the social, and the ethical and moral parts of our human personality. Such an unique combination makes knowledge, thought, talent and skills, choice and freedom possible. All these (including our genes and genetic compositions), will not determine and control who we are and who we will become. They all contribute to our specific personality and uniqueness. Our unique, non-repeatable, irreducible and irreplaceable individuality, cannot be fully understood and explained, unless we accept that our uniqueness comes from being uniquely shaped and moulded into the image of God (or some such superior being), who made us into this unique and historical (i.e., originated in specific combinations of space, time, motion and gravitation) composition of the body and soul, mind and matter, family, social and historical environments. We are an unique meeting point between soul and body, the corporeal and the spiritual, the physical and the social, that we call the human personality or individuality. Each of us, accordingly, is born with an unique destiny that forges and converges each one of us into an unique transcendent openness of possibility that translates (from a near infinite number of possibilities), into an unique combination of talents and skills, knowledge and ideologies, thoughts and actions, moral qualities and events, virtues and values. Our human personhood characterizes this profound unity between all our powers - bodily, mental, and emotional and spiritual – this unity defines us (Covey 2004). Human personhood, therefore, entails a dynamic unity of the activities of affection, cognition, and choice (Thomas Aquinas). The particular forms and patterns of interaction of these three activities congeal over time into certain more or less integrated self-structure of habits or virtues (or vices), which in turn generate or manifest as a combination we call our personality characteristics such as attitudes, beliefs, tendencies, motivations or psychological traits (Allport 1955).

Our Unique Sociality

We do not live, move and have our being in isolation. Because of our unique immanence and individuality we are social creatures, members of a common human species. We can sense, feel and manipulate the world around, as animals do. But, far more than animals, we have "knowledge," because the activity of knowing is dependent upon a deeper reality, that of sharing. Knowledge by its very essence is relational. Without sociality, there is no individuality. We are born and inserted into society. We cannot be personalized human persons in isolation. It is through our social contacts that we activate and develop the ability to be individual and social, to be ethical and moral. Our unique and essential human sociality can be applied, *mutatis mutandis*, to the corporation as a whole, since it is composed of real human persons, all of whom are radically social in being and becoming. Sociality can be built into our otherwise competitive and anti-social corporate personality and strategy. This is the foundation for corporate executive social spirituality.

Our Unique Transcendence

Etymologically (from Latin *ascendere* = to climb; transcendere = to go beyond, to surpass), transcendence implies going beyond one's sense and experience, emotions and feelings, knowledge and skills, capacities and limitations, in order to achieve excellence, moral integrity, and extraordinary heights of self-actualization. In Kantian philosophy, transcendence means going beyond sense data and hypothetical imperatives, to categorical moral imperatives inherent in the organizing function of the mind and the will, and which are necessary conditions for human knowledge. Accordingly, transcendentalism is a philosophy (attributed to 18th century German philosophers Kant, Hegel and Fichte) that proposes to discover the nature of reality, by investigating the process of thought, rather than the objects of sense experience. By extension, Emerson and other 19th century New England philosophers, defined transcendentalism as a search for reality through spiritual intuition.

Hence, given our individuality, sociality, immanence and transcendence, major values and responsibilities accrue. There is a multidirectional responsibility involved in being human. There is, additionally, a multidirectional responsibility involved in being an executive. We are responsible not only for what we are (immanence), but who we are (individuality), what we do (sociality), and what we have become (transcendence). That is, we are responsible for our individuality, sociality, immanence and transcendence, individually and collectively; that is, we are responsible to ourselves (individuality), to others, our community, society and culture (sociality), to the world and the universe we are immersed and living in (immanence), and to God who created us, and whose absolute transcendence we share, and to something beyond ourselves, society and the universe (transcendence). (Mascarenhas, 2012).

ETHICS

Ethical scholars distinguish between morality and ethics. *Morality* (from the Latin *moralitas*) is generally used to describe a *sociological phenomenon*, namely, the existence of a society with rules and standards of behaviour. The word ethics comes from the Greek word "ethos," which means "disposition, character, or fundamental values peculiar to a specific person, people, culture, or movement." Thus defined, ethics bears two important implications: a) as cultures change over time, ethics change; hence, ethics is a dynamic and not a static concept; b) as values change over time, ethics change across cultures; values define what we consider acceptable ways of working; hence, by its very definition, ethics has a "relativistic" and not absolute connotation; however, there is a base level of "black and white" ethics consistent across cultures (e.g., do not kill; do not cheat; do not lie). Nevertheless, there is a large spectrum of grey area in ethics, where values and cultures are involved (e.g., be non-hierarchical; be inclusive; be just; be contributing). It is the grey area that tests corporations, its leaders and chief executives. Values such as social compliance, industrial codes of conduct, consumer privacy, personal security, patent rights and duties, intellectual property rights and duties, and employee rights and duties may not be similar across countries and continents. As also, certain questionable strategies such as aggressive competitive practices, wash trading, insider trading, and other financial shenanigans, acceptable in certain countries may not be in others, thus creating conflict of values and interests. Most of the times, business executives will have to operate in this grey area that is full of personal conflicts and choices, each of which tests individual ethical sensitivities, decision abilities and personality characters (Narasimhan, 2011).

On the other hand, *ethics* (from the Greek word *ethikos*) generally refers to the rules and norms of specific kinds of conduct, or the code of conduct for specialized groups. Thus, we speak about ethics of doctors, ethics of the legal profession, code of ethics for the accounting profession, ethics of business executives, and so on, rather than morality of doctors, lawyers, accountants, and business executives (Boatright 2003: 22-23).

We also use the term ethics to denote the field of moral philosophy. Like logic, epistemology and metaphysics, ethics as a moral normative philosophy dates back to the time of ancient Greeks [e.g., Socrates (470-399 BC), Plato (427-347 BC) and Aristotle (384-322 BC)]. In this view, ethics as a philosophical endeavour, is the study of morality. Ethics studies morality; ethics presupposes the existence of morality and moral people who judge right from wrong (De George 1999: 19). Such a study, as argued earlier, can be descriptive or normative. While *descriptive ethics* is a scientific inquiry into the actual moral beliefs and behaviours of people, *normative ethics*, based on various philosophical theories and doctrines, prescribes what our beliefs and behaviour ought to be.

Raymond Niebuhr (1963: 48-55) argues that we use two fundamental metaphors to describe human activity: the *maker* and the *citizen*. As a maker (or artificer), we construct things according to an idea for the sake of an end; in this process, we create ourselves, our society, our world and our civilization, and we do this with purposeful freedom. As citizens, we are created, constrained, social, live in communities, and hence, bound by laws and duties, law and order; but we are still makers, and as makers we can choose to live in compliance of the law, learn to live in harmony with people, and choose to make our community, our city, our country, our world and our civilization. We rule ourselves while being ruled; we are internally free, while being ruled externally. Thus, human action is individual, transcendent, purposive and creative; but it is also immanent and social, contextual and situational, and hence bound by values, laws and ordinances. We use clusters of concepts in this regard: value, right and duty, good and evil, common good, ethical and moral, spiritual and religious, virtue and vice, truth and falsehood. As makers we create value; as citizens we subject value to being good and right; we do what is right in order to produce good; we realize value in order to become good. In this regard, the key metaphor in the cluster of related concepts is that of *duty*: the ethical and moral choice of the maker is to fulfil one's obligations as a citizen; we do good and avoid evil as specified by moral law.

We assume that, in general, business executive ethics or morality can be predicated about two components of executive conduct: 1) executive decisions, choices, actions or strategies; 2) executive intent, statements, declarations or reports.

MAJOR NORMATIVE ETHICAL THEORIES OR SYSTEMS

Executive behaviour or corporate conduct in general, and business executive decisions, actions and strategies in particular, may be characterized as involving a system of ethical "inputs," ethical "outputs," and an ethical "process" that converts inputs to outputs. Some of these inputs, processes and outputs have ethical content and hence, involve a decision process that has ethical elements and ethical consequences. Thus, if the outputs are good and beneficial to society, then the business executive must be praised and rewarded appropriately. If the outputs bring about harmful effects or costs to society, then the executive or the corporation responsible for them must accept "responsibility" for these cost burdens.

Deontology is the ethical theory that is primarily geared to analyze the ethics of inputs and process (i.e., the Act), and the duties and obligations associated with *responsibility*. The ethical theory of *teleology* judges the morality of an action primarily by its consequences. Third, the theory of *distributive justice* judges the morality of an action by both the act (for its capacity for distributing costs and benefits equitably across all people concerned), and the consequences (for their actual distribution of costs and benefits across all members of society affected by the act). The entire process of executive inputs, process and outputs can be further analyzed and enhanced by the ethical theories of responsibility, which in turn, are supported by the ethical theories of human personhood, ethics of virtue, ethics of trust, ethics of moral worth, and the ethics of moral reasoning.

CORPORATE GOVERNANCE

The 19th century saw the foundations laid for modern corporations – that was the century of the entrepreneur. The 20th century was the century of management – the phenomenal growth of management concepts and theories, management models and paradigms, management consultants and gurus, management schools, journals, books and teachers flourished in this century. The 21st century promises to be a century of corporate governance – the focus is swinging from production and profits to legitimacy and effectiveness of wielding power over corporate and government bodies, nationwide and worldwide (Tricker 2009: 7-8).

Currently, all of us are overwhelmed by the massive pandemic of corporate fraud, political corruption and bribery in the world, particularly in India. Ever since Satyam did self-whistle-blowing and declared near bankruptcy in January 2009, several major corporate and political scandals have emerged and featured by almost all media – companies such as 2G and 3G spectrum, the CWG scam of misguided Commonwealth Game biddings, the Adarsh Housing debacle, the de-notification of public choice land in Bangalore to favour one's family members, usurping agricultural land for questionable industrial uses in Uttar Pradesh, DLFs unsecured advances to Robert Vadra and Vadra's disproportionate accumulation of wealth to known sources of income and the like. Despite Anna Hazare, Kejriwal and the noble mission of their teams, the cascade of corporate and political scandals has not abated.

Several laws condemning and regulating corporate and political scams have mushroomed during the last two decades, notably the Cadbury Report in 1992, the Kumar Mangalam Birla Report in 2001, the Narayana Murthy Report in 2003, and the SEBI Report that summarized and accepted all these reports in most of their recommendations formulated under *Clause 49*. In the wake of Enron, the USA promulgated a very stringent law called the Sarbanes-Oxley Act of 2002. This Act definitely helped in creating a global awareness of corporate scams, set up more procedures and processes for an ethical and moral audit of corporations, but did not generate much compliance with the Act. Corporate fraud has continued unabated. In understanding, detecting and preventing corporate and political crimes of money laundering or fraudulent accounting practices, we need to study the concept, code, and models of corporate governance in relationship to ownership and control. Lack of good corporate governance that thrives on transparency and disclosure, responsibility and accountability, sound management, self-regulation and control, can inevitably lead to these scandals.

Simply stated, any governance is the exercise of three values or duties: *accountability, openness*, and *probity*. In the case of corporate governance (CG), these three duties whittle down to a) accountability to owners; b) honest open dealings within and outside the board, and c) transparency of risk-assessment and decision-taking process to the owners (Kumar 2010: 28).

The simplest definition of CG was provided by the Cadbury Report (1992): Corporate governance is the system by which businesses are directed and controlled. The definition of CG as provided in the preamble of the OECD (Organization for Economic Cooperation and Development) Principles is: Corporate governance … involves a set of relationships between a company's management, its board, its shareholders, and other stakeholders. CG also provides the structure through which the objectives of the company are set, and the means of attaining those objectives and monitoring performance are determined. This definition reflects the conformance-performance dichotomy of CG.

Turning to the Indian scene, one finds increasing concern about improving the performance of the Board. This is doubtless an important issue, but a close analysis of the ground reality in India would force one to conclude that the Board is not really central to the corporate governance malaise in India. The central problem in Indian corporate governance is not the conflict between management and owners as in the US and the UK, but conflict between the dominant shareholders and the minority shareholders. The Board cannot even in theory resolve this conflict. One can in principle, visualize an effective Board which can discipline management. At least in theory, management exercises only such powers as are delegated to it by the Board. But, how can one, even in theory, envisage a Board that can discipline the dominant shareholders from whom the Board derives all its powers? (Varma, 1997).

CONCLUSION

Our global financial crisis and other deviant behaviours cannot be easily stopped by laws and regulations; what we need is a radical conversion of heart and mind at the top. Any amount of reform in corporate governance (CG) in terms of unitary or two-tier boards, the proportion of independent non-executive directors (INEDs), the separation of Chairman and CEO, board committees, internal and external audit control systems, independent audit committees, and the like, have not drastically reduced corporate deviant behaviour. CG is not about structures; CG is a process, a management and a political process, that should be informed and ruled by clear mission, vision, mindset, ideals, goals and objectives that should primarily be directed in serving society at large, while providing meaningful employment, salaries, profits, wealth, growth and prosperity for all its stakeholders. *The original concept of the corporation was founded on trust, stewardship, and responsibility* (Tricker 2009: 392).

The corporate executive human act is a creative act made by a human person, made in the image of God. This is the great gift of human action: in every human action, the human person is imaging God, because he is creating social meaning, he is creating himself, he is creating the corporate organization, and hence, he is creating his social community. Thus, the corporate executive call is not just to act, to define ourselves, to exercise our freedom, and to create the world of meaning. The corporate executive call is all this and more: *to create meaning and become goodness*. It is not enough to say that the corporate executive acted freely and knowingly. He must be able to say that he acted freely and knowingly in such a way that he became more like the God in whose image he is made, and in doing so he empowers others to do the same (Rehrauer 1996: 121-122).

REFERENCES

Allport, G. (1955), Becoming, New Haven, CT: Yale University Press.

Boatright, John R. (2000), *Ethics and the Conduct of Business*, 3rd edition, Upper Saddle River, NJ: Prentice-Hall.

Bob Tricker (2011), Corporate Governance, Oxford University Press Inc., New York.

Covey, Stephen R. (2004), The 8th Habit: From Effectiveness to Greatness. New York: Free Press.

DeGeorge, Richard R. (1999), Business Ethics, 5th edition, Prentice Hall.
Häring, Bernard (1978), Free and Faithful in Christ, Volume 1, General Moral Theology, Middlegreen, Slough: St. Paul Publications.
Harré R. and J. Shorter (1983), "The Concept of Person," in Harré, R. and R. Lamb eds. The Encyclopaedia Dictionary of Psychology, Cambridge: MIT Press, 456.
Hildebrand, von D. (1953), Christian Ethics, New York: David McKay.
Jayanth Rama Varma(1997) Corporate Governance in India: Disciplining the Dominant Shareholder, Journal of the Indian Institute of Management, Bangalore.
Kumar, Satheesh (2010), *Corporate Governance*, New Delhi: Oxford University Press.
Mascarenhas, Oswald A. J. (1988a), "Can We Humanize Consumption? Tasks and Models," in 1988 AMA Winter Theory Conference: Proceedings, CA: San Diego.
_____ (1981), "Marx, and Corporate Social Responsibility," Management and Labor Studies, 7:2 (December), 265-281.
____ (1995), "Exonerating Unethical Marketing Executive Behaviors: A Diagnostic Approach," Journal of Marketing, 59:2 (April), 43-57.
Mascarenhas, Oswald A., Ram Kesavan and Michael D. Bernacchi (2008), "Buyer-Seller Information Asymmetry: Challenges to Distributive and Corrective Justice," Journal of Macromarketing, 28:3, (January), 68-84.
____ (1995), "Exonerating Unethical Marketing Executive Behaviors: A Diagnostic Approach," Journal of Marketing, 59:2 (April), 43-57.
____ (2012), The Foundation of Corporate Ethics: The Human Person.
____ (2012), Corporate Governance: Concepts, Codes and Models of Corporate Ownership and Control.
Mascarenhas, Oswald A. J. (2011) Business Transformation Strategies, Sage Publications.
Narasimhan, Laxman (2011), "Values in a Turbulent World," Xavier Labor Relations Institute (XLRI) 20th Annual JRD Tata Oration, XLRI Publications.
Niebuhr, Raymond H. (1963), The Responsible Self, San Francisco, CA: Harper & Row.
Niebuhr, Raymond H. (1964), The Nature and Destiny of Man. Volume I: Human Nature, New York: Charles Scribner's Sons.
Rehrauer, Stephen T. (1996), Responsibility and the Human Person: Its Nature and Attribution in Moral Theology and the Contribution of Psychological Theories of Attribution, Doctoral Dissertation, Madrid: Universidad Pontificia Comillas de Madrid.
Strawson, P. (1959), Individuals, London: Methuen.
The UK Cadbury Report (1992).
Thomas Aquinas: Summa Theologiae, Ia: 77-78, 84-85.

Whistle-Blowing in the Financial Institutions in Emerging Markets

Hilwani Hariri, Radiah Othman[1], Hasnah Haron[2], Said Bouheraoua[3] and Mohammad Talha[4]

Universiti Teknologi MARA, Malaysia
[1]Massey University, New Zealand
[2]Universiti Sains Malaysia
[3]International Shari'ah Research Academy for Islamic Finance (ISRA), Malaysia
[4]King Fahd University of Petroleum & Minerals, UAE

ABSTRACT

The aim of this article is to examine the establishment and implementation of whistle-blowing policies in full-fledged Malaysian Islamic Financial Institutions (IFIs) by surveying their websites and latest annual reports for 2009. The study found that only one (Bank Islam) out of the five full-fledged IFIs disclosed the whistle-blowing policy in their Annual Reports. None of them disclosed the policy on their websites, but they do have a Code of Ethics in their organizations. A survey of the middle-level managers revealed that they prefer internet, intranet or e-mails as the whistle-blowing communication channel. Surprisingly, the cost issue took precedence over safety and security issues, as the most preferred feature of whistle-blowing communication channel, stating that it should be free. Since whistle-blowing policy is generally in its infancy in Malaysia, more awareness and training must be provided for Malaysian IFIs to be able to benchmark with international standards. The findings of this research would be helpful for the regulatory and policy makers in monitoring the development and implementation of whistle blowing practices of Malaysian IFIs.

Keywords: *Whistle-Blowing, Malaysia, Emerging Market, Financial Institutions*

INTRODUCTION

PriceWaterHouseCoopers's Global Economic Crime Survey (2009) revealed that the financial and banking industry has had high levels of fraud over the last 10 years. The survey highlighted that financial services have experienced the largest increase in fraud (56 percent) as compared to 43 percent of the average global figure across all sectors, reporting an increase over the same period. It is reported that the financial services industry is one of the top four industries targeted by fraudsters, even though this industry has more robust and proactive anti-fraud measures and practices.

Malaysia, being one of the pioneers, enjoys a reputation in the Islamic finance and banking sectors within the region. It is quite worrying when the Islamic Financial Services Board (2010) highlighted that financial services providers lack sound corporate governance and disclosure practices. This might induce undesirable behavior, leading to unwanted economic crimes ranging from asset misappropriation, accounting fraud, corruption and bribery, money laundering and intellectual property infringement. Ideally, organizations that utilize effective ethical guidelines and compliance programs are much less vulnerable to economic crime (PriceWaterHouseCoopers, 2009). This can be leapfrogged, if the senior executives take active interest in fraud risks and demonstrate the highest ethical behavior, and having effective whistle-blowing policies in their organizations.

Whistle blowing can be defined as "an attempt by an employee or former employee of an organization to disclose what he or she believes to be wrongdoings in, or by the organization" (James, 1995, p. 409). Whistle-blowing is the disclosure of information, made in good faith and in the public interest, showing objectionable misconduct which is not otherwise known or visible (Gay & Simnett, 2010). Whistle blowing is an important way to prevent and deter fraud, waste, and abuse. According to Uys (2000), whistle blowing can be defined as "the disclosure of illegal, unethical or harmful practices in the workplace to parties who might take action."

In Malaysia, the Whistleblower Protection Act 2010 (The Act) has been duly approved in Parliament on 6 May 2010 and came into force on Wednesday, 15 December 2010. This Act is to be implemented by all enforcement agencies which include the police force, customs, immigration, Malaysian Anti Corruption Commission, and all ministries and departments under the federal and state governments with investigative and enforcement authority. The Act has been formulated to encourage informers to expose corrupt practices and other misconduct. This move would provide immunity to informers from civil or criminal charges. The Act is much needed and well-received by the public, who wants government to demonstrate its seriousness in combating corruption and other white-collar crimes.

According to the Act "Whistleblower." is "any person who makes a disclosure of improper conduct to the enforcement agency". Section 6(1) of the Act states that a person may make a disclosure of improper conduct based on his reasonable belief that any person has engaged, is engaging, or is preparing to engage in improper conduct, provided that such disclosure is not specifically prohibited by any written law. A disclosure of improper conduct may also be made, although the person making the disclosure may not be able to identify a particular person to which the disclosure relates, or although the improper conduct has occurred before the commencement of this Act [Section 6(2)]. However, it is relatively unknown how effective Malaysian Islamic financial institutions have been in establishing, enforcing whistle-blowing practices to combat corruption, misconduct and fraud.

The objective of this study is first to investigate the extent of awareness and practices of whistle blowing and the code of ethics among organizational members of the Islamic Financial Institutions in Malaysia to become whistle-blowers. Islamic Financial Services Board (2010) claims that the financial services industry is often targeted by fraudsters, therefore this study is vital and timely for the effective implementation of the Whistle-blowing Act which has been enacted last year. This study would provide evidence about the establishment and implementation of the Whistle-blowing policies in Malaysian Islamic Financial Institutions. The findings of this research would be helpful for the regulatory and the policy makers in monitoring the development and the implementation of whistle blowing practices of Malaysian financial institutions.

Literature Review

There were several cases of whistle blowing such as Maxwell Pensions Scandal (Personnel Today, 2002). An employee, Harry Templeton worked as a printer at the Scottish Daily Record and the Sunday Mail, newspapers owned by Robert Maxwell's Mirror Group. In 1985, Templeton was appointed as a trustee of the Mirror Group Pension Scheme. Templeton often found himself as the only trustee challenging Maxwell's misuse of pension funds, and this lead to him being fired in 1988. Maxwell vowed Templeton would never work in the print industry again.

Another well-known case of whistle blowing is WorldCom, one of the country's largest companies with over 20 million customers and 80,000 employees, has filed for bankruptcy. Cynthia Cooper, an internal auditor, began investigating some of the company's capital expenditures in May. She discovered bookkeeping entries that constituted what looked like the largest accounting fraud in US history.

Other similar case is at Enron, and this time, it was Sherron Watkins, Vice President of Corporate Development in Enron who sent a long memo to Chief Executive Officer, Kenneth Lay. In that memo, Watkins explained in detail to Lay, issues on Enron's incredibly complex special-purpose entities. Being an accountant, Watkins understood exactly what the problems were, and knew that something very bad was going on, something everyone else seemed to think was perfectly okay, and that public revelations would be disastrous. Even the accountants including Arthur Andersen had blessed the accounting treatment.

Another popular case that has received media attention and a Parliamentary inquiry was Dr Andrew Millar who as Director of Clinical Research for British Biotech, a leading UK biotech drug company. He was aware that preliminary results from trials of two key new drugs were not encouraging. Dr Millar became increasingly concerned that British Biotech's public statements on the prospects of these drugs were misleading. Although Dr Millar raised his concerns with British Biotech's directors with increasing anxiety, the directors remained optimistic about the potential of the drugs. When British Biotech discovered that Dr Millar had spoken to the directors, it dismissed Dr Millar and sued him for disclosing confidential information. Out of a job and feeling threatened by legal action, Dr Millar counter-sued for libel and wrongful dismissal (with financial backing from the British Medical Association). The conclusions for the final drug trials were published in 1999, and showed that the company's early statements had been seriously over-optimistic. Meanwhile, Dr Millar has been able to successfully pursue his medical career elsewhere.

Whistle-Blowing in Malaysia

In Malaysia, the much awaited Whistleblower Protection Act 2010 (Act 711) came into force on Wednesday 15 December 2010. The Act is to combat corruption and other wrongdoings by encouraging and facilitating disclosures of improper conduct in the public and private sector, to protect persons making those disclosures from detrimental action, to provide for matters disclosed to be investigated and dealt with, and to provide for other matters connected therewith.

Earlier the Securities Industy Act 1983 had been amended to provide a provision for an auditor to submit a report to the Securities Commission or the Bursa Malaysia, if he uncovered any misdeeds that breached the securities law, rules of the Bursa Malaysia or matters that adversely affected the financial position of the listed company. The Securities Commission of Malaysia described whistle-blowing as "the disclosure of information that one reasonably believes to be evidence of contravention of any laws or regulations or information that involves mismanagement, corruption or abuse of authority."

The Companies Act 1965 has also being amended by the Companies (Amendment) Act 2007 to include new provisions, whereby auditors of public listed companies and companies controlled by public companies are required to report to the Companies Commission of Malaysia, should they perceive that a serious offence involving fraud and dishonesty is being or has been committed. The same provision is extended to the officers of the company.

Whistle-Blowing Policy and Code of Ethics

Policies at the organizational level are important to encourage employees to report wrongdoings and ethical issues (Mathews, 1987). Several studies have recently examined the relationship between organization policies and whistle blowing issues. For example, Keenan (1990b) surveyed upper level managers about the policies and practices regarding wrongdoing, that is, whether the organization has a written policy, conducts regular reviews on what actions to take, and has a watchdog department or person concerned with the issue of whistle blowing. On perception about the adequacy of whistle blowing practices, he found that the existence of these policies and practices and lowered fear of retaliation were associated with positive perceptions about the adequacy of company encouragement of whistle blowing. He suggested that the whistle blowing policy should be adequately communicated and conducted regularly.

The main purpose of the Whistle Blowing Policy is to encourage employees to disclose any malpractice or misconduct of which they become aware. Also the whistle blowing policy should provide sufficient protection to the whistle blower and the employees who participate, or assist in an investigation, especially protection against adverse employment actions such as discharge, demotion, suspension, harassment, or other forms of discrimination, for raising allegations of business misconduct. The employee should be protected even if the allegations eventually are not proven. Most reported unethical behaviours are employee theft, conflict of interest, quality control issues, misuse of proprietary information, misuse of company assets and abuse of company expense accounts.

Some companies do not have a specific whistle-blowing policy, but they do have a Code of Ethics in place. Ethics may be defined as the set or code of moral principles that distinguish what is right from what is wrong (Schemerhorn, 2008, p. 32). Business ethics, are sometimes referred to as management ethics or organizational ethics, should be actively managed, emphasizing on common norms, values and standards. These must be set, communicated and enforced by all organizational members. The code of ethics should be comprehensive, encourage reporting of wrongdoing and distributed to all employees. It is important that all employees acknowledge periodically their compliance with the code of ethics. The code of ethics awareness program also needs to be conducted regularly.

Whistle-Blowing Channels

Whistle-blowing channels may be classified as internal or external (Callahan & Dworkin, 2000; Dworkin & Baucus, 1998; Miceli & Near, 1992; Near and Miceli, 1995; Dworkin & Callahan, 1991). This classification was based on the nature of the channels used to report, that is, the location of the recipient receiving a report of wrongdoing in an organization. External whistle blowing, which is one of the most typical forms of whistle blowing, uses external channels to report inadequate or illegal practices in an organization. The receivers of the information can be the anti-corruption or regulatory government agencies, mass media, and other parties external to the organization. On the other side, internal whistle blowing performs by using the reporting channels inside an organization.

The whistle-blowing process normally involves a two-stage process. The whistle-blower first reports the wrongdoing internally. If the matter is not resolved to the whistle blower's satisfaction, then he or she may decide to report the matter externally. In other cases, the whistle-blower may decide to report the wrongdoing to an external party right at the outset. This might occur, for example, if the whistle-blower perceived that the matter would not receive an appropriate response if reported internally, and that the only way to get an appropriate response was to report the matter to an external party.

Also to report externally rather than internally depends on a few factors, such as the retaliation experienced by the whistle-blower. The consequences of the report can also vary depending on the channel used to whistle-blow. Dworkin and Baucus (1998, p.1296) who investigated 33 whistle blowing cases, have classified whistle-blowers into internal and external, reported that external whistleblowers are likely to have more extensive experience of organizational retaliation than that of internal whistleblowers. are They concluded that the choice of internal or external reporting channels may significantly influence the organization's response to the whistleblower and the type of retaliation. External whistle blowing tended to cause greater damage to an employee's co-workers and the employer, than internal whistle blowing. On the other hand, internal whistle blowing could give more chance to the organization to avoid the negative consequences than the external one (Miceli & Near, 1988, p.267).

In order to justify one's own whistle blowing, an employee is often required to exhaust internal procedures that allow him or her to correct wrongdoings within an organization, before blowing the whistle on the outside (Grant, 2002). The external whistleblower, which was seen as a traitor by his or her employers and coworkers (Dworkin & Callahan, 1991), was more likely to be subjected to retaliation than the internal whistleblower. Due to the differences between these two types of whistle blowing, an employee's beliefs, which are mentioned in the theory of planned behavior, would be different.

Internal whistle blowing is the reporting of wrongdoing to sources within the organization, and normally the reporting is done to parties outside the chain of command, but inside the organization. This may include the internal auditor, board of directors, the audit committee, and a senior officer, such as the chief executive officer or designated complaint recipient within the organization (Finn, 1995). Some whistleblowers let the upper level of management know about it or their superior. However, reporting to co-workers (or peer reporting) is not classified as whistle-blowing (King, 1999). External whistle-blowing occurs when the complaint recipient is outside of the organization, for example, law enforcement agencies and regulators, professional bodies, external "watch dog" organizations and interest groups, and the media (Near and Miceli, 1995). External whistleblowers have less tenure with the organization, greater evidence of wrongdoing, and they tend to be more effective in changing organizational practices. External whistleblowers also experience more extensive retaliation than internal whistleblowers.

Whistle-Blowing Communication Channels

Communication channel deals with the mediums to be used in reporting wrongdoings either internally or externally. Common alternative reporting channels can be such as telephone hotlines, anonymous suggestion systems or ethics officers. A well-designed whistle blowing communication channel can be a powerful tool to report or uncover wrongdoing in an organization (American Institute of Certified Public Accountants, 2006).

The following are the common medium that can be used as whistle-blowing communication channels:

Communication Channel	*Benefit/Advantages*
Oral communication (including using telephone and fax as hotlines)	More suitable to communicate sensitive and confidential information. Confidentiality of the callers must be protected and the telephone must not have any tracking devices.
Face-to-face media	More personal, able to obtain immediate feedback.
Written media • Hardcopies such as flyers, bulletins, memos and letters. • Employee handbooks	• Appropriate for routine messages such as reminders, awareness campaign, recent amendments to whistle-blowing policies. • Whistle-blowing policies adopted by the organisation.
Web media	Using web which has sufficient free-form areas and is configured correctly.

Research Methodology and Design

Research design is the framework, comprehensive plan or procedure for conducting a research study for fulfilling the research objectives and answer research questions (Churchill, 2001; Collis & Hussey, 2003; Cooper & Schindler, 2006). There are three types or purposes of research design: exploratory research, descriptive research and casual research / hypothesis testing / analytical or predictive research (Churchill, 2001;Collis & Hussey, 2003; Sekaran, 2003). Research methods, on hand refer only to the various means by which data can be collected and / or analysed. Data collection methods such as focus groups, interviews, observations, questionnaires, diaries, each has its own advantages and disadvantages (Collis & Hussey, 2003). Table 1 highlights the research methods used in previous studies on whistle-blowing.

The questionnaire for this study was developed based on literature review, exploratory interviews / focus groups and previously tested and validated measureable variables from earlier empirical studies. Data was collected using a self – administered questionnaire approach for focus groups with key informants (pre-testing) was conducted. Focus group is a small group discussion about some research topic, led by a moderator who guides the discussions surrounded by the participants (Zikmund,Babin, Carr, & Griffin, 2003).

Table 1: Research Methods and Whistle-blowing Studies

Research Methods	*Literature Source*
Survey	• Hwang, Staley, Chen, & Lan (2008) • Ponnu, Naidu, & Zamri (2004)
Case study	• Cross (2005)
Grounded theory	• Guiral, Rodgers, Ruiz, & Gonzalo (2010)
Experimental studies	• Hopman & Leeuwen (2009)

Pre-testing and pilot testing of the questionnaire was conducted during the month of December, 2010 and January, 2011 respectively. Field testing is important to establish the validity of research and the survey questionnaire and is also used to improve questions, format, and the scales in order to upgrade the level of reliability of the instrument. The pre-testing and pilot testing conducted proved to be important in developing the final version of the questionnaire.

- Focus group (pre-testing) with key informants in Hotel Concorde on 29 October 2010 to improve the design, content and layout of the questionnaire.
- Pilot testing with 19 lecturers in the Faculty of Accountancy, Universiti Teknologi MARA on 16 December 2010 till 30 January 2011.

The pilot test was conducted because of several reasons: (a) to make respondents understand the question meanings (b) to get appropriateness of response categories for both muslim and non-muslims (c) to know the effectiveness of data capture. Feedback evaluation forms were composed from the respondents to help amend the final questionnaire.

Data Analysis and Findings

The first part of this chapter discusses the findings of the exploratory survey in the Islamic banks' website. This study will identify the location and disclosure extensiveness on the whistle-blowing policy and other information, especially on whistle-blower protection information, channel of communication and other related information.

The second part of the chapter discusses the results of the analysis of the questionnaire using descriptive statistical analysis. To determine that all respondents were representative of the research population , a non – response bias test was carried out using t-test for differences in mean and ch9i-square test for independence, to compare survey responses between early replies (representative group for replies) and late replies (representative group for non – replies). Descriptive statistics such as frequency and cross tabulations were used to test the response rate and to analyse demographic information of the survey responses. T-test and chi-square test were also carried out to ensure that the pattern of answers by the survey respondents was independent, regardless whether they were working in the headquarters offices or branch offices. The responses to the questionnaire were coded and the Statistical Package for the Social Sciences (SPSS) version 12.1 software.

Whistle-Blowing Respondents

There are five full-fledged Islamic banks in Malaysia, two are locals, Bank Islam, and Bank Muamalat. The other three are foreign Islamic banks which include Kuwait Finance House (Malaysia) Berhad, Al-Rajhi Banking and Investment Corporation (Malaysia) Berhad and Qatar Islamic Bank. Qatar Islamic Bank owns a majority of shares in Asian Finance.

The websites of these banks were surveyed to find out whether they have disclosed the whistle-blowing policy of their organizations. The latest annual reports (2009) were also examined, if such information was not available on the website.

Bank Islam

Bank Islam disclosed their *whistle-blowing policy* in their Annual Report 2009. It was stated that the whistle-blowing policy was established to prevent employees and/or external parties from conducting fraud, wrongdoings, malpractices or any unlawful act, including breach of policies and procedures; fraud, embezzlement, corruption or dishonesty; actions which could cause physical danger to another person, or give rise to the risk of damage to properties/ assets and others. This whistle-blowing policy was located under the Ethics, Integrity and Trust section in the Annual Report 2009 of Bank Islam at http://www.bankislam. com.my (accessed on 12 August 2010).

However, there were no specific guidelines on the procedures for a specific employee or stakeholder to blow the whistle. All frauds and non-fraud related irregularities were advised to be directed to the Audit and Examination Committee (AEC). However, there was little information on how to report any fraud cases or assurance for safety and security for the whistle-blower.

Bank Muamalat

At the time of the study, the website of Bank Muamalat did not have any disclosure on whistle-blowing policy. There was no indication of whistle-blowing practices in the organization. However, under the Sha'riah Committee section of the website, there was a statement that one of their roles was to advise the Bank to consult Sha'riah Supervisory Council (SAC), Bank Negara Malaysia (BNM) on any matters which had not been resolved or endorsed by the SAC or BNM. This policy can be found in the Sha'riah Committee section in the Annual Report of 31' March 2010 (http://www.muamalat. com.my), (accessed on 13 August 2010).

Kuwait Finance House (Malaysia) Berhad

From the website, Kuwait Finance House (Malaysia) Berhad did not specify any whistle-blowing policy. However, in ensuring that the bank's business operates in good manner, there was an Audit Committee report (Internal audit and internal control activities) disclosed under Statement of Corporate Governance section in its Annual Report 2009 (http://www, kfhonline.com.my/kfhmb), accessed on 16 August 2010,

"The Audit Committee was responsible for the bank's system of internal controls and its effectiveness to manage the bank's risks within an acceptable risk level and profile, and to achieve the policies and business objectives set by the bank. The internal controls should be able to provide reasonable assurance against material misstatement of management and financial information, and records or against financial losses or fraud. The Board regularly reviewed the process in order to comply with the regulatory guidelines for directors on internal control, Islamic financial institutions and the Statement on Internal Control."

The Board received and reviewed management reports on a regular basis. In addition to the financial statements, reports on monitoring of compliance with banking laws, Bank Negara Malaysia's (BNM) and other central bank's guidelines on financing, capital adequacy and other regulatory requirements, as well as monthly progress reports on business operations, are tabled before the Board at periodic meetings. The bank had also put in place policies, guidelines and authority limits imposed on the Executive/Managing Director and management within the bank of the day-to-day banking and financing operations, extension of credits, investments, acquisitions and disposal of assets.

Al-Rajhi Banking & Investment Corporation (Malaysia) Berhad

There was no whistle-blowing policy stated in the Annual Report of Al-Rajhi Banking & Investment Corporation (Malaysia) Berhad in 2009. However, there was a Sharia Group, whose responsibility is to make sure that the bank conducts its business in harmony with the precepts of Islamic Sharia (http://www.alrajhibank.com.sa/ Aboutus/pages/Shariaa Group, accessed on 16 August 2010).

According to the website, the objective of the Sharia Group was to participate in the realization of the bank's Islamic banking strategy by supporting the plans and policies necessary for the bank's compliance with the precepts of Islamic Sharia, in the conduct of its business transactions. The Sharia Group had stated their Sharia policy, and one of the rules and guidelines stated it at was strictly forbidden to act in violation of any decisions of the Sharia Board.

Qatar Islamic Bank

There is no specific information about whistle-blowing practices, or any policy about them in the Qatar Islamic Bank (QIB) annual report. In fact, QIB still did not have any website for its operations in Malaysia. Nonetheless, QIB stated that it had a Shari'a Supervisory Board (SSB) under The Shari'a Supervision section, in the Annual Report 2009. This Board consisted of eminent scholars who were globally renowned in the field of commercial and financial Islamic transactions. Shari'a Supervisory Board established the Executive Committee, to ensure that all the transactions at QIB are performed in strict compliance with the Shari'a guidelines.

Besides that, QIB also had a Shari'a Audit Department (SAD). SAD's roles and responsibilities were to review the transactions of the bank. It was also involved in the training of the bank's employees, in order to make sure that they understand the Shari'a guidelines that they had to abide within the Islamic banking industry. SAD aimed to preserve the inherent identity of the Islamic banking industry, by ensuring that all the transactions performed by the bank were in strict compliance with the directives and guidelines of the Shari'a Supervisory Board (http://www.qib.com.qa/, accessed on 16 August 2010).

Demographic Statistics of Respondents

The respondents were asked to state their organization, ethnicity, gender, academic qualifications and job position.

Table 2: Demographic Statistics

Characteristic of Respondents	*Results*	
	Frequency	*Percentage*
Ethnicity		
Malay	16	94.1
Other	1	5.9
Gender		
Male	12	70.6
Female	5	29.4
Academic qualification		
First Degree	8	47.1
Post Degree	8	47.1
Other	1	5.9
Job position		
Sha'riah Supervision Committee/Shari'ah	12	70.6
Department's Employment	5	29.4

After much attempts, only 17 questionnaires were returned for this study. When contacted, the other respondents were either not willing to participate, or were advised by their immediate superiors not to participate due to confidentiality and sensitivity of the information to be provided for this study. A majority of the respondents were from the

Islamic Financial Institution (94 percent). Twelve of them (70 percent) were in the Shari'ah Supervision Committee or Shari'ah Departments Employee; while the other five (29 percent) of the respondents held other positions in the organization. With regards to their education level, eight (47 percent) of the respondents were first degree holders, other eight (47 percent) were post degree holders, while one (6 percent) of the respondents possessed others qualifications. This sample comprised of twelve (70 percent) male and five (29 percent) female respondents; where sixteen (94 percent) of the respondents were Malay, while one (6 percent) of the respondents was from other ethnics.

Table 3: Respondents' Experience

Age	31-35 years
Years of service in current position	1- 5 years
Years of service in the current industry	1- 5 years
Years of experience	6-10 years

Overall, the age of the respondents was in the range 31 to 35 years old, and the respondents experience was in the range 6 to 10 years. The length of service in the current position and the length of service in the current industry was 1 to 5 years.

Reporting Channel

The respondents were asked to indicate the preferred reporting channel for reporting wrong doings.

Table 4: Channel Reporting

Channel Reporting of Wrongdoing in your Workplace	*Results*	
	Frequency	*Percentage*
Internal Channel	14	82.4
Both External And Internal	3	17.6

More than 80 percent of the respondents choose an internal channel for reporting of wrongdoing in their workplace. The remaining 17.6 percent preferred to use both external and internal channels to report wrongdoing in their workplace.

Further analysis of respondents who choose an internal reporting channel revealed that the statement "I would tell my immediate superior about it" had the highest mean of 6.39 (SD=1.08) as compared to other statements. The other three preferred internal reporting channels are whistle blowing channels (Mean = 4.07; SD = 2.30), top management (Mean = 3.79; SD = 2.19) and internal auditor (mean = 3.79; SD = 2.22). The respondents are not required to answer statements (e) and (f) in their cases.

Table 5: Reporting Channel

	Mean (SD)	
	Internal Channel	*Both External and Internal Channel*
I would tell my immediate superior about it	6.36 (1.08)	5.33 (1.52)
I would report it to the internal auditor of my organization	3.79 (2.22)	3.67 (0.57)
I would inform top management about it	3.79 (2.19)	4.33 (0.57)
I would use whistle blowing channels to report	4.07 (2.30)	3.67 (1.52)
I would report it to the appropriate authorities outside the organization	Not required	3.00 (1.73)
I would inform the media	Not required	3.33 (2.51)

Some respondents chose both external and internal reporting channels. In terms of reporting channels, the majority preferred reporting to their immediate superiors, with the highest mean of 5.33 (SD = 1.52). This is similar to those respondents that choose an internal reporting channel. Other preferred reporting channels were "top management" with mean of 4.33 (SD = 0.57), "internal auditor" 3.67 (SD = 0.57), "whistle blowing channels" 3.67 (SD = 1.52), "media" 3.33 (SD = 2.51) and lastly, "appropriate authorities outside the organization" 3.00 (SD = 1.73). Please note that standard deviation (SD) may be due to numbers of respondents (n = 3).

In both instances, the most preferred reporting channel was to report to the immediate superior.

Whistle-Blowing Policy

The respondents were also requested to indicate whether their organization has a whistle blowing policy.

Sixty five percent of the respondents indicated that the whistle-blowing policy was available in their organizations, while 11.8 percent stated that whistle blowing policy was not available in their organizations, while 23.5 percent of the respondents did not know the availability of the whistle blowing policy in their organizations.

Table 6: Whistle-Blowing Policy

Is There any Whistle Blowing Policy in Your Organization	*Results*	
	Frequency	*Percentage*
No	2	11.8
Yes	11	64.7
Do not know	4	23.5

The respondents were then asked about the nature of the whistle-blowing policy, i.e, whether the policy provides sufficient protection to the whistle-blower, encourages reporting of wrongdoing, has been adequately communicated, and whether the awareness program is conducted regularly. They were asked to indicate the extent of their agreement with the statements on a scale of 1(strongly disagree) to 5(strongly agree). Table 4.7 presents the statements on the nature of the whistle-blowing policy and the respondents' responses. Most of the respondents agree that the whistle blowing policy provides sufficient protection to the whistle blower with the highest mean of 4.09 (SD=0.53). They almost agree that the whistle blowing policy encourages reporting of wrongdoing (mean=3.82; SD=0.60). They were quite neutral to the statements that the whistle-blowing policy had been adequately communicated (mean=3.64; SD=0.80) and that the whistle blowing awareness program had been conducted regularly (mean=3.09; SD=0.83).

Table 7: Nature of Whistle-Blowing Policy

Is there any whistle blowing policy in your organization	*Yes (n=11)*
The whistle blowing policy provides sufficient protection to the whistle blower	4.09 (0.53)
The whistle blowing policy encourages reporting of wrongdoing	3.82 (0.60)
The whistle blowing policy is adequately communicated	3.64 (0.80)
The whistle blowing policy awareness program is conducted regularly	3.09 (0.83)

Similar analysis was also conducted for respondents who indicated that "whistle blowing policy" in their organizations was not available, or that they did not know whether the policy was available in their organisations. They were asked whether the whistle blowing policy should provide sufficient protection to the whistle-blower; should encourage reporting of wrongdoing; should adequately communicate and that whistle blowing policy awareness program should be conducted regularly. The group who said that the policy was not available in their organisations generally agreed on all the statements with mean of 3.50 (SD = 0.70).

The group who did not know the availability of whistle blowing policy in their organization had different opinions on the statements. They were fairly neutral that the whistle-blowing policy should provide sufficient protection to the whistle blower (mean = 2.75; SD = 2.06) as compared to other statements. They disagreed that whistle-blowing had encouraged reporting of wrongdoing (mean = 2.50; SD = 1.73), whistle-blowing policy had been adequately communicated (mean = 2.25; SD = 1.50) and that the whistle blowing policy awareness program had been conducted regularly (mean = 2.00; SD = 1.15).

Code of Ethics

Our preliminary survey revealed that some organisations did not have a whistle-blowing policy, but they did have, a Code of Ethics in place to deal with wrongdoings in their organisations. Therefore, in addition to whistle-blowing policy, the respondents were also asked about the availability of the Code of Ethics in their organizations.

The respondents were first cross-checked to examine whether their organizations had both a whistle-blowing policy and Code of Ethics, or either of the policies. Table 8. showed that only nine respondents had both the whistle-blowing policy and Code of Ethics in their organisations. Two respondents who did not (or not sure) have whistle-blowing policy, but they did have a Code of Ethics in place.

Table 8: Whistle-Blowing Policy vs Code of Ethics

Is there a whistle-blowing policy in your organization	*Is There A Code of Ethics in Your Organization?*	
	Yes	*No/don't know*
Yes	9	2
No/ Do not know	2	1
Total	11	3

There were also two respondents who did not (or not sure) have Code of Ethics, but they had a whistle-blowing policy in their organisations. Only one respondent did not (not sure) have both the whistle-blowing policy and Code of Ethics.

Table 9: Code of Ethics

Is There A Code Of Ethics In Your Organization	*Results*	
	Frequency	*Percentage*
No	1	5.9
Yes	15	88.2
Do Not Know	1	5.9

With regard to the code of ethics only, 88.2 percent of the respondents indicated that the Code of Ethics are available and while another 11.8 percent indicated that the Code of Ethics was not available in their organization. The remaining 5.9 percent of the respondents indicated that they did not know if the Code of Ethics was available.

Table 10: Availability of Code of Ethics

Is there a code of ethics in your organization	*Yes (n=15)*
The code of ethics encourages reporting of wrongdoing	3.47 (1.06)
The code of ethics is distributed to all employees	4.13 (1.06)
All employees need to acknowledge periodically their compliance with the code of ethics	3.53 (1.06)
The code of ethics awareness program is conducted regularly	2.80 (0.86)

They were asked to indicate the extent of their agreement with the statements on a scale of 1(strongly disagree) to 5(strongly agree). The results revealed that the respondents agreed that the code of ethics is distributed to all employees (mean = 4.13; SD = 1.06). They also generally agreed that "all employees need to acknowledge periodically their compliance with the code of ethics" (mean = 3.53; SD = 1.06), and "Code of Ethics encourage reporting of wrongdoing" (mean = 3.47; SD = 1.06). However, they fairly disagree that "the Code of Ethics awareness program is conducted regularly (mean = 2.80; SD = 0.86)."

Similar analysis was also conducted with respondents who indicated that the "Code of Ethics" in their organizations was not available, or that they did not know whether the Code was available in their organisations. They were asked whether the Code of Ethics should encourage reporting of wrongdoing; should be distributed to all employees; employees should acknowledge periodically their compliance with the Code and whether the Code of Ethics awareness program should be conducted regularly. The group who said that the policy was not available in their organisations, strongly agree with all the statements with mean of 5.00. Similar response was identified for the group who did not know about the availability of the Code in the organization. All of them indicate their agreement on all statements with a mean of 4.00.

Whistle-Blowing Communication Channels

The respondents were also requested to indicate the preferred whistle-blowing communication channel.

With regard to whistle-blowing communication channels, the majority of the respondents prefer the usage of internet, intranet or e-mails as the whistle-blowing communication channel (76.5 percent) as compared to mail letters (47.1 percent), telephone (41.2 percent), others (17.6 percent) and fax (5.9 percent).

Further analysis was conducted on the respondents opinion regarding the preferred features of whistle blowing communication channels. As shown in Table 4.11, the most preferred feature was "the communication channel is free of charge," followed by, it would not disclose the whistle blower identity, easily accessible, not complicated, provides anonymous reporting of wrongdoing, handled by an expert, and lastly, it is handled by an independent external body.

Table 11: Method of Whistle-Blowing Communication Channel

Whistle- Blowing Communication Channel		*Results*	
		Frequency	*Percentage*
Telephone (T)	Y N	7 10	41.2 58.8
Internet, Intranet or E-mails (I)	Y N	13 4	76.5 23.5
Fax (F)	Y N	1 16	5.9 94.1
Mail letters (M)	Y N	8 9	47.1 52.9
Others (O)	Y N	3 14	17.6 82.4

Table 12: Features of Whistle-Blowing Communication Channels

	Mean	*Standard Deviation*
The communication Is free of charge	4.06	0.65
The communication channel would not disclose the whistle blower identity	3.88	0.78
The communication channel is easily accessible	3.82	0.63
The communication channel is not complicated	3.76	0.66
The communication channel provides anonymous reporting of wrongdoing	3.35	0.70
The communication channel is handled by the experts	3.35	0.49
The communication channel is handled by an independent external body	3.06	0.74

LIMITATIONS OF STUDY AND FUTURE RESEARCH

The sample of the study is very small which is a major limitation of this study. Though great efforts have been taken to personally distribute and collect the questionnaires, most of the respondents were either not willing to participate, or were advised by their superior not to participate in the study. This indicates that the whistle-blowing policy is generally in its infancy stage in Malaysia, and the IFIs might not be willing or ready to disclose that they did not have it yet. Larger studies in the future might produce different results as perceptions of right versus wrong, justice, morality, and loyalty may differ very much in different countries (Vogel, 1992) or different contexts. Overall, we hope that the findings of this research would be helpful for the regulatory and the policy makers in monitoring the development and the implementation of whistle blowing practices of Malaysian IFIs.

REFERENCE

Alrajhi(http://www.alrajhibank.com.sa/Aboutus/pages/ShariaaGroup, accessed on 16 August 2010).

American Institute of Certified Public Accountants, 2006 available from http://www.aicpa.org/

Bank Islamhttp://www.bankislam.com.my (accessed on 12 August 2010).

Bank Muamalat(http://www.muamalat.com.my), (accessed on 13 August 2010).

Callahan, E. S., & Dworkin, T. M. (2000). The state of state whistleblower protection. American Business Law Journa, 38, 99-175.

Churchill, G. A. (2001). Basic Marketing Research. Forth Worth: The Dryden Press.

Collis, J., & Hussey, R. (2003). Business Research: A Practical Guide for Undergraduate and Postgraduate Students (2nd Edition ed.). Basingstoke: Palgrave Macmillan.

Cooper, D. R., & Schindler, P. S. (2006). Marketing Research. New York: McGraw–Hill.

Cross 2005.

Dworkin, T. M., & Baucus, M. S. (1998). Internal vs. external whistleblowers: A comparison of whistleblowing processes. *Journal of Business Ethics, 17*(12), 1281-1298.

Dworkin, T., & Callahan, E. (1991). Internal whistle-blowing: Protecting the interests of the employee, the organization and society. *American Business Law Journa, 29*, 267-308.

Finn, D. (1995). Ethical decision making in organizations: a management employee organization whistle-blowing model. *Research on Accounting Ethics, 1*, 291-313.

Gay, G., & Simnett, R. (2010). Auditing assurance and services in Australia (4th ed.). North Ryde,N.S.W.: McGraw-Hill.

Grant, C. (2002). Whistle blowers: Saints of secular culture. *Journal of Business Ethics, 39*(4), 391-399.

Guiral, A., Rodgers, W., Ruiz, E., & Gonzalo, J. (2010). Ethical Dilemmas in Auditing: Dishonesty or Unintentional Bias? Journal of Business Ethics, 91(1), 151-166.

Hopman, P., & Leeuwen, E. V. (2009). Who Do We Inform? The Role of Status and Target in Intergroup Whistle-blowing. Group Processes & Intergroup Relations, 12(5), 605-618.

Hwang, D., Stanley, B., Chen, Y. T., & Lan, J.-S. (2008). Confucian culture and whistle-blowing by professional accountants: an exploratory study. *Managerial Auditing Journal, 23*(5), 504-526.

Islamic Financial Services Board (2010) http://www.ifsb.org/.

James, 1995.

King, G. (1999). The implications of an organization's structure on whistleblowing. Journal of Business Ethics, 20(4), 315-326.

Kuwait Finance House (Malaysia) Berhad(http://www,kfhonline.com.my/kfhmb), accessed on 16 August 2010,

Miceli, M. P., & Near, I. P. (1988). Individual and Situational Correlates of Whistleblowing. *Personnel Psychology, 41*, 267-281.

Miceli, M., & Near, J. (1992). *Blowing the Whistle*. New York: Lexington Books.

Near, J. P., & Miceli, M. P. (1995). Effective whistle-blowing. *Academy of Management Review, 20*(3), 679-708.

Near, J. P., & Miceli, M. P. (1996). Whistle-blowing: Myth and reality. *Journal of Management, 22*(3), 507-526.

Personneltoday (2002). Blowing the whistle. Retrieved from personneltoday website: http://www.personneltoday.com/Articles/02/12/2002/16508/Blowing-the-whistle.htm

Ponnu, C. H., Naidu, K., & Zamri, W. (2007, 26-27 April). *Whistle-Blowing As Planned Behaviour: A Survey Amongst Executives In The Banking Sector In Malaysia.* Paper presented at the Proceedings of the 5th International Business Research Conference, Dubai.

PricewaterhouseCoopers, 2009

Qatar Islamic Bank (http://www.qib.com.qa/, accessed on 16 August 2010).

Schemerhorn, J. R. (2008). *Management*. Hoboken, NJ: Wiley.

Sekaran, U. (2003). Research methods for business: A skill building approach.: John Wiley & Sons, Inc.

Uys, T. (2000). The politicisation of whistle-blowers: a case study. *Business Ethics: A European Review, 9*(4), 259-267.

Websites:

Whistleblower Protection Act 2010 http://www.bheuu.gov.my/

Zikmund, W. G., Babin, B. J., Carr, J. C., & Griffin, M. (2010). Business Research Methods (8th Edition ed.). Canada: South-Western, Cengage Learning.

Footprints of Corporate Governance of BSE Companies

Sunaina Kanojia and Harleen Kaur Bindra[1]
Delhi School of Economics, Delhi
[1]Janki Devi Memorial College, Delhi

ABSTRACT

Despite the fact that corporate governance is considered to be the seed of corporate excellence and long term survival, it has still not taken firm roots in Indian Inc. It has been over two decades since the first Adrian's code of corporate governance were announced, however the complete synthesis of those codes in corporates is yet to be seen. Perhaps there is a need to ascertain the evidence of corporate governance codes on the performance of companies, to analyze the lag in the desired framework. The present study attempts to unearth the impact of imbibing the codes and principles of corporate governance, empirically. The utmost intrinsic variables presumed as independent variables have been regressed with financial stability as a dependent variable to scan the footprints of corporate governance in the thirty companies comprising BSE sensex.

Keywords: *Corporate Governance, Corporate Excellence, Net Worth, Financial Stability*

INTRODUCTION

Corporate governance is all about promoting corporate fairness, transparency and accountability of managers and the board of directors[1]. Corporate governance has narrowly been defined as the relationship of a company to its shareholders (agency theory), however, more broadly, it is a relationship to society, i.e., towards employees, creditors, suppliers and local communities where the corporation operates (stakeholder's theory).[2] Adequate disclosures, transparency, ethical conduct of business can lead to higher returns, attracting more investors and long term sustainability to achieve corporate excellence. Managers, while

---

[1] Business get in corporate governance http://busimess.gov.in corporate-governance\concept_objectives. php as on may 2012

[2] Simms Marsha E & Gregory Holly J (1999). "Corporate Governance: What It Is And Why It Matters" 9th International Anti-Corruption Conference. Pp 2

making decisions have to consider the expectations of all the stakeholders, and they should bear in mind that they are trustees and not owners of capital, this is what corporate governance theories are about.[3] The aim of corporate governance is to bring a distinction between personal and corporate funds, so as to attain the long term objectives like growth, value of firm etc. Good corporate governance leads to corporate excellence, thereby strengthening the economy, socio-economic development as the economic health of a nation depends substantially on how sound and ethical businesses are[4]. Corporate governance mechanisms are considered necessary to resolve problems like the existence of agency problems, managers expropriating the resources of a firm at the ultimate expense of shareholder, and moreover it leads to an increase in profitability, revenues, share value, performance that satisfies stakeholders and by building the brand image. Studies in the Indian context have revealed that corporate governance variables do contribute to the bottom line. Kanojia (2010), Upadhyaya and Sriram (2010), Gomper et al., (2003), and Claessens (2003) highlighted that corporate governance variables effect the financial parameters of listed companies in different sectors. Following the results of these researches, the present article aims to find evidence in companies constituting the BSE Sensex.

REVIEW OF LITERATURE AND FORMULATION OF HYPOTHESIS

The struggle for efficient internal management control is the centre of the corporate governance debate in Europe since 1602 (Hopt and Leynes, 2004), where the internal corporate control is related to the way boards manage an organization in a better and efficient way[5]. Further, Harris and Raviv (1976), Jensen and Meckling (1976), Holmstrom (1979) and Shavell (1979) initiated seminal research, and applied the agency theory in the management of corporations. Several studies examine corporate governance generally. Lawrence D.Brown and J. Mack Robinson (2004) found that better governed companies are more profitable. Bauery R, et al., (2003) found a positive relation between variables and the firm's value. Jackling and Johl (2009) study the association between the board structure and firm performance in large Indian firms. Largely, it has been found that there exists a strong relation between governance structure, agency problems, and a firm's performance level. Most of studies indicate better governed companies are more profitable, and have higher firm value, especially in countries with weak legal environments. Then internal control

[3] Thomas Donald son and Preston Lee E. (1995) "The Stakeholder Theory of the Corporation: Concepts, Evidence, and Implications" The Academy of Management Review, Vol. 20, No. 1 (Jan., 1995), pp. 65-91. Accessed on 4 may 2012

[4] Cherupalli Kiran Kumar. (2008) "corporate governance" http://www.articlesbase.com/accounting-articles/corporate-governance-637944.html as on 8 july 2012

[5] Kanojia, S (2010), "Active Board Monitoring and Performance of Banks: A Study of Public and Private Sector Banks", Corporate Governance Beyond Boundaries, MacMillan Publishers India Ltd, pp 212-223

mechanisms, of corporate governance are less effective than external mechanisms, as the board and managers are likely to have a more positive effect on performance when they have a significant financial interest in the firm. Further, concentration of largest shareholders has a positive effect on performance, and that of others is insignificant or negative. Prior studies of Mace (1971), Pfeffer (1972), Lipton and Lorch (1992) and Jensen (1993) highlighted contrasting results of board size and effective, monitoring. It has been empirically tested that large boards are generally less effective, as compared to smaller boards, due to communication and coordination advantages, Lipton and Lorch (1992); Jensen (1993); and Yermack (1996). Gompers.et al., (2003) found that firms with strong shareholders' rights have superior valuations, better margins and improved sales growth. Further, Claessens (2003) suggests a relationship between corporate governance and improved performance of an enterprise is not only from better governance variables, rather it is the other way round that better performance creates demand for better governance.

Good corporate governance refers to the way in which companies are directed and controlled. The board is mainly responsible for this function, that performs their duties with the support of the management and staff, in line with law and stakeholders benefits. It is about commitment to values, ethical business conduct, and exercise of powers in a responsible way[6]. One of the emerging issues nowadays in the field of management research is the impact of corporate governance on the financial aspects of the firm. This impact holds more importance in developing countries like India, because it can provide good leverage to the profits figures, as investors here follow more of value strategy, i.e. people are willing to pay more for corporate governance, as it reduces risks and attracts further investments. The present article aims to find evidence of the causal relationship between corporate governance variables and a firm's long term sustainability in case of the BSE 30 companies. The objective of the article is to study and highlight the impact of corporate governance on a company's quantitative variables. Further, it intends to examine the relation between corporate governance variables, company's net worth and the top line.

The hypotheses created for the purpose are:

H_{o1} : Ceteris Paribus, board size, board composition, duality and independent non executive chairmanship does not affect the financial net worth of the sample companies.

H_{a1}: Ceteris Paribus, board size, board composition, duality and independent non executive chairmanship significantly affect the financial net worth of the sample companies.

---

[6] Sharma, J.P. *"emerging issues in company law"*, an easy approach to company and compensation law (pg 303-308).

H_{o2} : Ceteris Paribus, board size, board composition, duality and independent non executive chairmanship does not affect the financial net sales of the sample companies.

H_{a2} : Ceteris Paribus, board size, board composition, duality and independent non executive chairmanship significantly affect the financial net sales of the sample companies.

METHODOLOGY

The present article attempts to analyze the impact of corporate governance variables- board size and board composition on the financial parameters of the BSE 30 companies constituting the sensex. The data for analysis has been collected from the annual reports of the companies and the PROWESS database. For analyzing the data so collected, Pearson's correlation, descriptive statistics and multiple regression analysis under ordinary least square has been used. The variables of corporate governance taken in the study are board size, board composition, duality and independent non-executive chairman. For the purpose of exploring the financial health of companies, the net worth as an indicator of long term survival and net sales as the top line have been regressed using multiple regression analysis. To check the consistency of these variables, Pearson's correlation method has been used. Corporate governance variables are taken of the 30 companies creating the BSE index for the period of (2009-2011). i.e., three years after the crisis. This data holds importance due to the fact that these companies are under obligation to give their corporate governance details to the exchange authorities, and forming the base of the BSE INDEX shows their importance. These companies have high earnings levels, so their corporate governance practices can give a very fair and vital idea of the impact of corporate governance on the financial aspect of companies in the Indian context.

The variables taken are explained as follows:

- *Board size*: It shows the total number of executive and non executive directors on the board. Board size generally ranges from 5 to 30 in many companies. Board size is a very crucial element which effects the board's decisions, and hence corporate performance as well. There are many theories given by different researchers which say that the firm's performance is affected by a smaller or bigger board size, whereas, some say there isn't any such kind of relationship between the two. That is why we take board size as our variable, and check whether it affects a firm's net worth in any way possible, or not.
- *Board composition*: This shows the number of non executive directors on the board. The board consists of two types of directors- executive and non executive. Executive directors are responsible for the day to day working of the company. But, a

mechanism is required to see whether these directors work in the interests of the shareholders or not. They are in a position to affect the company's performance tremendously. The nonexecutive board is appointed to provide independent/ unbiased judgment on the executive board's decisions. The effectiveness of this mechanism can help improve the firm's performance levels. Generally, it has been found that a firm's performance is not affected by the board composition. In a few previous studies, it was shown that if the same board continues for long, then generally there is no impact of their existence on the firm's performance and executive monitoring.

- *Duality*: The corporate governance codes and standards emphasize avoiding practicing duality, i.e., holding the Chairmanship and Managing Director position by one person. Separation of Chairman and Managing Director leads to better corporate governance. Therefore, duality has been checked in all the thirty companies as a binary variable.
- *Chairman's independence*: A decade back, it was a common feature in almost every company to have an executive chairman, however the persistent recommendation of various committees of corporate governance has lead to the independence of the chairman. The independence of the chairman being a non executive director is desired for better corporate governance. To bring objectivity in the board operations, corporates have realized its significance and started practicing it.
- *Firm's net worth*: For a company, this is known as shareholders' (or owners') equity, and is determined by subtracting liabilities on the balance sheet from assets. Net worth of a firm's business is the value of all assets, minus the value of all liabilities at the carrying value (which is the value as expressed on financial statements). It has been taken as the independent variable in the regression equation. Here the values of this variable have been found from the annual reports of the companies. We have taken the log of this variable.
- *Sales* : Here defines the natural log of net sales of that year.

Testing of Hypotheses

Model 1 for H_{01} : Ceteris Paribus, board size, board composition, duality and independent non executive chairmanship does not affect the financial net worth of the sample companies.

H_{a1}: Ceteris Paribus, board size, board composition, duality and independent non executive chairmanship significantly affect the financial net worth of the sample companies.

$$FNW= a + (b1*BS + b2* BC +b3*CI +b4*DU) \qquad \text{Model 1}$$

Model 2 for H_{o2} : Ceteris Paribus, board size, board composition, duality and independent non executive chairmanship does not affect the financial net sales of the sample companies.

H_{a2} : Ceteris Paribus, board size, board composition, duality and independent non executive chairmanship significantly affect the financial net sales of the sample companies.

FS= a + (b1*BS + b2* BC +b3*CI +b4*DU) Model 2

Where,
BS= Board size
BC= Board composition
CI= Chairman's independence
DU= Duality
FNW= Firm's net worth (in log)
FS= Firm's net sales (in log)

While calculating for duality and Chairman's independence, binary variables were taken:

Duality: 0 when both Chairman and Managing Director are the same and one when Chairman and Managing Director are different.

Chairman's independence: 0 when Chairman is an Executive Director and one when Chairman is a Non-Executive Director.

There said hypnoses have been tested in the next section of the articles with the help of Pearson's Correlation and OLS for multiple regression analysis.

Analysis and Findings

The descriptive statistics of corporate governance variables for all the 30 BSE index firms are given in Table 1 to present the broad parameters.

Table 1: Descriptive Statistics of Corporate Governance Variables

Variable	*Mean*	*Median*	*Standard deviation*	*Minimum*	*Maximum*	*Range*
Board Size	13.02	13	3.054	6	20	14
Board Composition	9.00	9	2.513	4	14	10
Chairman's Independence	0.43	0	0.498	0	1	1
Duality	0.67	1	0.474	0	1	1

Statistics in Table 1 show that the mean and median board size is 13 in the 30 companies for the period of three years from 90 observations. As per the recommendations of various committees on corporate governance, 13 directors on an average are considered a very large size for a board. It has been observed that it ranges from 9 to 16 normally, whereas the range of the board in the sample companies has been 6-20. The variability in board size is given by its standard deviation which is 3.504. At the same time, it was seen that the board comprises of 9 non executive directors on an average, which shows a range is 4-14, i.e., differs by 10, so it may be concluded that the corporate governance clause 49 requirements are seriously met by these companies. Therefore, it may be concluded from the range of the board size that some companies have a large board, while others prefer to have a smaller board. Hemalin and Weisbach (1998) and Bhagat and Black (1999, 2002) suggested that companies alter their board size, followed by financial results. Companies who need diverse experience and have sufficient profits for expansion, prefer a larger board. The Chairman is independent in 43 percent cases, but if it has to be decided about the Chairman's independence on the board, and in general he is an Executive Director. Further, in case of duality, i.e., whether the Chairman is also the Managing Director of the company or not, the mean is 67 percent exhibiting that generally both of them are different. The duality is favoured for improved corporate governance, as it brings objectivity in the total control mechanism.

In order to regress the corporate governance variable on net worth and net sales, the correlation coefficient has been checked. The results shown in Table 2 explore the degree of association between the variables, and exhibit that there exists a positive correlation between, a firm's net worth and board size and board composition, whereas, it is negatively correlated with duality and the Chairman's independence variables. Board composition and board size are also highly correlated with each other, followed by high correlation between the Chairman's independence and duality variable. Further, it shows that there exists a positive correlation between a firm's net sales, board size and board composition, and negative correlation with duality. The result of the correlation matrix reveals that the problem of multic collinearity does not exist among the set of variables.

Table 2: Correlation Matrix of Financial Net Worth, Sales and Corporate Governance Variables

		FNW	*FS*	*BC*	*DU*	*BS*	*CI*
FNW	Pearson Correlation	1	.558**	.086	-.285**	.134	-.101
	Sig. (2-tailed)		.000	.420	.007	.208	.345
	N	90	90	90	90	90	90
FS	Pearson Correlation	.558**	1	.270*	-.259*	.237*	.052
	Sig. (2-tailed)	.000		.010	.014	.025	.629
	N	90	90	90	90	90	90
BC	Pearson Correlation	.086	.270*	1	.094	.821**	-.099
	Sig. (2-tailed)	.420	.010		.377	.000	.355
	N	90	90	90	90	90	90
DU	Pearson Correlation	-.285**	-.259*	.094	1	-.111	.618**

	Sig. (2-tailed)	.007	.014	.377		.297	.000
	N	90	90	90	90	90	90
BS	Pearson Correlation	.134	.237*	.821**	-.111	1	-.309**
	Sig. (2-tailed)	.208	.025	.000	.297		.003
	N	90	90	90	90	90	90
CI	Pearson Correlation	-.101	.052	-.099	.618**	-.309**	1
	Sig. (2-tailed)	.345	.629	.355	.000	.003	
	N	90	90	90	90	90	90

**. Correlation is significant at the 0.01 level (2-tailed).
*. Correlation is significant at the 0.05 level (2-tailed).

Table 3: Result of OLS for Net Worth

Variables	*Coefficients*	*Tolerance collineraity statistics*	*Vif*
Intercept	4.107	-	-
Board size	.092	.269	3.711
Board composition	.064	.287	3.489
Chairman's independence	.174	.552	1.811
Duality	-.388	.586	1.706

Significace Level= .05

Table 4: Model Summary

R^2	.111
ADJ R^2	.069
P VALUE	.039

The result of the regression analysis run for model 1 has been shown in Tables 3 and 4. The analysis indicates that the intercept is 4.107, and the independent variables- board size, board composition, duality and Chairman's independence have their coefficient values at .092, .064, –.338 and. 174 respectively, which shows that 1 percent increase in the independent variable leads to the coefficient's amount increase in net worth for example, 1percent increase in board composition leads to .064 increase in net worth. The R square statistic shown in Table 4, suggests that 11.1 percent of the variance in net worth can be predicted from the variables of the board size, board composition, duality and Chairman's independence. Whereas, the adjusted R square is .069 which shows that even if more variables are added to the equation, this much of variance prediction is not by chance. With the p value at .039 which is lesser than .05, we may reject the null hypothesis. Therefore, we may say that Ceteris Paribus, board size, board composition, duality and independent Non

Executive Chairmanship significantly affect the financial net worth of the sample companies. Further, the variables have VIF and tolerance value within the prescribed limits, showing no cause for multicolinearity. Since all VIF values are lesser than 10, and all tolerance values are greater than .20, so there is no cause for multicolinearity existence. As seen from earlier table, the MRA results indicate that the firm's net worth is found to be affected by corporate governance variables. The overall model is significant at 95 percent interval. If the ADJ R^2 increases with adding more independent variables, then it indicates that the dependent variable has been affected by the independent variables and error term is minimal.

The other hypothesis of the study H_{02} : Ceteris Paribus, board size, board composition, duality and independent Non Executive Chairmanship does not affect the financial net sales of the sample companies has been analyzed in the following section.

FS= a + (b1*BS + b2* BC +b3*CI +b4*DU).............................Model 2

Table 5: Result of OLS for Net Sales

Variables	*Coefficients*	*Tolerance collineraity statistics*	*Vif*
Intercept	3.752	-	-
Board size	.031	.269	3.711
Board composition	.341	.287	3.489
Chairman's independence	.442	.552	1.811
Duality	-.561	.586	1.706

Significace Level= .05

Table 6: Model Summary

R^2	.268
ADJ R^2	.233
P VALUE	.001

The figures in Tables 5 and 6 show the results of regression for model 2. It indicates that the intercept is 3.752 and the independent variables- board size, board composition, duality and Chairman's independence have their coefficient values at .031, .341, –.561 and. 442 respectively which shows that 1 percent increase in independent variable leads to the coefficient's amount increase in net sales for example, 1 percent increase in board composition leads to .341 increase in net worth. Further, the R square statistic shows that 26.8 percent of the variance in net sales can be predicted from the variables board size, board composition, duality and Chairman's independence. Whereas, the adjusted R square is .233, which shows that even if more variables are added to the equation, this much of variance prediction is not by chance. The p value is .001 which is lesser than .05, showing the group of independent variables is statistically significant, and we may reaccept the alternate hypothesis that Ceteris Paribus, board size, board composition, duality and independent Non Executive Chairmanship significantly affect the financial net sales of the sample companies. In addition to this, the variables have VIF and tolerance value within the limits, showing no cause for multi collinearity. Since all VIF values are lesser than 10, and all tolerance values are greater than .20, so there is no cause for multi collinearity existence.

As observed in Table 6, the MRA results indicate that the firm's top line is found to be affected by corporate governance variables. The overall model is significant at 95 percent interval. The adjusted r^2 value shows that 23.3 percent of variation in net worth could be explained by corporate governance variables, board size, board composition, duality and Chairman's independence.

SUMMARY AND CONCLUSION

The present study attempts to find evidence for a relationship between a firms's net worth, net sales, board size, board composition, duality and independent Non Executive Chairmanship on the BSE sensex by using multiple regression analysis. The descriptive statistics highlighted that some companies have a large board, while others prefers to have a smaller board. The result is parallel with Hemalin and Weisbach (1998) and Bhagat and Black (1999,2002), who suggested that companies alter their board size, followed by financial results. Companies who need diverse experience, and have sufficient profits for expansion, prefer a larger board. In addition, the Chairman is independent in 43 percent cases, but if it has to be decided about the Chairman's independence on the board, in general he is an Executive Director. Further, on an average duality stands for 67 percent exhibiting that generally both the Chairman and Managing Directors are different. The duality is favoured for improved corporate governance, as it brings objectivity in the total control mechanism. The correlation analysis highlighted a positive correlation between board size, board composition and firm's net worth whereas, a negative correlation with duality and Chairman's independence. By means of multiple regression analysis, the results of prior studies conducted on US based firms and S&P 1500 companies were found to be true, in case of the sensex companies. The regression results show that corporate governance variables do affect the net worth and net sales of the company, though the variations in net worth which can be predicted from variable board size, board composition, duality and Chairman's independence when adjusted gives a rate of 6.9 percent and 26.8 percent respectively. Subsequent research can be done by including a wider dataset of stock exchanges, as suggested by the adjusted R square. Therefore, the corporate governance variables must be engrossed in the corporate control system to deliver long term sustainability of corporates with excellence.

REFERENCES

Bauery Rob; Gaunsterz Nadja; Ottenx Roger. (2003), "Empirical Evidence on Corporate governance in Europe the Effect on Stock Returns, Firm Value and Performance", http://papers.ssrn.com/sol3/papers.cfm?abstract_id=444543&http://papers.ssrn.com/sol3/papers.cfm?abstract_id=444543&rec=1&srcabs=286440. November 23, 2011.

Bhagat S.& B. Black (1999), " The Uncertain Relationship between Board Composition and Firm Performance", Business Lawyer, 54, pp. 921-963.

Bhagat S.& B. Black (2002), "The non correlation between Board Independence and Long Term Financial Performance, Journal of Corporation Law, 27, pp. 231-274.

Brown Lawerence D; Robinson J.Mack. (2004), "Corporate governance and firm performance",.http://papers.ssrn.com/sol3/papers.cfm?abstract_id=586423&rec=1&srcabs=286440, on December 20, 2011.

Claessens.S (2003), "Corporate Governance and Development", Global Corporate Governance Forum, The International Bank for Reconstruction and Development.

Gompers. P Ishii.J, MetrickA (2003), "Corporate Governance and Equity Prices, The quarterly Journal of Economics, 118 (1), pp.107-156.

Harris, M and Raviv A (1978), "Some Results on Incentive Contracts with Application to Education and Employment, Health Insurance and Law Enforcement, American Economic Review, 8(3):pp.20-30.

Holmstrom. B (1979), "Moral Hazard and Observability, Bell Journal of Economics, 10 (2), pp.74-91.

Jensen .M and Meckling. W (1976), "Theory of Firm: Managerial Behavior, Agency Cost and Ownership Structure", Journal of Financial Economics, 3(2): pp.305-360.

Jensen.M(1993), " The Modern Industrial Revolution, Exit and the Failure of Internal Control System", Journal of Finance, 48, pp.831-880.

Lipton.M & J.W.Lorch, (1992), "A Modest Proposal for Improved Corporate Governance, Business Lawyer, 1, pp. 59-77.

Mace.M.M (1971), "Directors Myth and Reality, Boston: Harvard Business School Press.

Pfeffer.J(1972), "Size and Composition of Corporate Boards of Director: The Organization and its Environment", Administrative Science Quarterly, 17, pp.1829-1853.

Shavell.S (1979), "Risk Sharing and the Incentive in the Principal and Agent Relationship", Bell Journal of Economics, 10(1), pp.55-73.

Yermack.D (1996), "Higher Market Valuation of Companies with a Small Board of Directors", Journal of Financial Economics, 40, pp. 185-212.

Boards and Audit Committees: An Empirical Study of Companies Listed in the BSE Sensex

M.D. Saibaba and Padma Srinivasan[1]

Dayananda Sagar Academy of Technology and Management, Bengaluru

[1]*RV College of Management, Bengaluru*

ABSTRACT

Boards form an important element of corporate governance mechanisms interfacing both with the internal and external stakeholders. Accordingly, they have a critical role to play in monitoring and implementing the corporate governance process. Research evidence shows that practices beyond mandatory compliance lend credence to the governance process, and investors accord premium valuations to such firms. This study is about board independence, board meetings, audit committee independence, audit committee meetings and CEO duality. 30 Indian companies listed in the BSE sensex have been considered for the years 2009-10 and 2010-11. An index, based on these non-mandatory parameters have been computed, and we find a positive relationship between the index and the financial measure ROA.

Keywords: *Index, Corporate Governance, Boards, ROA, Tobin's Q, MVBV*

INTRODUCTION

Regulatory reforms enunciated in the SOX Act, 2002 have had a far-reaching impact in corporate governance history (Byrnes 2003). Regulations stipulated in the SOX Act, 2002 have been the forerunner for all the regulatory amendments of almost all countries of the world which have adopted the Anglo Saxon model of corporate governance. Black and Khanna (2007) observed that governance reforms in India, Clause 49, resembles the US Sarbanes Oxley Act. In India, SEBI's Clause 49 of the listing agreement has been revised on the basis of Narayana Murthy's committees' report, which in a way mirrors the SOX ACT. The revised clause came into force in 2006. In subsequent years, the governance landscape has been dotted with scandals resulting in a few minor changes, but the substance of the earlier reforms remain unaltered, which points out to the robustness of these regulations. In recent years, many Indian companies have been issuing ADR/GDRs and cross listing on foreign bourses. From a CG perspective, there is need for convergence (between Indian and foreign regulations) for such a cross country approach. However, survey conducted by Yoshikawa and Rasheed (2009) show that the convergence is seen more in form than in substance. They are echoing the views of Khanna et al. (2006) who similarly report evidence of formal convergence at the country level, but find actual corporate governance practices to remain heterogeneous at the firm level. This brings us to the role of firm-level corporate governance practices, particularly the top Indian firms listed on the bourses. Notwithstanding the regulations, progressive boards have a strategic role to play in the operations of firms, and the strategies reflect good corporate governance processes. Boards also play an active role in monitoring and implementing the CG practices (Lange and Sahu, 2008). Against this backdrop, the present study of board practices becomes relevant.

This article is focussed on the board structures of firms listed on the BSE SENSEX. The study is about board size, number of independent directors, board meetings, audit committee's independence, audit committee's meetings and CEO duality. These aspects are structured in the form of an index. The financial performance measures are ROA, Tobin's Q and MVBV. The index is regressed with the lead values, and current values of financial measures to partly address the issues of endogeneity. Results show that the index is positively related to ROA, which is considered as a proxy for firm performance. With respect to other financial measures, the relationship is positive, but not significant.

The rest of the articles is organized as follows. The next sections deal with literature review, followed by methodology and then analysis.

LITERATURE REVIEW

Voluntary Adoption of Corporate Governance Practices

This article reviews recent research on corporate governance, with special focus on emerging markets. Research evidence shows that better corporate governance practices, particularly voluntary ones, provide firms with greater access to financing, lower cost of capital and better operating performance, and equitable treatment of all stakeholders (Claessens and Yurtogly, 2012; Brown and Caylor, 2006).

Many researchers have linked actual corporate governance practices of firms to their market valuation, and firm performance. An influential study about US firms by Gompers et al., 2003 found that the valuations of firms who adopt voluntary corporate governance mechanisms are higher, and their cost of capital is low. Similar evidence is observed for European firms by Bauer et al., 2003, and in India by Balasubramanian et al., (2010).

The improvement in valuations is derived from several channels. In the Korean context Joh (2003) finds that at the firm level, better corporate governance leads to improved rates of return on equity, sales leading to growth and premium firm valuations. Black et al. (2012), report similar results for Brazil and contend that different practices are adopted in different countries, for different types of companies. Bruno and Claessens (2010a) find that, irrespective of weak or strong legal protection, individual firms adopting specific practices improves firm valuation. This implies that the approach to governance can be flexible, and firms can follow both top-down and bottom up approaches. In this context, the role of the boards in corporate governance is vital, and they have a critical role to play.

Boards

Boards constitute an important corporate governance mechanism. The corporate board is juxtaposed between the principals (owners) and executive management. The Cadbury report (1992), emphasized the role of the board in corporate governance. Since then, all the regulatory enactments have enhanced their role. Good corporate boards which adopt corporate governance practices beyond the mandated ones, are accorded premium valuations by investors (Aggarwal and Willamson, 2006).

Several studies find a strong connection between board composition and market valuations of emerging market companies. Findings suggest that companies with boards comprised of a higher fraction of outsider/independent directors usually have a higher valuation. Black et al. (2006a) report that Korean firms with 50 percent outside directors have higher Tobin's Q. Board size has been argued to relate to the voluntary formation of an audit committee (Bradbury, 1990) and audit committee activity (Menon & Williams, 1994).

Board Independence

Researchers Lo et al., 2010; Chen et al., 2006 find that stronger board structures with greater independence reduces the likelihood of fraud and expropriation through related party transactions. Board size, board meetings frequency and board independence are all associated with audit committee meetings frequency (Raghunandan & Rama, 2007; Sharma et al., 2009). Right from the reports of The Cadbury Committee (1992), the Greenbury Committee (1995), the Hampel Committee (1998), the Higgs Committee (2003), etc., all have mandated independent directors on the board. Continuing this trend, similar emphasis can be seen in the SOX Act and Clause 49 of the listing agreement, since the relationship with the firm is fiduciary in nature. The objective behind such recommendations is to ensure that the boards discharge their duties, balancing the interests of all stakeholders.

Independence of the Audit Committee

The primary purpose of the board's audit committee is to oversee the financial reporting process of a firm. The committee oversees a company's audit process and internal accounting controls. In 1999, the Blue Ribbon Committee sponsored by the NYSE and NASDAQ made recommendations about the independence of audit committees. Klein (1998) finds a negative relation between audit committee independence, and earnings management. This finding is consistent with the idea that a lack of independence impairs the ability of boards and audit committees to monitor management. A generic four dimensional framework (composition, resources, authority and diligence) has been drawn by DeZoort et al. (2002), with respect to benefits and effectiveness of audit committees. According to them, while the composition reflects independence, the other three relate to the inputs for the corporate governance processes adopted by firms.

Meetings of the Audit Committee

Meetings frequency is one of the indicators of proper monitoring. Yige et al., (2012) find evidence that board independence increases, as audit committees meet more frequently. They further contend that audit committee meetings and board of director independence are complements in corporate governance, not substitutes. Research findings of Xie et al., (2003) show that frequent meetings of the audit committee indicates greater diligence. Profitability and growth are positively related to audit committee meetings frequency (Raghunandan & Rama, 2007; Sharma et al., 2009). Better quality financial statements (transparency; disclosures; fraudulent financial reporting; reduced levels of discretionary current accruals) are associated with more frequent audit committee meetings (Abbott et al., 2000; Beasley et al., 2000). Similar evidence of lesser earnings management is observed by Kang et al., 2011. Such firms have fewer financial restatements contend Abbott et al., 2000.

Reputational capital is important for accounting firms given the repeat nature of their business. The Big 5 accounting firms (Price- Waterhouse Coopers, Ernst & Young, Arthur Andersen, Deloitte & Touche, and KPMG) were long viewed as surrogates for audit quality. However, in the wake of the accounting revelations and the demise of Arthur Andersen and the recent scandals in India, it is unclear whether these **'Big'** firms indeed provide higher-quality audit services than other firms.

SCORING METHODOLOGY

Selection of the Parameters

Board Independence

'1' is assigned in case the number of independent directors on the board is more than the mandatory requirement (1/3 of the board size in the case of CEO-non duality; 50 percent in the case of CEO duality) and '0' otherwise

CEO Duality

'1' is assigned in case of CEO-non duality. '0' otherwise.

No of Meetings of the Board

'1' is assigned if the number of meetings held by the board is more than 4; '0' otherwise.

No of Meetings of the Audit Committee

'1' is assigned if the number of meetings held by the audit committee is more than 4; '0' otherwise.

Totally Independent Audit Committee

'1' is assigned in case all the members of the audit committee are independent; '0' otherwise.

The maximum score for a firm will be 5, and the minimum can be 0, implying that the firm is complying with only the provisions contained in Clause 49 of the listing agreement.

Bsimacim Index

This index summarizes, firm wise, scores for the parameters listed earlier. The maximum score is 5 and the minimum is 0.The values are computed for 30 firms for the years 2010-11 and 2009-10 separately. The suffix indicates the corresponding year.

The hypotheses set are:

H_1: The index is not positively associated with firm performance proxied by ROA

ROA 10-11 = β1 ebit/sales '11+ β2BSIMACIM INDEX10-11+β3 Log assets+β4 Log brd ind+β5Log Acmtgs+β6Log brd mtgs+β7Log brd siz

H_2: The board's activities (measured by index for the year 2009-10) do not influence the financial performance measured by ROA for the year 2010-11.

ROA 10-11 = β1 ebit/sales '11+β2BSIMACIM INDEX9-10+β3 Log assets+β4 Log brd ind+β5Log Acmtgs+ β6Log brd mtgs+β7Log brd siz

Bhagat and Bolton (2008); Brown and Caylor (2006); Kumar (2004) have considered ROA as one of the financial measures.

The hypotheses were tested using linear regression.

All the index scoring was done by manual compilation.

Sources of Data: Company annual reports, Moneycontrol.Com, India Infoline.Com etc.

The period of study is 2009-10 and 2010-11.The accounting year ending 31 March is considered as reference.

The scope of study covers 30 firms listed on the BSE SENSEX.

Table 1: Description of Valuables Used in the Regression

Variables used in the regression	*Description*
Rota -Ebit/ Assests '11	Ratio of profit before interest and taxes
Log Brd Siz	Natural logarithm of number of members constituting the Board
Log Brd Ind	Natural logarithm of number of independent members in the Board
Log Brd Mtgs	Natural logarithm of number meetings of the Board
Log Acmtgs	Natural logarithm of number meetings of the Audit committee
Assets'11	Book value of assets of the firm for the year ending 31st March of the year
Ebit/Sales '11	Ratio of Earnings before Depreciation and Taxes/Sales or Income as the case may
BSIMACIM INDEX9-10	The index constituting the parameters listed above
Log sales	Natural logarithm of sales or income of a firm
Log assets	Natural logarithm of book value of the assets owned by the firm

ANALYSIS

We examine the relation between firm performance measured by ROA and the index, during the years 2009-10 and 2010-11. To analyze the impact of the index on firm performance, regressions were run with different performance variables such as board size, board independence, audit committee composition, meetings etc., as dependent variables and index as explanatory variables. The results of the same are shown in the following tables:

Table 2: Descriptive Statistics of Different Variables for the Year 2010-11

Descriptive Statistics			
	Mean	*Std. Deviation*	*N*
EBIT/ ASSESTS '11	0.288697	.2496727	30
BSIMACIM INDEX10-11	3.20	1.669	30
Log brd siz	1.089291	.1082507	30
Log brd ind	0.813921	.1330955	30
Log brd mtgs	0.868039	.1782221	30

Log Acmtgs	0.787921	.1524645	30
Log assets	4.490469	.6158472	30
ebit/sales '11	0.335082	.2490537	30

Table 2 reports the descriptive statistics for the variables used in the study. For brevity, only data for the year 2010-11 has been shown.

Table 3: Correlation Matrix of ROA and Other Independent Variables used in the Multiple Regression for the Year 2010-11

Pearson Correlation	*ROA '11*	*BSIMACIM INDEX10-11*	*Log brd siz*	*Log brd ind*	*Log brd mtgs*	*Log Ac mtgs*	*Log assets*	*ebit/ sales '11*
ROA '11	1.000							
BSIMACIM INDEX10-11	.002	1.000						
Log brd siz	.122	-.321	1.000					
Log brd ind	-.015	-.198	.815	1.000				
Log brd mtgs	-.201	-.185	.073	-.011	1.000			
Log Acmtgs	-.169	.263	.105	-.088	.566	1.000		
Log assets	-.616	.010	.252	.310	.475	.355	1.000	
ebit/sales '11	-.174	-.117	.206	.163	-.197	-.205	.196	1.000

The table reports the results of correlation coefficients of OLS regression

The values of Durbin Watson is approximately two implying the reliability of the results of regression or interpretation.

The coefficient value of the index is significant at 10 percent level while that of log brd size and log assets are positive and significant at 10 percent and 1 percent respectively. The variance inflation factor is less than 10 in all the variables considered (Myers, 1990)

Table 4

Model Summary

Model	*R*	*R Square*	*Adjusted R Square*	*Std. Error of the Estimate*	*Change Statistics*					*Durbin-Watson*
					R Square Change	*F Change*	*df1*	*df2*	*Sig. F Change*	
1	.721[a]	.520	.368	.1985218	.520	3.410	7	22	.013	1.977

a. Predictors: (Constant), ebit/sales '11, BSIMACIM INDEX10-11, Log assets, Log brd ind, Log Acmtgs, Log brd mtgs, Log brd siz; b. Dependent Variable: EBIT/ ASSESTS '11

Table 5: Cross sectional regression: In this regression, the index value of the years 2009-10 are regressed with the lead values of other variables of the year 2010-11.

The table reports the regression results of ROA on other variables ***, (**) and (*) indicate significance at (1 percent), (5 percent) and (10 percent) level

Variables	*Unstandardized Coefficients*		*Standardized Coefficients*	*t*	*Sig.*	*Correlations*			*Collinearity Statistics*	
	B	*Std. Error*	*Beta*			*Zero-order*	*Partial*	*Part*	*Tolerance*	*VIF*
(Constant)	.359	.513		.701	.491					
BSIMACIM INDEX10-11	.037	.029	.246	1.776	.095*	.002	.263	.188	.588	1.701
Log brd siz	1.349	.709	.585	1.903	.070*	.122	.376	.281	.231	4.336
Log brd ind	-.417	.557	-.222	-.749	.462	-.015	-.158	- .111	.247	4.045
Log brd mtgs	.347	.315	.247	1.102	.283	-.201	.229	.163	.432	2.315
Log Acmtgs	-.353	.378	-.216	-.935	.360	-.169	-.196	- .138	.410	2.441
Log assets	-.293	.080	-.721	- 3.636	.001***	-.616	-.613	- .537	.554	1.806
ebit/sales '11	-.083	.169	-.083	-.494	.626	-.174	-.105	- .073	.771	1.297

Table 6: Correlation Matrix of ROA and other independent variables used in the multiple regression for the year 2010-11 except for the index values(t+1). The index values used in this set of regressions relates to the year 2009-10.

Pearson Correlation	*EBIT/ ASSESTS '11*	*Log brd siz*	*Log brd ind*	*Log brd mtgs*	*Log Acmtgs*	*assets'11*	*ebit/sales '11*	*BSIMACIM INDEX9-10*	*Log sales*	*Log assets*
EBIT/ ASSESTS '11	1.000									
Log brd siz	.122	1.000								
Log brd ind	-.015	.815	1.000							

Log brd mtgs	-.201	.073	-.011	1.000						
Log Acmtgs	-.169	.105	-.088	.566	1.000					
assets'11	-.319	.088	.230	.487	.287	1.000				
ebit/sales '11	-.174	.206	.163	-.197	-.205	-.092	1.000			
BSIMACIM INDEX9-10	.002	-.321	-.198	-.185	.263	-.052	-.117	1.000		
Log sales	.000	.380	.303	.453	.400	.403	-.377	-.016	1.000	
Log assets	-.616	.252	.310	.475	.355	.737	.196	.010	.586	1.000

Table 7

Model Summary										
Model	*R*	*R Square*	*Adjusted R Square*	*Std. Error of the Estimate*	*Change Statistics*					*Durbin-Watson*
					R Square Change	*F Change*	*df1*	*df2*	*Sig. F Change*	
1	.937[a]	.878	.823	.1050515	.878	15.979	9	20	.000	1.967

a. Predictors: (Constant), Log assets, BSIMACIM INDEX9-10, ebit/sales '11, Log brd ind, Log Acmtgs, Log brd mtgs, assets'11, Log sales, Log brd siz; b. Dependent Variable: EBIT/ ASSESTS '11

The values of Durbin Watson is approximately two implying the reliability of the results of regression or interpretation

Table 8: The table reports the regression results of ROA on index, Log sales, Log assets, Log brd size, Log brd independence, Log brd meetings, Log audit committee meetings, and Margin. ***, (**) and (*) indicate significance at (1%), (5%) and (10%) level.

Coefficients										
Model	*Unstandardized Coefficients*		*Standardized Coefficients*	*t*	*Sig.*	*Correlations*			*Collinearity Statistics*	
	B	*Std. Error*	*Beta*			*Zero-order*	*Partial*	*Part*	*Tolerance*	*VIF*
(Constant)	.387	.296		1.309	.205					
Log brd siz	.530	.427	.230	1.241	.229	.122	.267	.097	.178	5.622
Log brd ind	-.326	.309	-.174	-1.055	.304	-.015	-.230	-.082	.225	4.441
Log brd mtgs	.175	.168	.125	1.043	.310	-.201	.227	.081	.423	2.362

Log Acmtgs	-.268	.201	-.164	-1.336	.197	-.169	-.286	-.104	.406	2.461
assets'11	8.450E-7	.000	.782	5.581	.000***	-.319	.780	.436	.311	3.218
ebit/sales '11	.699	.137	.698	5.088	.000***	-.174	.751	.398	.325	3.080
BSIMACIM INDEX9-10	.040	.015	.267	2.580	.018**	.002	.500	.202	.571	1.752
Log sales	.642	.094	1.083	6.844	.000***	.000	.837	.535	.244	4.101
Log assets	-.800	.079	-1.973	-10.082	.000***	-.616	-.914	-.788	.159	6.271

The coefficient of BSIMACIM INDEX9-10 is positive and significant at 5 percent level while that of log assets and log sales are positive and significant at 1 percent level.

Tobin's Q and MVBV are considered as proxies for financial performance by many researchers. Hence, these have been considered in this study. Multiple regressions using these as dependent variables were run and the results of the same are tabulated as follows:

Table 9: The Table reports the results of regression of Tobin's Q on the index of the year 2010-11

Pearson Correlation	*Tobin's Q*	*Log brd siz*	*Log brd ind*	*Log brd mtgs*	*Log Acmtgs*	*Log sales*	*Log assets*	*ebit/sales '11*	*BSIMACIM INDEX10-11*
Tobin's Q	1.000	-.040	-.128	-.216	-.217	-.143	-.575	-.028	.040
BSIMACIM INDEX10-11	**0.040**	-.321	-.198	-.185	.263	-.016	.010	-.117	1.000

The coefficient value of the index is 0.040 which is positive. The 't' statistics are reported in the Table 10.

Table 10: The table reports the 't' values of multiple regression using Tobin's Q as the dependent variable and other variables as independent. For brevity only the values pertaining to the index have been shown.

Coefficients											
Model		*Unstandardized Coefficients*		*Standardized Coefficients*	*t*	*Sig.*	*Correlations*			*Collinearity Statistics*	
		B	*Std. Error*	*Beta*			*Zero-order*	*Partial*	*Part*	*Tolerance*	*VIF*
1	(Constant)	6.067	10.411		.583	.566					

BSIMACIM INDEX10-11	.534	.562	.188	**.950**	**.353**	.040	.203	.143	.581	1.720
a. Dependent Variable: Tobin's Q										

It can be seen that the coefficient of the index is positive but not significant. Hence, the conclusive inference cannot be drawn.

Table 11: The table reports the results of regression of MVBV on the index of the year 2010-11

Pearson Correlation	*MVBV11*	*BSIMACIM INDEX10-11*	*Log brd siz*	*Log brd ind*	*Log brd mtgs*	*Log Acmtgs*	*Log sales*	*Log assets*	*ebit/sales '11*
MVBV11	1.000	.084	-.019	-.027	-.316	-.330	-.189	-.501	.053
BSIMACIM INDEX10-11	**0.084**	1.000	-.321	-.198	-.185	.263	-.016	.010	-.117

It can be seen that the coefficient value of the index 0.084 is positive but not significant. Hence conclusive inference cannot be drawn. The't' statistics are reported in the Table 12.

Table 12: The Table reports the 't' values of multiple regression using MVBV as the dependent variable and other variables as independent. For brevity only the values pertaining to the index have been shown.

Model	***Coefficients***									
	Unstandardized Coefficients		*Standardized Coefficients*	*t*	*Sig.*	*Correlations*			*Collinearity Statistics*	
	B	*Std. Error*	*Beta*			*Zero-order*	*Partial*	*Part*	*Tolerance*	*VIF*
(Constant)	8.051	11.558		.697	.494					
BSIMACIM INDEX10-11	.734	.624	.254	***1.176**	**.253**	.084	.249	.194	.581	1.720

*It can be seen that the coefficient of the index is positive but not significant and hence conclusive inference cannot be drawn.

CONCLUSIONS

This article has investigated the relative impacts of the mandatory and the voluntary aspects of the board and audit committee processes. The study provides preliminary evidence on the association between the non mandatory attributes of boards and audit committees, and financial performance. The index captures the essence of these attributes. The inference is based on the results of OLS regressions of the index, with the financial measure of ROA and other variables.

The hypothesis 'index is not positively associated with firm performance proxies by ROA' is rejected, since there is a positive and significant relationship between the index and financial performance measured by ROA.

The hypothesis 'board's activities (measured by index for the year 2009-10) do not influence the financial performance measured by ROA for the year 2010-11' is also rejected, since there is a positive and significant relationship between the board's activities (measured by index for the year 2009-10) and the financial performance measured by ROA for the year 2010-11.

When the firm value proxies are measured by Tobin's Q and MVBV ratios, the relationship is found to be positive, but not significant. Hence, conclusive inference cannot be drawn, which needs further study.

REFERENCES

Abbott, L. J., S. Parker, G. F. Peters, and K. Raghunandan (2000). The effects of audit committee activity and independence on corporate fraud. *Managerial Finance* 26 (11): 55-67.

Aggarwal, R and Williamson, R. (2006). Did New Regulations Target the Relevant Corporate Governance Attributes? *McDonough School of Business,* http://ssrn.com/abstract=859264.

Balasubramanian, N., Black, B. S and Khanna, V. (2010). Firm Level Corporate Governance in Emerging Markets: A Case Study of India. *Emerging Markets Review* 11, (2010), 319-340.

Bauer, R., Gunster, N. and Otten, R. (2003). Empirical evidence on corporate governance in Europe. *Journal of Asset Management, forthcoming.*

Beasley, J. V. Carcello, D. R. Hermanson and P. D. Lapides. (2000). Fraudulent financial reporting: Consideration and industry traits and corporate governance mechanisms. *Accounting Horizons (December)*: 441-454.

Birkett, B. S. (1986). The recent history of corporate audit committees. *The Accounting Historians Journal* 13, (2), 109-124.

Bhagat, S and Bolton, B. (2008). Corporate Governance and Firm Performance. *Journal of Corporate Finance*, 14, (3), 257-273.

Black, B., Jang, H., Kim, W. (2006a) Does corporate governance predict firms' market values? Evidence from the Korean market. *Journal of Law, Economics, and Organization* 22, 366-413.

Black, B.S, Carvalho, A.G and Gorga, E. (2012). What Matters and for Which Firms for Corporate Governance in Emerging Markets? Evidence from Brazil (and Other BRIK Countries). *Journal of Corporate Finance (forthcoming)*.

Black, B.S and Khanna, V.S. (2007) Can Corporate Governance Reforms Increase Firm Market Values? Event Study Evidence from India. *Journal of Empirical Legal Studies* 4, 749-796.

Black, B.S., and Kim, W. (2012). The Effect of Board Structure on Firm Value: A Multiple Identification Strategy Approach Using Korean Data. *Journal of Financial Economics 103.*

Bradbury, M. E. (1990).The incentives for voluntary audit committee formation. *Journal of Accounting and Public Policy* 9, (1), 19-36.

Brown, L. D and Caylor, M.L. (2006). Corporate Governance and Firm valuation. *Journal of Accounting and Public Policy*, 25, (4), 409-434.

Bruno, V and Claessens, S. (2010a). Corporate governance and regulation: Can there be too much of a good thing? *Journal of Financial Intermediation,* 19, 461-482.

Byrnes, N., Dwyer, P and Thornton, E. (2003). Who's making the Grade: A Performance review for CEOs, Boards, Analysis and Others? sites.google.com/site/.../cg.../Corporate Governance and Firm Performance. Pdf accessed: 7th Sept, 2012.

Chen, G., Firth, M., Daniel N. G, and Rui, O.M. (2006). Ownership structure, corporate governance, and fraud: Evidence from china. *Journal of Corporate Finance,* 12, 424-448.

Claessens, S and Yurtoglu, B. (2012). Corporate Governance in Emerging Markets: A Survey. SSRN-id1988880[1]

Dadalt, P.J (2003) Earnings management and corporate governance: the role of the board and the audit committee. *Journal of Corporate Finance*, 9, (3), 295-316.

DeZoort, F. T., Hermanson, D. R., Archambeault, D. S, and. Reed, S. A. (2002). Audit committee effectiveness: A synthesis of the empirical audit committee literature. *Journal of Accounting Literature* 21: 38–75.

Gompers, Paul A., Joy L. Ishii, and Metrick, A. (2003). Corporate Governance and Equity Prices. *The Quarterly Journal of Economics*. 118, (1), 107-155.

Joh, S.W. (2003). Corporate governance and firm profitability: Evidence from Korea before the economic crisis. *Journal of Financial Economics* 68, 287-322.

Kang, W., Kilgore. A. and Wright .S. (2011). The Effectiveness of Audit Committees for low and mid-cap firms. *Managerial Auditing Journal,* 26, (7), 623-650.

Kiel, G. C and Nicholson, G. J. (2003). Board Composition and Corporate Performance: How the Australian Experience informs Contrasting Theories of Corporate Governance. *Corporate Governance: an International Review*, 11, (3), 189-205.

Khanna, T., Kogan, J and Palepu, K.G. (2006). Globalization and Similarities in Corporate Governance: A Cross-Country Analysis. *Review of Economics and Statistics*, 88, (1), 69-90.

Klein, A. (1998). "Firm Performance and Board Committee Structure," *Journal of Law and Economics*, 41(1), 275-299.

Kumar, J. (2004). Does Ownership Structure Influence Firm Value? Evidence from India. *The Journal of Entrepreneurial Finance and Business* 9, (2), 61-91.

Lange, H and Sahu, C. (2008). Indian Board Structure and Size: The Impact of Changes to Clause 49 in India. In C. Long (Chair), Corporate governance in China and India. Research symposium by Wiley-Blackwell and Old Dominion University, Virginia Beach, VA. Pdf accessed: 1st, September 2012.

Lo, A.W.Y., Wong, R and Firth, M. (2010). Can Corporate Governance Deter Management from Manipulation Earnings? Evidence from Related-Party Sales Transactions in China. *Journal of Corporate Finance*,16, 225-235.

Menon, K., and Williams, J. O. (1994). The use of audit committees for monitoring. *Journal of Accounting and Public Policy* 13 (2): 121–139.

Myers, R. (1990). *Classical and Modern Regression with Applications*. 2nd edition. Boston, MA: Duxbury Press.

Raghunandan, K. and Rama, D.V. (2007). Determinants of audit committee diligence. *Accounting Horizons,* 21 (3): 265-279.

Sarbanes-Oxley Act 2002 (Corporate and Auditing Accountability, Responsibility, and Transparency Act of 2002). United States Congress. Washington. D.C.

Sharma, V., Naiker,.V and Lee, B.(2009). Determinants of Audit Committee Meeting Frequency: Evidence from a Voluntary Governance System. *Accounting Horizons* 23(3):245-263.

Xie, B., Davidson, W.N. and Dadalt, P.J. (20030. Earnings Management and Corporate Governance: The Roles of the Board and the Audit Committee. *Working Paper*, Southern Illinois University.

Yoshikawa, T and Rasheed, A. (2009). Convergence of corporate governance: Critical review and future directions. *Corporate Governance: An International Review* 17, 388-404.

Yige Ma., Kilgore A and Wright, S. (2012) The voluntary formation of an Audit committee; Financial markets and Corporate governance http://ssrn.com/abstract=1980484

Cadbury Committee, 1992. The Report of the Committee on the Financial Aspects of Corporate Governance (London).

Greenbury Report, 1995.

Hampel Committee's Report, 1998.

Hicks committees report on Corporate Governance, 1991.

Report of the SEBI Committee on Corporate Governance – Narayana Murthy Committee, 2003.

Should Unlimited Liability be Fastened on Shareholders?

Sayobani Basu and Priti Sinha
National Law University, Odisha

ABSTRACT

Unlimited liability was generally rejected after 1850 and one of reasons was that the law failed to distinguish clearly between tort and contract when it came to shareholder liability. Securing unlimited liability on shareholders entails detailed involvement by them, so as to supervise unanticipated actions by the management in order to minimize risks and this is possible for shareholders who invest fractions of their earnings in the share market. The question is whether there is any reason to prefer unlimited shareholder liability over limited shareholder liability for corporate torts, and if is there, is there any state which should adopt the concept of unlimited shareholder liability for corporate torts.

Keywords: *Unlimited Liability, Shareholders, Corporate Torts*

The reasons that would discourage investment under a regime of unlimitedly ability are the same ones that ought to discourage investments under a regime of limited liabilities. A shareholder does not invest to lose even the initial investment. One invests in the belief that one will derive a profit, from appreciation of shares, or from dividends. One selects one's investment after having concluded that the investment is one that will make money, not lose it. This is the same calculation that one would perform if there were unlimited liability." - Stephen B. Presser

INTRODUCTION

A company is a separate legal entity having its own corporate personality, which is completely separate and distinct from its stakeholders. It has its own rights and obligations; can sue and be sued; borrow and lend, make contracts, buy, own and dispose properties. It can sue for tort committed against it, and can also commit tort. It has a perpetual existence, as the company remains impassive by change of shareholders and directors, except at the time it is being wound up by law.[1] The most distinguishing feature of a company is the type of liability the shareholders have. It can be a limited liability company, where the shareholders are liable to the amount unpaid on shares held by them.[2] The limited liability was first introduced by the Limited Liability Act, 1855 which provided that the liability of a shareholder would be not beyond the amount remaining unpaid on his shares.[3] From toxic torts to poison pills, no corporate undertaking is unaffected by the workings of one of corporate law's bedrock principles: limited liability.[4] In companies with unlimited liability, there is no limit on the liability of members which extends to the company's debts and liabilities. However, liability risks, if left unchannelled or not controlled, ordinarily attaches to the corporation, rather than to its stakeholders. According to proponents of the limited liability regime, if shares carried unlimited liability and shareholders were liable for debts and liabilities of the company, there will develop concentrated ownership structures in which only a handful of people would own all the stock.[5] However, it is has been contradicted by arguing that markets can still thrive under unlimited liability, since most importantly the type of unlimited liability rule adopted is significant[6]. This is also the result of the concept of 'shareholder's paradise' – where they are able to ruthlessly pursue 'shareholder value' without any corresponding responsibility on the part of shareholders, for the losses arising out of corporate failure, or the damage caused by corporate activities or malfeasance[7]. Thus, this has led to the belief that shareholders should be unlimitedly liable, particularly for the tortious liabilities of companies. The call for a return to unlimited liability amounts to taking the separate corporate personality less seriously, since it seeks to eradicate the problem of corporate irresponsibility and unaccountability, by identifying corporations more closely with their shareholders, encouraging a shift towards the concept of 'the company' as an aggregation of people.[8]

---

[1] Dr. Muhammad Khalid Malik, "*International Aspects of Corporate Law and Governance*",[2005] School of Law, the University of Warwick, UK < http://www.dgtrdt.gov.pk/Research/limited-liablity.pdf> accessed 4 April 2012

[2] Mulla

[3]The Limited Liability Act 1855 was an Act of the United Kingdom, Parliament that first allowed limited liability for corporations that could be established by the general public in the UK.

[4]RD Kahan, 'Shareholder Liability for Corporate Torts: A Historical Perspective'[2009] 97[4] Georgetown LJ < http://papers.ssrn.com/sol3/papers.cfm?abstract_id=1269181 >accessed 8 April 2012

[5]

[6] H Hansmann and R Kraakman, 'Toward Unlimited Shareholder Liability for Corporate Torts' [1991]100 [7] Yale LJ 1879

[7]Paddy Ireland, 'Limited Liability, Shareholder Rights And The Problem Of Corporate Irresponsibility'[2010]34 Cambridge Journal Of Economics 837–856 < http://Cje.Oxfordjournals. Org/Content> Accessed 08 April 2012

[8] Ibid

UNLIMITED SHAREHOLDER LIABILITY

In case of unlimited shareholder liability, the shareholders are liable for the payment of any outstanding claims if the firm defaults on its obligations. On a default, corporate assets are liquidated, and any unsatisfied claims will have to be met by them. On the other hand, if the shareholders are limited liable, they are liable to the amount unpaid on shares held by them, and the creditors are in a risky position, since there is the possibility that the firm will default on its obligations.[9] This chapter will begin with a brief history of unlimited shareholder liability mentioning the case of the US company, American Express which had stock with unlimited liability for 115 years (1850-1965) and subsequently, deal with the pros and cons of unlimited shareholder liability, the economic analysis of the same to be compared with limited shareholder liability and also, discuss whether the disadvantages of limited shareholder liability in closely-held firms can be solved by converting to unlimited shareholder liability.

Unlimited liability carries the potential of calls on wealth in excess of the investor's purchase price, investors of "modest means" would refuse to participate in the stock market, if shares carried unlimited liability.[10] The institution of limited liability incorporation has been credited with playing a key role in American industrial development, like one scholar has claimed that this system was "indispensable" for marshalling large quantities of capital responsible for economic growth.[11] The establishment of a new regime of unlimited liability kindled the debate of merits and demerits of unlimited and limited liability. Proponents of limited liability state that it is a necessary condition for markets to function, and a change in the rules to unlimited liability would mean that a liquid securities market would "be unlikely to exist."[12] This means that if shareholders have unlimited liability in regard to the company's debt, then the corporate world will have a concentrated ownership structure, with power limited in a few hands which have the monetary strength to tackle all kind of debts, including torts and contractual obligations. Some scholars like Henry Hansmann and Reinier Kraakman[13] contend that markets can still thrive under unlimited liability as they say, it only matters what type of unlimited liability rule is adopted. Others believe that unlimited liability will either be unenforceable (because it would be too costly to enforce), or will simply be circumvented by modern financial instruments and organizations.[14]

---

[9] Jain D K and Jain I, '*Guide to Private limited Company*'(1st edn LBH Publishers 2011)
[10] P Z Grossman, 'The Market for Shares of Companies with Unlimited Liability: The Case of American Express' [1995] 24 [1] The Journal of Legal Studies 63
[11] Ibid 64
[12] Ibid 64
[13] Hansmann and Kraakman (n 2) 1879
[14] Grossman (n 5) 64

A US company, American Express Company, was originally chartered in 1850 under the statutes governing unlimited liability joint stock associations, and became a limited liability corporation in 1965. So the company traded for 115 years with stock that carried unlimited liability. The company carried parcels and high-value items such as financial paper, offering a complete warranty on contents which meant that the company had potentially significant liabilities. Initially, there were 1,500 shares outstanding (par value US $150,000), divided among 39 shareholders and therefore, monitoring of management practices was not tough, but this changed in 1869, as a result of 180,000 shares with a large number of shareholders. The company retained this form until 1965, when it finally became a limited liability corporation. because (1) the informational advantages of unlimited liability had more or less disappeared, and (2) it seemed too much a relic of the past and a new management team wanted a more forward-looking approach.[15] There was a regular market for American Express stock during the period of unlimited liability, as their stock was traded regularly and consistently, with a large pool of investors participating.[16] Throughout the period, the number of shareholders averaged about 25,000, implying that the average shareholder owned less than 85 shares, and only one Ralph Owen, controlled a significant block of shares-about 10 percent of the total. Although no records have been kept of the wealth of shareholders, but probably given the size of the pool, that some shareholders were of modest means. However, no one could possibly have known if other shareholders were wealthy or not. Evidence strongly suggests that the shares were not perceived to be particularly risky.[17] In 1963, American Express certified that a company called Allied Crude Vegetable Oil Refining Corporation possessed more than 800 million pounds of soybean oil which Allied could use as a loan collateral, and that American Express had been deceived, and Allied was using the money to try to corner the futures market in soybean oil. Allied declared bankruptcy, and it was revealed that its loans totalled about US $150 million, twice American Express's net assets. The company still carried unlimited liability status, and US buyers of the stock included the Dreyfus Fund and investor Warren Buffett although the share price did fall by 43 percent, but a large drop would have occurred whether the stock was limited or unlimited, and the actual after-tax cost to settle the claims was US $31.6 million. Unlimited liability did not lead either to concentration, illiquidity, or perverse pricing. More importantly, even without modern financial instruments, an unlimited liability company will freely trade among domestic buyers, even when there are many alternatives in limited liability corporate stock. The case of American Express strongly supports the premise, that unlimited liability does not

[15] ibid 75

[16] American Express was always placed among the stocks that were widely held and actively traded.

[17] As per the capital asset pricing model [CAPM (Ri - Rf) = a + P(Rm - Rf)], the value of p is substantially less than one (approximately 0.5) and significant at the 1 percent level. This implies that the stock was viewed as significantly less risky than the market for the period.

disrupt the functioning of markets for company shares, and the earlier case study contests some of the objections raised to the regime of unlimited liability.

Unlimited Shareholder Liability and Corporate Torts

Limited liability is, at its core, a method of protecting shareholders from claims against the corporation in which they are invested.[18] Shareholders with limited liability are immune from personal liability to the extent of the amount unpaid on shares held by them. The beginning of the application of the doctrine of limited liability to corporate torts can be traced back to judicial opinions discriminating between contract claimants and tort claimants. In their efforts to distinguish between the two claimants, the judges ended up leaning towards the contract claimants, rather than the tort claimants.[19] Prior to 1855, joint stock companies commonly sought to limit their shareholders' liability to voluntary creditors by contractual means, thus providing evidence that limited liability is the appropriate default rule for contractual obligations.[20] In *Clinton Mining &r Mineral Cc. v. Beacom,*[21] the corporation had wrongfully obtained ore from the plaintiff's property, and despite a statute providing that each stockholder shall be personally and individually liable for the 'debts' of a corporation to the extent of his unpaid stock, it was held that 'debts' does not include the liability of a corporation for a tort and therefore, not recoverable under the statute.[22] This judgment was passed in 1920 and clearly signals that a corporation to incur liability for corporate torts was against the accepted opinion. The reason given in the judgment was that the statute-makers could not have intended to hold shareholders for debts they could not have conceived the corporation incurring, at the time they entered a contract relation in becoming subscribers for stock.[23] Therefore, it does not come within the scope of 'liability arising out of contract.' Keeping in mind the nature of corporate tort of not being able to apprehend, and the unlikely possibility of the tort taking place not to mention the 'uncertain sum' to be incurred as damages, the concept of being liable for corporate torts did not win popular votes, specially by the shareholders. Corporations owned by affluent shareholders, yet too impoverished to meet their tort liabilities, are the inevitable products of present-day incorporation laws.[24]Grotesque accidents, mass torts, environmental abuses, accounting frauds, and other instances of corporate wrongdoing sparked the debate, and each new scandal breathes wind

[18] Kahan (n 1) 1088
[19] ibid
[20] Hansmann and Kraakman (n 2) 1924
[21] [I920]266 Fed. 621
[22] 'Corporations: Liability of Stockholders under a Statute Making Them Liable for "Debts" DoesNot Include Liability for Torts' [1921] 19 [3] Michigan LR 341
[23] ibid
[24] 'Should Shareholders Be Personally Liable for the Torts of Their Corporations?' [1967]76[6] Yale L J 1190

into its embers.[25] Limited liability creates negative externalities, encouraging harmful and sometimes tortious corporate behavior like nonadherrence to the norms of basic risk mitigating precautions etc., in cases of debts and liabilities incurred by the company by virtue of contracts or otherwise, the shareholders have been held responsible on the basis of doctrines like 'piercing the corporate veil' or 'alter ego,' but these doctrines will hardly render any help in case of torts, as it is not a question of deceiving.[26] In the case of Lininger v. Botsford,[27] the issue for the California Court of Appeals was whether the term "liability" imposed on shareholders of corporations their proportional share of the "liabilities" of their corporation, over and above the unpaid part of their shares, extended to torts of the corporation. It was held that the term "liability" included claims *ex delicto*, and therefore the share-holders must be held liable in this case. The case serves to emphasize that the confusion and lack of discrimination which characterize the discussion of this question in all the texts, and most of the judicial opinions have been by no means dispelled even at this late date.[28] The first element of the confusion is that statutory liability is vague, on the one hand, with common law liability, where there is no question that the shareholder is liable for claims *ex delicto* of the corporation; and on the other hand, with penal liability for failure to perform some statutory corporate duty, where it is equally clear that no liability exists, unless by the express terms of the statute.[29] In *Heacock & Lockwood v. Sherman,*[30] the plaintiff brought an action against two shareholders[31] of the Buffalo Hydraulic Association as the plaintiff's horse fell while crossing a bridge apparently due to improper maintenance of the bridge. The judge of a bench trial awarded him US $50 in damages, but the defendants appealed and in a jury trial, the verdict was in favour of the plaintiff and US $85 in damages. The defendants pursued the matter by suing upon a writ of error, and the Supreme Court granted the writ reversing the lower court order.[32] The charter of the corporation provided that no stockholder shall be obliged to pay more in the whole, than the amount of the stock he may hold in the said company, at the time the debt accrued. Then, the Justice Associate of the Supreme Court opined, that notwithstanding an exception to limited liability in the corporation's charter, shareholders could not be held liable for corporate torts. The court conveniently read 'all debts contracted by the said corporation' to cover only claims *ex contractu* and not claim *ex*

---

[25]Kahan (n1)1089

[26] Dine J and Koutsias M, '*Company Law*' (6th edn Palgrave Macmillan 2007)

[27] 163 Pac. 63

[28] E B H, 'Statutory Liability of Shareholders on Tort Liabilities against the Corporation' [1917]15[8]Michigan LR 665

[29] Ibid

[30] 14Wend. 58 (N.Y. Sup. Ct. 1835).

[31] The charter,Buffalo Hydraulics Association provided that any person(s) having any demand against the said corporation, may sue any stockholder(s), in any court having cognizance thereof, and recover the same with costs.

[32] Kahan (n 1) 1099

delicto.' This decision had a measurable impact on other courts, and there was widespread universal agreement that an action in tort could not be brought against individual shareholders of a solvent corporation.[33] Nevertheless, in the five decades that followed, the rule of shareholders not being liable for corporate torts spread across the nation, and there was no doubt that a tort was not a "debt" for which shareholders could be held liable.[34] Hence, there was hardly any acceptance to hold shareholders liable for corporate torts, based on the reasoning that a tort cannot come in the ambit of a 'debt,' since shareholders couldn't possibly have envisaged the same when they subscribed to the shares of the corporation. The debate was revived in *Walkovszky v. Carlton*[35] prior to which limited liability was the general rule. In this case, the plaintiff was struck by a cab owned by a corporation in which the defendant was the sole shareholder. The defendant was the sole shareholder of not only that particular cab corporation, but nine other cab corporations as well, and carried only the state mandated minimum amount of automobile liability insurance, regularly paying himself dividends out of the corporation's shares. Because Seon was thinly capitalized, Walkovszky sought to recover from Carlton and the nine other corporations whose stock he owned on the theory of "enterprise liability." The court rejected the theory, and held that the plaintiff had not stated a cause of action against Carlton in his individual capacity. The decision was not agreeable to many, as it seemed inequitable because had the defendant formed only one corporation and not got dividends, then the plaintiff could have recovered more than the insurance minimum. The court took the defense that inequity issues were to be dealt with the legislature and not the judiciary. The dissenting opinion was that Carlton's use of the corporate form was "designed solely to abuse corporate privilege at the expense of the public interest," and should not allow him to avoid liability. Tort victims cannot foresee their injuries, thus, assuring prohibitive transaction costs and therefore, they cannot bargain with the corporation to either create incentives for the corporation to avoid the tort in the first place, or provide for sufficient compensation for the victim.[36] Therefore, contract creditors can demand premiums for limited liability, but tort creditors cannot, and this is inequality resulting in the unfortunate lack of justice in favour of the victims. By the middle of the nineteenth century, however, these rules were relaxed, and it was easier for individual plaintiffs to recover from corporations due to doctrines like the last clear chance and *res ipsa loquitur.*[37] At the same time, state legislatures began to impose strict liability on large corporations, particularly for violating newly prescribed safety regulations. As a result of the changes and developments in torts, "the relaxation of tort doctrine," the limited liability rule was changing to establish an equilibrium level of liability. The fact that the areas of contract,

[33] Ibid 1085

[34] California was an exception since it recognizes 'liabilities' and 'debts' - Kahan (n 1)1085 footnote 93

[35] 223 N.E.2d 6 (N.Y. 1966)

[36] Kahan (n 1) 1085

[37] "the thing speaks for itself."

tort and corporate were affected and influenced by each other was recognized slowly. Changes in technology, knowledge, liability rules, and procedures for mass tort litigation have for the first time raised the prospect of tort claims, that exceed the net worth of even very large corporations.[38] Environmental harm, such as oil spills or the release of toxic materials, are one potential source of massive liabilities; hazardous products and carcinogens in the workplace are others.[39] Till now, we can see that shareholder liability is the main problem in corporate tort liability, and the boundaries of contractual rights are not being respected in torts as well. The efficiency of the capital markets would be seriously damaged if shareholders were exposed to personal liability for corporate torts. So, now even if unlimited liability could be imposed on corporate shareholders without seriously interfering with the capital markets, the broad potential scope of enterprise liability under prevailing liability rules and damage measures, constitutes an independent reason for favouring limited liability.[40] If unlimited liability is forced on shareholders, then the market would be governed by only that section of shareholders who would be willing to take the risk of very large losses in case of low probability accidents not covered by insurance. Of course, the risk is slightly decreased by monitoring management and maintaining safety regulations, but the risk remains as the loss continues to be impossible to be assessed and envisaged. Some courts believe that a tort victim's recovery depends on whether shareholders have observed the statutory formalities before the accident makes compensation turn on circumstances purely fortuitous to the tort claim. Furthermore, shareholders can avoid liability simply by being careful, which is to say, simply by retaining adequate counsel.[41] More graphically, the concept of unlimited liability seems to engender in the minds of many the image of small passive shareholders with modest means, being suddenly and unexpectedly thrown into personal bankruptcy when the few shares of publicly-traded stock they own, bring upon them massive personal liability for some corporate tort.[42] Such a scenario need not continue in case of unlimited liability as by keeping a balance and checks, the courts have to determine which costs are efficiently and equitably borne by a corporation and its shareholders, and which are not. The courts should appropriately consider the structure of particular corporate defendants in determining the extent of their tort liability under an unlimited liability regime.[43] With unlimited liability, courts would be forced to consider the appropriate scope of enterprise liability more thoughtfully, in the full awareness that limited liability would not automatically constrain any tendency toward excessive liability. Courts could not award generous damages under the illusion that only corporations, and not individuals, would bear the resulting costs. In

[38]Hansmann and Kraakman (n 2) 1880
[39] ibid
[40] ibid 1916
[41] Yale LJ (n 19) 1197
[42] Hansmann and Kraakman (n 2)1917
[43] ibid 1917

England, prior to 1844, manufacturing firms had difficulty obtaining corporate charters and large manufacturing firms were commonly formed as unincorporated joint stock companies with transferable shares. Indeed, an active public market in the shares of such companies developed as early as the seventeenth century.[44] Between 1844 and 1855, joint stock companies were permitted to be incorporated, but had to retain unlimited liability, and only after 1855 was incorporation with limited liability generally available.[45] However, prior to 1855, joint stock companies generally sought to limit their shareholders' liability only to voluntary creditors by contractual means. This means that limited liability was the most apt rule for contractual obligations. The US freely granted corporate charters by the beginning of the nineteenth century, and for the first several decades of that century, a number of states imposed unlimited liability on manufacturing corporations. California imposed unlimited *pro rata* liability by statute on the shareholders of both domestic and foreign corporations from statehood in 1849 until 1931, evidently without crippling industrial and commercial development.[46] This suggests that unlimited liability is administrable, and that corporations can survive and prosper under it. Moreover, in the past, unlimited liability regimes for joint stock companies often employed joint and several rather than *pro rata* liability. If such a regime is viable, then a practice involving unlimited liability only in tort, and with *pro rata* liability, is not exactly impossible. So, the fact that unlimited liability can survive along with economic and commercial development is not inadmissible. Past experience permits the observation that extensive corporate development is at least compatible with unlimited liability. However, we see that unlimited liability was generally rejected after 1850, and one of reasons was that the law failed to distinguish clearly between tort and contract when it came to shareholder liability. It is also an established fact, that contractual obligations are far more important than the occasional problem of corporate tort, as torts that would bankrupt a publicly-traded firm were presumably rare.

APPLICATION OF UNLIMITED LIABILITY RULE

There are two rules of unlimited liability which are possible, out of which the first is a rule of joint and several liability, under which each shareholder is personally liable to the extent that it exceeds the value of the firm's assets. The second is a rule of *pro rata* liability, under which each shareholder is personally liable in proportion to her equity ownership of the firm. The chapter will explain these two rules, compare the two, and also find out which of the two is feasible for both contractual obligations faced by corporations and corporate torts. So, say, if the tort damages exceed the company's assets by US $100 million and a shareholder holds

[44] ibid 1924
[45] ibid
[46] ibid

10 percent of the of the shares of the company, then under the joint and several rule, he will be potentially liable for US $100 million and US $10 million under the *pro rata* rule. So, clearly shareholders with moderate share holdings would prefer the *pro rata* rule. The choice between joint and several and *pro rata* rules resurrects, in a new form, the tradeoff between perverse incentives and transaction costs that underlies the choice between unlimited and limited liability.[47] As compared to the *pro rata* rule, the joint and several rule has the advantage of deterring judgment-proof shareholders from externalizing tort costs.[48] The choice between the rules depends on the type of firm, as in whether a jointly-held firm, or a publicly-held firm. In a publicly held firm, one is sure to find shareholders of moderate means may be of a 'passive' nature, and the rule of *pro rata* would certainly be apt in this case. In fact, a public corporation will usually have managers, a large number of passive shareholders, a market for freely-trading stock, substantial assets, and potential tort liability that may not only exceed the firm's assets, but that may not be fully insurable at any premium etc. Obviously, given these factors, it will be tough to run an efficient market with unlimited liability on a joint and several basis. The price of deterring risk-shifting under the joint and several rule, is to increase further the transaction costs imposed by unlimited liability on a jointly-held firm. When insurance is unavailable, the joint and several rule forces the firm's full tort losses on its wealthy shareholders, and thus exacerbates the problem of asymmetrical stakes among investors. The *pro rata* rule is clearly the superior alternative for publicly-held corporations.[49] The advantage of promulgating a single rule for all corporations makes the case for the *pro rata* rule compelling for closely-held firms as well.[50] Proportional liability also supports diversification, although, any loss would be a related to the amount invested, owning all of the shares in a given corporation would make the risk unlimited, but owning shares in several corporations increases the risk of loss due to bankruptcy, but diversifying holdings limits the size of any one loss.[51] The proposed rule of *pro rata* shareholder liability merely makes sure that shareholders, upon investing in a corporation, are put on notice that they risk substantive liability not just up to the amount they invest, but rather, up to their *pro rata* share of all tort damages assessed. The claim that unlimited liability might distort share prices, or prevent shareholders from diversifying risk is persuasive only under a joint and several liability rule, and clearly under a *pro rata* rule, shares would have the same expected value for all shareholders. Unlimited liability is claimed to generate excessive monitoring of both management and shareholders by all participants in public corporations, but this claim would come into the picture only if each shareholder were liable for all corporate debts, as

[47] Hansmann and Kraakman (n 2)1893

[48] ibid

[49] ibid

[50] ibid

[51] G G Sollars, 'An Appraisal of Shareholder Proportional Liability' Journal of Business Ethics'[2001] 32, [4] Journal of Business Ethics 340

they would be under a joint and several rule as in that case, the risks burden of each individual share-holder or creditor would depend in part on fluctuations in the aggregate wealth of all shareholders.[52] This would not be a problem under the rule of *pro rata* liability, as a shareholder's risk would depend only on the size of his respective investment, rather than on the wealth of other shareholders. Furthermore, contract creditors would not rely on the wealth of shareholders at all.

The choice of whether to implement the *pro rata* rule, or the joint and several rule, is not only related to the type of firm, but also on the type of timing rule on the basis of which shareholders become liable after a tort occurs. There are two types of rules i.e., an "occurrence" rule, under which liability attaches to persons who are shareholders at the time a tort occurs, is the most difficult rule for shareholders to evade, but also the most difficult to administer and a "judgment" rule that attaches residual liability only to those persons who are shareholders at the time of judgement, is the simplest to administer, but creates widespread opportunities for evasion.[53] The disadvantage of the occurrence rule is that it is very difficult to pinpoint and identify the exact shareholders at a specific time of the occurrence of the tort, therefore, this rule is difficult to administer, but in case of judgement rule, the rule is at a disadvantage since it gives enough time to shareholders to evade. The task of apportioning excess liability among all investors who held shares in an affected company at any time during this period would be an administrative nightmare, in a case where harm occurs gradually over a period of ten years.[54] Henry Hansmann and R.Kraakman proposed the "information-based rule"-under which liability would attach to shareholders at the earliest of the following moments: (1) when the tort claims in question were filed; (2) when the corporation's management first became aware that with high probability, such claims would be filed; or (3) when the corporation dissolved without leaving a contractual successor.[55] The "liability date," might be established either by corporate management by making an announcement accepting responsibility on behalf of all current shareholders for likely future claims arising from the conduct in question, and the incentive for the management would be a desire to preserve an orderly market for the company's stock," disclosure obligations under the securities acts, or a liability date could be judicially established on the initiative of tort plaintiffs.

One of the criticisms of unlimited liability is that small shareholders over large shareholders might discourage investment, intermediaries, such as mutual funds, and lead wealthy shareholders to abandon risky industries. Under unlimited liability, investing in a diversified financial intermediary, such as a mutual fund, would protect investors from

[52] ibid 1906
[53] ibid 1896
[54] ibid
[55] Ibid 1897

personal liability in fact, but not in law. To deter wholesale evasion, an unlimited liability regime must permit liability to pass through intermediary entities to the ultimate beneficiaries of share ownership.[56] Thus, participants in investment companies, no less than the shareholders of parent corporations and holding companies, would themselves face *pro rata* liability if the intermediary's assets failed to satisfy its assessment under the *pro rata* rule.[57] Unlimited liability might encourage wealthy shareholders to "over diversify" by eschewing large stock positions, hence reducing the frequency of control transactions, and depriving all shareholders of the services of sophisticated monitors.[58] Under a *pro rata* rule, however, this is minor in relation to the beneficial incentive effects of unlimited liability. If collection from dispersed shareholders is feasible, there would be little reason for wealthy shareholders to prefer less risky firms, or for small share holders to withdraw from mutual funds. If anything, investing in a broadly diversified portfolio such as a mutual fund would become more attractive for small shareholders.

EXISTING NORMS AND FUTURE PROSPECTS OF UNLIMITED SHAREHOLDER LIABILITY

Under a regime of unlimited shareholder liability, however, there are persuasive reasons to give all contract creditors priority over tort creditors as a default option, but such a rule would provide strong protection-stronger than under limited liability for both contract creditors and tort creditors. Upon bankruptcy, contract creditors would be able to collect against all of the firm's assets under the proportional liability rule, without the risk of being forced to share in the firm's value with tort claimants. But tort creditors, in turn, would also be better off, since they could proceed against shareholders when the firm's remaining assets were insufficient to satisfy their claims. A specialized market in retroactive insurance will have to arise shortly after the adoption of an unlimited liability regime. Such a market would permit old shareholders to insure against the contingency that a tort judgment might ultimately exceed the net value of the firm. Under the prevailing priority rule, tort creditors come after the secured contract creditors and participate *pro rata* with general contract creditors.[59]

India has established tort principles like primarily negligence, nuisance and strict/absolute liability and have employed the same to hold companies accountable for their wrongdoings. Tort law in India is based in common law, but is not codified and thus, has developed in a slow and haphazard manner creating difficulties in implementation. Companies can be held liable for torts committed by their agents or servants "to the same

[56] ibid 1905
[57] ibid
[58] ibid 1904
[59] Hansmann and Kraakman, (n 1) 1927

extent as a principal is liable for the torts of his agent, or an employer for the torts of his servant, when the tort is committed in the course of doing an act which is within the scope of the powers" of companies.[60]

Mass torts, and a multiplicity of victims, pose both substantive and procedural problems as identifying individual victims, and the extent of injury and loss caused to each of them makes a situation of mass tort difficult and challenging.[61] The tort law in India has not yet embraced, for instance, epidemiology or presumption of causation as evidentiary tools to fix liability in mass torts.[62] The judiciary usually relies on reports of fact-finding committees, or statutory bodies, to hold companies accountable. There has not been much progress in mass tort litigation in India since there are not many mass tort cases. For example – in the Bhopal gas tragedy case, the government enacted the Bhopal Gas Leak Disaster (Processing of Claims) Act in which section 3 vested in the central government an "exclusive right to represent, and act in place of every person who has made a claim arising out of the Bhopal disaster in order to acquire speedily, effectively and equitably justice. The victims could have invoked class action, but thanks to the Indian political scenario, this law severely curtailed the right of victims to participate in civil litigation. According to a study published in the *Journal of Management Science*, stock prices respond positively to defensive activities by management, rather than accommodative moves by managers towards the victims, which, explains how managers while trying to deflect lawsuits suppress their personal human reactions towards a tragedy and try to deny all responsibility.[63] The Dow Chemical Company successfully took over Union Carbide after which Union Carbide became a wholly-owned subsidiary, although a separate entity, but Dow claimed that the stockholders and the Union Carbide did not have any responsibility in the tragedy.[64]

Indian law allows companies as well as its officers to be held criminally liable for specified wrongs. However, prosecuting and convicting companies and their officers is not easy in practice.[65] The court order also quashed pending criminal proceedings against UCC and Union Carbide India Ltd. (UCIL), although the Supreme Court upheld the settlement

[60] Singh GP, *'Ratanlal & Dhirajlal's the Law of Torts'* (23rd edn Wadhwa – Nagpur 1997)34

[61] Singh GP, *'Ratanlal & Dhirajlal's the Law of Torts'* (23rd edn Wadhwa – Nagpur 1997)

[62] ibid

[63] The increase in the stock prices was explained as a result of restructuring and recapitalization of the company before the sell-off. Nair M, 'Bhopal Gas Tragedy – A Social, Economic, Legal and Environmental Analysis' [2005]. <SSRN: http://ssrn.com/abstract=1977710> 7

[64] ibid

[65] The Bhopal case exemplifies this after the civil suit was dismissed from the US court, legal proceedings began in India and, in February 1989, a court-approved settlement was reached. The settlement order of the Supreme Court read: "The aforesaid payments [US$470 million] shall be made to the Union of India as claimant and for the benefit of all victims of the Bhopal gas disaster [...] and not as fines, penalties, or punitive damage."

award, it agreed to reinstate criminal charges against UCC-UCIL and their personnel, but the criminal proceedings moved very slowly.[66] Companies in India enjoy separate legal personality, but it is not generally easy to convince courts to pierce the veil which causes hardship to the victims of corporate human rights abuses, because on various occasions, it becomes necessary for them to sue a parent company, even though the actual violation might have resulted from the acts of its subsidiaries.[67]

The Bhopal case demonstrates very clearly how difficult, time consuming and resource-intensive the quest to impose criminal liability on a company can be, even in a situation where the conduct was within the purview of criminal law provisions, and there was a strong public demand for justice. Gaining access to internal corporate documents, which might provide critical evidence, is often not possible and the task of criminal prosecution becomes more challenging if an overseas parent company is involved, over which the courts might not be able to secure effective jurisdiction.[68]

CONCLUSION

Limited liability can be an extremely rough check, as it is on either of the extreme sides of restricting liability excessively or not enough in others paving the way for stockholders to take advantage opportunistically. Historically, the doctrine of limited liability was meant to protect shareholders from corporate contract liability, but not from tort liability. However, shareholder liability limited, by third party costs like corporate torts is an illustration of inefficient convergence towards the shareholder model of corporate governance, driven by economic forces around the world. What we can see from the entire project is that initially there were two problems, i.e., whether corporate torts come in the ambit of 'debts' of the corporation, and also we were not able to differentiate and give equal importance to both contract and tort creditors. By now, there has been a growing consensus on the fact that upholding the interests of the shareholders serves the greater aim of corporate enterprises to serve society as a whole, and we should follow the shareholder model which favours the main control over the corporation should be in the hands of the shareholder class, with the managers of the corporation, burdened with the obligation of managing the corporation in the interest of the shareholders. There is no doubt that limited liability has certain advantages namely:

---

66 Nair (n 55) 6

67 When the Indian government decided to sue UCC, the parent company incorporated in the US, it relied, among others, on the enterprise principle. S Deva , 'Access to Justice: Human Rights Abuses Involving Corporations – India' [2012] ISBN 978-92-9037-153-6 International Commission of Jurists (ICJ) < Available at SSRN: http://ssrn.com/abstract=2034813>58

68 ibid 59

- Limited liability decreases the need for monitoring due to agency problems atleast in comparison to unlimited liability.
- Limited liability reduces the costs of monitoring the wealth of other shareholders which is again in comparison to unlimited liability.
- Limited liability gives managers incentives to act efficiently by promoting the free transfer of shares and reduces the costs of determining the "true" value of a share.
- Limited liability allows more efficient diversification and facilitates the corporation's optimal investment decisions.

But, proportional liability manages to have almost the same advantages like the wealth of other shareholders is irrelevant to determining the liability of any given shareholder, reduces the need for monitoring, although not to as great a degree etc. As explained in the chapters, unlimited liability will not discourage shareholder investment, and even in the case of publicly-held corporations, unlimited liability would not burden capital markets, although it would lower share prices to reflect the full social costs of corporate activities. Of course, in the regime of unlimited liability, shareholders may attempt to evade tort liability by hiding assets, or by exploiting the limitations on personal liability offered by bankruptcy law, but to create a check on this, we need to come up with potential strategies to prevent evasion. Unlimited liability might not be the ultimate solution to the whole lot of problems, but the rule of limited liability might have to be abandoned in favour of the tort system. But all said and done, if one focuses on the procedure of instituting the regime of unlimited liability, one might view the whole task to be difficult, as proper insurance instruments and other features of the corporate world would have to be changed in order to facilitate this regime.

References

Adrian Cadbury' Report of the Committee on The Financial Aspects of Corporate Governance' [1992] London: Gee and Company

Adrian Cadbury' Corporate Governance and Chairmanship: A Personal View [2002] Oxford: Oxford University Press

CII. *Desirable Corporate Governance:A Code.* 1998. http://www.nfcgindia.org/ desirable_ corporate_governance_cii.pdf (accessed April 04, 2012).

Conde, Richard Alock and Casper. "Socially and Environmentally Responsible Business Practices: An Australian Perspective." *The Corporate Governance Law review* 1 (2005): 329.

'Corporations: Liability of Stockholders under a Statute Making Them Liable for "Debts" Does Not Include Liability for Torts' [1921] 19 [3] Michigan LR 341

'Should Shareholders Be Personally Liable for the Torts of Their Corporations?' [1967]76[6] Yale L J 1190

Bittlingmayer, George, 'The Market for Corporate Control (including Takeovers' http://encyclo.findlaw.com/5640book.pdf <accessed April 05, 2012>

Burkart M, Gromb D and Panunzi F, 'Large Shareholders, Monitoring, and the Value of the Firm' [1997] 112[3] The Quarterly Journal of Economics, 693

Carr J L and Mathewson G F, 'Unlimited Liability as a Barrier to Entry' [1988] 96[4] Journal of Political Economy 766

E B H, 'Statutory Liability of Shareholders on Tort Liabilities against the Corporation' [1917]15[8] Michigan LR 665

Grossman P Z, 'The Market for Shares of Companies with Unlimited Liability: The Case of American Express' [1995] 24 [1] The Journal of Legal Studies 63

Halpern P, Trebilcock M and Turnbull S, 'An Economic Analysis of Limited Liability in Corporation Law', [1980] 30[2] Toronto LJ 117

Hansmann H and Kraakman R, 'Toward Unlimited Shareholder Liability for Corporate Torts' [1991]100 [7] Yale LJ 1879

Hansmann H and Kraakman R, 'A Procedural Focus on Unlimited Shareholder Liability'[1992] 106[2] 106 Harvard LR 446

Hansmann H and Kraakman R, 'The anatomy of Corporate law: A comparative and functional approach'[2004]Oxford Univ. Press 1

Imanalin A, 'Rethinking Limited Liability' (LLM thesis, School of Law, the University of Warwick2011)<http://www.cslr.org.uk/index?option=com_journal&task=article&mode=pdf &format=raw&id=123> accessed at 08 April 2012

Ireland P, 'Limited Liability, Shareholder Rights And The Problem Of Corporate Irresponsibility' [2010]34 Cambridge Journal Of Economics 837–856 < http://Cje.Oxfordjournals. Org/Content> Accessed 08 April 2012

Jensen, Eugene fama and Michael. "Separation of Ownership Control." *Journal of Law and Economics* 26, no. 2 (June 1983): 301-325.

Kahan R D, 'Shareholder Liability for Corporate Torts: A Historical Perspective'[2009] 97[4] Georgetown LJ < http://papers.ssrn.com/sol3/papers.cfm?abstract_id=1269181 >accessed 8 April 2012

Kraakman R, 'Corporate Liability Strategies and the Costs of Legal Controls' [1984] 93[5] Yale LJl 857

Livermore S, 'Unlimited Liability in Early American Corporations'[1935] 43 [5] Journal of Political Economy, 674

Macey, Jonathan R. "The Concise Encyclopedia of Economics." *Market for Corporate Control.* http://www.econlib.org/library/Enc/MarketforCorporateControl.html (accessed April 04, 2012).

Mallin, Christine A. *Corporate Governance.* 2. 2007

Malik M K, 'Limited Liability' (LLM thesis, School of Law, the University of Warwick 2005-2006)

McConnell, Diane K. Denis and John J. "International Corporate Governance." *The Journal of Financial and Quantitative Analysis* 38, no. 1 (March 2003): 1-36.

Jackson, Martin Hopner and Gregory. *An Emerging Market for Corportae Control?* http://www.mpi-fg-koeln.mpg.de/pu/mpifg_dp/dp01-4.pdf (accessed April 05, 2012).

Millon D, 'Piercing the Corporate Veil, Financial Responsibility and the Limits of Limited Liability' [2003] Washington & Lee Public Law Research paper No.03-13< http://ssrn.com/abstract=451520> accessed 8 April 2012

Moll D K, 'Minority Oppression & the Limited Liability Company: Learning (or Not) from Close Corporation History' [2005] 40 Wake Forest LJ 883

Reed, Darryl. "Corporate Governance Reforms in Developing Countries." *Journal of Business Ethics* 37, no. 3 (May 2002).

Shleifer A and Vishny R W, 'Large Shareholders and Corporate Control' [1986] 94[3] Journal of Political Economy 461

Sollars G G, 'An Appraisal of Shareholder Proportional Liability' Journal of Business Ethics'[2001] 32, [4] Journal of Business Ethics 329

UK:Committee on Corporate Governance. "The Combined Code: Principles of Good Governance and Code of Best Practice." 2000.

United Nations Conference on Trade and Development. "Selected Issues in Corporate Governance:Regional and Country Experience."

Westphal J D and Zajac E J, 'The Symbolic Management of Stockholders: Corporate Governance Reforms and Shareholder Reactions' [1998] 43[1] Administrative Science Quarterly 127

Warren E H, 'Torts by Corporations in Ultra Vires Undertakings' [1925]2 [2] Cambridge LJ 180

Nair M, 'Bhopal Gas Tragedy – A Social, Economic, Legal and Environmental Analysis' [2005]. <SSRN: http://ssrn.com/abstract=1977710>

Zhao, Franklin Allen and Mengxin. *The Corporate Governance Model of Japan: Shareholders are not Rulers.* 2007. http://finance.wharton.upenn.edu/~allenf/download/Vita/Japan-Corporate-Governance.pdf (accessed March 20, 2012).

Theoretical and Operational Concerns of Corporate Governance in Pakistan

Malik M. Hafeez
The Islamia University Bahawalpur, Pakistan

ABSTRACT

The primary concept of corporate governance is with those who provide capital to companies, and its aim is to improve returns by providing market stability. However, the political slogan of public-private partnership has become popular, without implementing the theoretical dynamics of corporate governance. The UK has been an exporter of corporate legal concepts and innovations since the inception of corporate norms, not only in continental Europe and emerging economies, but also around the world. The British model of corporate governance struck a chord in many overseas countries; it has provided a yardstick against which standards of corporate governance in other markets are being measured. The ideas developed by the Cadbury Committee and its successors committees, have received ample importance in continental Europe and the rest of the jurisdictions, particularly in emerging economies such as China, India, Pakistan and those countries which have old colonial ties with the UK. The variations of the corporate governance structure and arrangement appears in different models, but the issue of managerial accountability is common everywhere. The corporate governance system in Pakistan, including the code of corporate governance based on 'shareholders primacy theory' that involves investors in managerial accountability of listed companies through effective and reliable disclosure to maintain good governance of listed companies and long-term market stability. In Asian economies, family dominated ownership has been playing an influential role, and requires competitive corporate and regulatory structure. Therefore, the regulatory authority, policy makers and the corporate community should also be clear that the new corporate legal framework in Pakistan should be attractive for investors, as well as provide security to the non-shareholder stakeholders through the services mechanism.

Keywords: *Corporate Governance, Dispersed Share-Ownership, Regulatory Authority, Corporate Monitoring, Family Owned-Corporations, Institutional Shareholders*

INTRODUCTION

Public offering of shares of large corporations has led to the dispersion of share-ownership in the hands of individuals and institutions. The corporate reality of dispersed ownership realized the separation of control from ownership. The significant increase in corporate activities, with the reality of dispersed share-ownership and separation between control and ownership, has raised corporate governance issues. However, in the UK, managerial opportunism and unaccountable management opened a debate on industrial democracy with employees' participation as the solution to early corporate governance issues. In 1979, public sector reforms based on market solutions, privatization of public industry, and reforms in the pension sector, healthcare, social welfare, removal of employment protection as well as removal of barriers of capital in-flows and out-flows changed the nature of corporate governance. These reforms replaced industrial democracy by shareholders primacy. Therefore on the one hand, investors as shareholders were expecting profits from the business and on the other hand, directors, as shareholders' agents, were managing the companies' business to gain profits.

The potential conflicts of interest among corporate participants led to the need for good corporate governance. The conflicts of interest resulted in agency problems, as Berle and Means (1932) indicated through separation of ownership from control, and arises due to corporate actors which have different objectives and imperfect information. Corporate governance mechanisms have direct concern with company law that provides discretion to the company management, while corporate governance shapes a framework for the exercise of this discretion by distributing powers between directors and shareholders.

Dispersed ownership, insufficient expertise and lack of professional commitment, created the need for specialised and professional management, that can develop and implement corporate strategies on its own, to achieve corporate aims and objectives. However, the lack of permanent supervision on the part of shareholders gave birth to the professional and skillfull independent boards of directors, to run the affairs of the companies and monitor the executive. In the bigger picture of dispersed share-ownership, professional managers run the companies' affairs with discretionary powers. Although discretionary powers may be conferred upon the management of the company through companies' legislation, in the UK they are being delegated through the company's constitution, which has been taken from common law corporate practices.

At the end of the 20th century, the ownership structure of large corporations significantly changed, and institutions became the major shareholders. Therefore, corporate scandals such as Polly Peck, BCCI and Maxwell, and financial reporting irregularities compelled business communities, market, and regulators to realize the importance of good corporate governance. They thought that an appropriate use of discretionary power could resolve the agency issues, with an effective system of corporate accountability and transparency through responsible corporate monitoring. Therefore, soft law practices on the basis of 'comply or explain' approach were introduced, in the form of code of best practices and the combined code. Responsible monitoring of the self-regulatory code was part and parcel of the British model to achieve good corporate governance. Later on, the self-regulatory code was transformed into the UK' Code and the Stewardship Code. The Stewardship Code provides guidelines for responsible monitoring, by putting the stewardship responsibility on the shoulders of the major shareholders.

Later on, corporate collapses, stock markets' crisis, managerial opportunism and dispersed ownership, forced institutional investors who have significant shares' ownership in listed companies, to become an active monitor of their investee companies. Although individual direct-share ownership in investee companies is relatively small, but institutional shareholders make their investments on behalf of individual investors. The concentration of share-ownership in the hands of a group of institutions empowers them to exercise control over management, by envisaging them stewardship obligations. The stewardship theory is an alternative to the agency theory, to fill the gap of stewards' obligations in existing corporate scenarios, where ownership and control is concentrated in the hands of institutions.

The UK has been an exporter of corporate legal concepts and innovations since the inception of corporate norms, not only in continental Europe and emerging economies, but also around the world. The British model of corporate governance struck a chord in many overseas countries; it has provided a yardstick against which standards of corporate governance in other markets are being measured. The ideas developed by the Cadbury Committee and its successors committees, have received ample importance in continental Europe and the rest of the jurisdictions, particularly in emerging economies such as China, India, Pakistan and those countries which have old colonial ties with the UK. The variations of the corporate governance structure and arrangement appears in different models, but the issue of managerial accountability is common everywhere.

The corporate governance system in Pakistan, including the code of corporate governance based on 'shareholders primacy theory,' that involves investors in managerial accountability of listed companies through effective and reliable disclosure to maintain good governance of listed companies and long-term market stability. The primary concept of corporate governance is with those who provide capital to the companies, and its aim is to improve their returns by providing market stability. However, the political slogan of public-private partnership has become popular without implementation of the theoretical dynamics of corporate governance. Therefore, this is the time to formulate the policy of corporate governance that should be competitive for corporate stability and investments. The regulatory authority, policy makers and corporate community should also be clear that the new corporate legal framework in Pakistan should be attractive for the investors, as well as provide security to the non-shareholder stakeholders through the services mechanisms.

The Security Exchange Commission of Pakistan (SECP) is a regulatory body like the Financial Services Authority (FSA) in the UK and the Security Exchange Commission in the USA. The SECP as a 'competent regulatory authority' controls and formulates the framework for stock exchanges of the country, laid down the listing rules for listed companies and supervises them. However, it is difficult for the SECP to monitor governance issues of listed companies on a regular basis, through effective engagement with the management of companies. Good corporate governance through effective compliance with the code on corporate governance requires regular and day-to-day monitoring through effective engagement, with the board of listed companies to resolve agency issues and minimize agency costs.

EFFECTIVE COMPLIANCE WITH THE CODE'S PROVISIONS THROUGH RESPONSIBLE MONITORING

Compliance with the provisions of the new code is self-regulatory, except where explicitly stated otherwise. The self-regulatory compliance of the code requires responsible monitoring through regular engagement with the companies' management, to examine that how did the management apply the provisions of the code, and what are the explanations in case of non-compliance with, or depart from the code. It is pertinent to mention, that without responsible monitoring, the compliance of the code is considered as a formality to adopt the 'box-ticking' approach for the satisfaction of the Regulatory Authority. Therefore, three monitoring mechanisms to resolve the agency issue, and minimise agency costs are going to be practiced around the world.

Enlightened Shareholder Value/Shareholder Supremacy Approach

In the UK, the Company's Act 2006 provides an innovative concept of "social corporation" to the corporate world, that is influential around the world. In the 'enlightened shareholder value' context, the directors are responsible for promoting the success of the company for the benefit of the members as a whole. However, the British model expects that in addition to the 'enlightened shareholder value' approach, the directors should have regard to pluralist factors relating to the impact of companies' operation on the community and the environment[1]. The directors' duty to promote the 'success of the company,' gives regard to shareholders' interest primarily and rest of the corporate constituency.

The 'shareholder supremacy approach' put the monitoring responsibility on the shoulders of the shareholders, who are considered either as the ultimate beneficiaries of corporate stability, or sufferer of corporate failure. The shareholders are not only responsible for

[1] The Company Act 2006, s. 417

appointing the board of directors, but also to make them accountable. In dispersed share-ownership of listed companies around the world, it was difficult for individual shareholders to monitor the management of their investee companies regularly, because the monitoring cost was more than their returns. Therefore, different approaches relating to effective corporate monitoring and to managing agency issues has been adopted around in the world financial markets.

Pluralist Approach

The 'pluralist approach' requires that directors are responsible for ensuring that a company is behaving like a 'good citizen'.[2] The British model expects, that in addition to the 'enlightened shareholder value' approach, the directors should have regard to pluralist factors relating to the impact of companies' operations on the community and the environment[3]. The directors' duty to promote the 'success of the company' gives regard to shareholders' interest primarily, and rest of the corporate constituency.[4] However, the Company Law Steering Committee considered the interests of the corporate constituency, and therefore proposed to 'enlighten shareholder value' and to use 'pluralistic' approaches.'[5] Later on, the pluralistic approach was rejected by the Committee in favour of the 'enlightened shareholder value' approach on grounds that deficiencies of the legal relationship between the company and its constituency can be overcome, and are made better by getting changes in other areas of the law and public policy, or in best practice, rather than by making mandatory changes in the Company Act. In fact, the 'pluralistic approach' recognises the role of all stakeholders in the corporate sector and corporate governance. The 'pluralistic approach' or stakeholder theory is not new, but successfully working in Germany, Japan and China since ages.

Monitoring Role of Major Shareholders

In the early 20th century, the shares of larger companies were publicly traded through stock exchanges, not only in the UK but also around the world. The trading of shares to the publicly listed companies increased and spread geographically. Consequently, the link between a company's shareholders and management became remote. The dispersed share-ownerships of listed companies led to the divergence between ownership and control – corporate ownership being vested in the shareholders, and control in the hands of directors. The separation of ownership and control caused a divergence between owners' and managers' interests, without

[2] LE Talbot, *Critical Company Law*, (Routledge Cavendish 2008) 145-152

[3] The Company Act 2006, s. 417

[4] The Company Act 2006, s. 172

[5] The 'enlighten shareholder value' approach, without altering the priority of shareholders value, requires that the interest of, and relationships with, all stakeholders should be considered by supporting corporate actions to further those interests or relationships.

keeping any effective check on management powers.[6] The dispersion of shares in listed companies not only led to the proxy-voting system, but also gave greater power to management rather than the shareholders, because proxy-voting tended to be exercised pro-management.[7] Therefore, managers were monitored and made accountable in order to stop them from pursuing their own economic self-interests at the expense of others, who have stakes in the company.[8]

The dispersed ownership of major public companies created a significant gap between remote individual shareholders and the executive-management of the companies.[9] Therefore, agency costs and managerial opportunism increased, due to dispersion of share-ownership. The new managerial era in the corporate sector started when management became powerful, without the reign of corporate accountability. However, the use of managerial unfettered powers in their own interests at the cost of the company, made the investors vigilant that they should monitor managerial opportunism and make them accountable for the protection of their capital.

The British model of corporate governance has an 'outsider' or 'arms-length' system of ownership and control.[10] An 'outsider' typology indicates a dispersed ownership structure of corporations among institutional investors and individual shareholders, while an 'arms-length' signifies that investors hardly intervene in the day-to-day affairs of their investee companies. Therefore, an 'arms-length or outsider' corporate structure suffers unavoidable 'agency costs' that arise from self serving managerial behaviours.

The fundamental objective of the corporate governance framework is to improve the accountability of corporate managers through investors.[11] In the early 1930s, individual investors had 80 percent of the securities traded on the London Stock Exchange, but now the ownership structure of public listed companies has significantly changed, and institutional investors have become the dominant players of the British financial market.[12] Institutional investors by virtue of their size and power, are ideal monitors of their investee companies.[13] Good corporate governance is possible by institutional investors' activism, wherein their

[6] D. D. Prentice and P.R.J. Holland, *Contemporary Issues in Corporate Governance*, (Oxford 1993) 27 ; Helen Garten, 'Institutional Investors and the New Financial Order' (1992) 44 Rutgers Law Review 585 at 593-603

[7] D. D. Prentice and P.R.J. Holland, (n. 6) 27

[8] Paul L. Davies, 'Institutional Investors in the United Kingdom' in D. D. Prentice and P.R.J. Holland (eds.) *Contemporary Issues in Corporate Governance* (Oxford 1993) 74-75; D. D. Prentice and P.R.J. Holland, (n. 6) 27

[9] The Berle and Means work (1932 & 1967) realised the significance of corporate power and drew attention of corporate community and regulators to understand the problems of corporate governance.

[10] Brian R. Cheffins, 'Corporate Governance Reform: Britain as an Exporter' Corporate Governance and the Reform of Company Law, 2000 Hume Papers on Public Policy 8(1) 9-11

[11] Brian R. Cheffins, (n. 10) 11

[12] Brian R. Cheffins, *Corporate Ownership and Control: British Business Transformed*, (Oxford 2008) 344-45

[13] The companies in which institutional shareholders invest are called their portfolio or investee companies.

responsible monitoring behaviour can force the management to concentrate on long-term corporate performance, which would not only enhance efficiency, but also maintain long-term corporate stability.[14]

The overwhelming rise of institutional shareholders and their subsequent role in corporate governance have significant importance. Although they work in a very competitive environment, their duties towards their beneficiaries or clients require them to avoid risks. Today institutional investors own 88.7 percent equity holdings in publicly traded companies that gives them a significant role in corporate governance and corporate control. In the wake of the recent corporate crisis that have shaken the corporate sector, most of them believe that institutional investors can and must play their role for the improvement of their investee companies for the long-term stability of financial markets.[15] The main types of institutional shareholders in the UK are insurance companies, pension funds, mutual-fund or pooled fund (unit trusts, and investment trusts), banks, and charities. Many institutional shareholders engage the services of investment managers, who take investment decisions and construct portfolios on their behalf.[16]

The board of directors has a vital role in corporate governance, by providing the company with leadership and drive. Their corporate actions are subject to laws, regulations, and the disciplines of the market place, as well as the shareholders in a general meeting. The shareholders are responsible to appoint the directors and auditors and make them accountable. The financial reporting system requires their accountability by the shareholders for the progress of the company. Auditors report to the shareholders for a company's financial matters, by keeping an external and objective check on the directors' financial statements.

The corporate monitoring and accountability of management is necessary to protect members of the public, who provide capital for investment and hoping for returns against certain types of wrong-doings including deliberate fraud, incompetent and unrealistic corporate decisions. The significant growth of institutional share-ownerships has made them a key actor of corporate governance with concentrated holdings, possessing the expertise to exercise control over corporate management. The institutional dominance of the equity market would not only force a change in the governance of public corporations, but effectively monitor and resolve the arising conflicts between corporate managers and shareholders.[17]

The increased quantity of financial assets came in the hands of a decreased number of institutional investors. Consequently, corporate control shifted towards institutions. The

[14] Lilian Miles, 'The Role of Institutional Shareholders in Corporate Governance: Recent Developments in the UK'2003 Scottish Law & Practice Quarterly 8(3) 204-216

[15] Lilian Miles, (n.14) 204-06

[16] Lodewijk Van Setten, *The Law of Institutional Investment Management*, (Oxford 2009) 6-20

[17] Helen Garten, 'Institutional Investors and the New Financial Order' (1992) 44 Rutgers Law Review 585-674 at pp. 587

control of institutional clout could offer to challenge the factual basis of "separation between ownership and control," rather than remain a silent partner of corporate management. The significant shift of corporate control and ownership in the hands of a group of institutions make them the stewards of the corporate sector. Greater institutional power is regarded as the potential to be a positive force in corporate governance to improve operating efficiency, employee productivity, shareholder value and corporate stability.[18]

However, the UK played a pioneering role in the development of a self-regulatory corporate governance framework.[19] British corporate failures in the 1980s (i.e. Maxwell, Polly Peck, and BCCI) commissioned the Committee on the Financial Aspects of Corporate Governance which launched the Cadbury Report (1992), that marked the start of corporate governance in the UK. The Cadbury Report recommended a 'Code of Best Practices' that provides a corporate arrangement of the company board of directors and accounting system, to diminish the risks and failures of corporate governance.[20]

The Cadbury Code initiated a debate about the British model of corporate governance, that subsequently commissioned the Greenbury and Hampel Committees on different aspects of corporate governance; their reports and recommended codes, enabled the emergence of the Combined Code that set out self-regulatory standards for good corporate governance.[21] The Combined Code, without any amendment, was operative through the Stock Exchange Listing Rules since 1998 to 2004, and later on it was updated by the Higgs Committee Recommendations.

The British model of corporate governance provided an innovative self-regulatory approach for listed companies on the basis of 'comply or explain' principle. The disclosure of compliance or non-compliance is mandatory for the companies to mention in their annual reports how they applied the provisions of the code, or reasons of non-compliance by indicating the reasons of any area of non-compliance in the light of their own particular circumstance. The operational flexibility of the 'comply or explain' approach, encourages companies to adopt the general spirit of the code, rather than the letters.[22]

---

[18] Helen Garten, (n. 17) 589; Michael C. Jensen, 'Eclipse of the Public Corporation'(1997) Harvard Business Review at pp. 5-10 available on http://papers.ssrn.com/sol3/papers.cfm?abstract_id=146149# accessed on March 2011

[19] Sridhar R. Arcot, 'In Letter but not in Spirit: An Analysis of Corporate Governance in the UK' (2006) 1-38 available on http://www.lse.ac.uk/FMGPersonalPages/sridharArcot/CGPaper1.pdf accessed on March 2011

[20] Sir Adrian Cadbury, 'Report of the Committee on the Financial Aspects of Corporate Governance' (1992) available on http://www.ecgi.org/codes/documents/cadbury.pdf Accessed on January 2011

[21] The Combined Code: Principles of Good Governance and Code of Best Practice (2000), Derived by the Committee on Corporate Governance from the Committee final Report (1998), and from the Cadbury and Greenbury Reports, available on http://www.ecgi.org/codes/documents/combined_code.pdf

[22] Sridhar Arcot, 'Corporate Governance in the UK: Is the Comply or Explain approach working?' (Social Sciences Research Network (SSRN) on-line), (2009) 1-29 available on http://papers.ssrn.com/sol3/papers. cfm?abstract id=1532290&rec=1&srcabs=1511904 accessed on 2011

The voluntary compliance with the code provided an unique opportunity for corporate actors to avoid a 'box-ticking' approach. This was a mandatory regime that neither provided space for any sound deviations of the company from the rule, nor did it foster investors' trust. The voluntary compliance with the code, coupled with mandatory disclosure requires shareholders' monitoring through their active engagement with their investee companies for the true functioning of the British model of corporate governance. This aims to secure company assets from managerial opportunism, and to provide long-term corporate stability.[23] Therefore, the Combined Code is widely regarded as an international benchmark for good corporate governance practices unlike the Sarbanes-Oxley Act 2000.[24]

Over the past two decades, from the inception of the Cadbury Code, all recommendations, the Combined Code 2002 and its successor code on corporate governance such as the UK Corporate Governance Code and the Stewardship Code, have continuously advocated active shareholders involvement in the affairs of public listed companies. For instance, the primary focus of the Cadbury Code was the supervision of executive decision-making through the board of directors and institutional investors, wherein they are required to play a monitoring role for the improvement of corporate governance.

The Cadbury Report (1992) encouraged systematic and active engagement of institutional investors with the management of their investee companies, by making positive use of their voting rights, as well as taking a positive interest in the composition of boards and the committees. The Hampel Committee endorsed and encouraged the Cadbury recommendations for institutional investors' engagement through dialogue between companies and major shareholders, and further recommended that pension fund trustees and their fund managers should formulate long-term investment policy.[25]

The Combined Code addressed the role of institutional investors by incorporating the Principle C.1, which requires dialogue between the board and shareholders, and Principle E.2 sets out reciprocal guidance for institutional investors' active engagement with their investee companies.[26] Although the Higgs Report (2003) focused on the role of outside directors, various new provisions in relation to the engagement of institutional shareholders with their investee companies, also incorporated in the Combined Code as recommended by the Report.[27] For instance, the revised Combined Code 2003 required that the Chairman of the

---

[23] FSA Handbook 2010, Listing Rules, L. R. 9.8.6 available on http://www.fsa.gov.uk/pubs/hb-releases/rel64/rel64lr.pdf accessed on 2011

[24] The Sarbanes-Oxley Act 2002, s. 302, 303, and 906, indicate the mandatory and rule based approach of the US model of corporate governance rather than principle based approach.

[25] Ronnie Hampel, 'Committee on Corporate Governance Final Report'(1998) 40-48 available on http://www.ecgi.org/codes/documents/hampel.pdf accessed 2011

[26] The Combined Code 2000, Principle C.1 & E.2

[27] Derek Higgs, 'Review of the role and effectiveness of non-executive directors' (2003) 67-70 available on http://www.berr.gov.uk/files/file23012.pdf accessed on 2011

board should maintain sufficient contact with major shareholders to understand their concerns, and the annual report should state how many steps have been taken by the board to understand the views of major shareholders.

Institutional investors are required to apply the principles issued by the ISC on the responsibilities of institutional shareholders for monitoring their investee companies.[28]The incorporation of these provisions in the Combined Code sponsored an initiative of institutional investors' activism in the corporate governance landscape, that provided an official endorsement for institutional investors' intervention in their investee companies. Paul Myners issued a government commissioned report (2001) that expressly indicated the concerns about the fund-managers' passivity in monitoring and their unwillingness to actively engaged with their portfolio companies. Therefore, Myners proposed that a duty should be imposed on the UK-based pension fund to make use of shareholders' voting rights where appropriate, as a responsible corporate monitor.[29]

The recent global banking crisis (2007-09) affected the British banking industry, in which Britain's largest banks, HBOS/Lloyds TSB, and RBS received government support through a bail-out policy for survival, while others such as Northern Rock and Bradford Bingley were completely nationalised. Institutional investors were identified as one of the culprits of British corporate failure, because they failed to perform their fundamental responsibility of effective scrutiny and monitoring the decisions of the boards and management. They did nothing to prevent the executives of financial institutions from making huge bonuses, and benefits. The Walker Report (2009) identified the passive and perfunctory role of institutional investors, relating to the monitoring of their investee companies.[30]

Major shareholders such as pension-funds, insurance companies, investment trusts, banks, charities and unit-trusts owe stewardship obligations, because they have significant share-ownership with the advantage of limited liability under company law. Resultantly, the Walker Report recommended and characterised the 'ISC's Code on the Responsibilities of

---

[28] The Institutional Shareholders' Committee (ISC) is a forum for interaction and cooperation for the Associations of Investment Companies (AIC), the Association of British Insurers (ABI), the Investment Management Association (IMA), and the National Association of Pension Funds (NAPF). ISC issued guidance in 2002 for Institutional investors to monitors the performance of their investee companies through regular dialogue with companies where appropriate, necessary intervention, and evaluate the impact of their own monitoring activism and report to their clients and beneficiaries. The ISC revisited and updated its principle on the 'Responsibilities of Institutional Shareholders and their Agents' in 2005 and designated it as an ISC Code. In November 2009, ISC again revised its principle and issued its promised code i.e. the Code on the Responsibilities of Institutional Investors.

[29] Paul Myners, *Institutional Investment in the United Kingdom: A Review*, London, HM Treasury, (2000) 14 at Para 79 available on http://archive.treasury.gov.uk/pdf/2001/myners_report.pdf accessed on January 2011

[30] David Walker, A Review of Corporate Governance in UK Banks and others Financial Industry Entities: Final recommendations, London, HM Treasury, (2009) 68-89 available on http://webarchive.nationalarchives.gov.uk/+/http://www. hm-treasury.gov.uk/d/walker_review_261109.pdf accessed on 2011

Institutional Investors'[31] as a Stewardship Code, that would provide guidance to institutional investors for the effective and responsible monitoring of their investee companies. The Financial Reporting Council (FRC), which was already responsible for revision and consultation of the Combined Code, took up the responsibility of the Stewardship Code.[32] The FRC, after the consultation document, issued the Stewardship Code 2010, and revised 'the UK Corporate Governance Code 2010, (i.e., new version of the Combined Code).[33]

The Stewardship Code consists of seven principles, namely disclosure policy regarding discharge of stewardship responsibilities, policy on managing conflicts of interests, the monitoring of investee companies, appropriate collective actions, voting and disclosure of voting activity, and a periodic report on stewardship and voting activities, which are drafted and incorporated by the FRC on a similar footing as 'the ISC's Code on the Responsibilities of Institutional Investors[34]'. Institutional investors and their agents are required to perform their stewardship commitments on the bases of the 'comply or explain' approach, similar to the self-regulatory approach of the Combined Code and the ISC's Code.[35]

In sum, the lack of permanent supervision on the part of shareholders, gave birth to professional and skillfull independent boards of directors, to run the affairs of companies and monitor the executive. Later on corporate collapses, stock markets' crisis, managerial opportunism and dispersed ownership, forced institutional investors who have significant shares' ownership in listed companies, to become active monitors of their investee companies. Although individual direct shareholding in investee companies is relatively small, but institutional shareholders make their investments on behalf of individual investors. The concentration of share-ownership in the hands of a group of institutions, empowers them to exercise control over management by envisaging stewardship obligations. The stewardship theory is an alternative to the agency theory, to fill the gap of stewards' obligations in existing corporate scenarios, where ownership and control is concentrated in the hands of institutions.

---

31 Institutional shareholders' Committee Code on the Responsibilities of Institutional Investors (ISC's Code), (2009) available on http://institutionalshareholderscommittee.org.uk/sitebuildercontent/sitebuilderfiles/ ISCCode 161109.pdf accessed on March 2011

32 Financial Reporting Council, *Consultation on a Stewardship Code for Institutional Investors*, London, FRC, (2010) available on https://www.frc.org.uk/images/uploaded/documents/Stewardship%20Code%20C onsultation %20January%2020101.pdf accessed on 2011

33 The provisions relating to role of institutional investors and their engagement with their investee companies by following the principles of the ISC's Code were omitted in the new version of the UK Corporate Governance Code 2010.

34 Financial Reporting Council, The Stewardship Code 2010, London, FRC, available on http://www.frc.org.uk/images/uploaded/documents/UK%20Stewardship%20Code%20July%2020103.pdf accessed on 2011

35 Financial Reporting Council, *Implementation of the UK Stewardship Code 2010*, London, FRC, 2010, available on http://www.frc.org.uk/images/uploaded/documents/Implementation%20of%20Stewardship% 20Code% 20 July%2020103.pdf accessed on 2011

Application of Stakeholder Theory

The German corporate governance model has significant importance due to a two-tier board, the supervisory and management boards, and employees' representation on a supervisory board on the principle of codetermination.[36] The management board is responsible for running the affairs of the company, while the supervisory board plays a monitoring role to ensure that the management board is managing the company in a competent and efficient manner.[37]

In Germany, the dual board and codetermination are not new. The dual-board was introduced by the General German Commercial Code of 1861. It was made compulsory in 1870 for large corporations. The supervisory codetermination was introduced in 1922 by an amendment of the Works Councils Act 1920. The workers representative members of the supervisory board were elected for their reserved seats through a secret ballot by the entire workforce.[38] This democratic right of employees' participation in the supervisory board was abolished in 1934 and again revived by agreement, between the British occupational forces and German trade unions, for management and labour to work together. The system of parity in employee representation in the supervisory board was introduced in the mining, iron and steel industry by the Codetermination Act of 1951, with the concept of the 'neutral person' as Chairman of the board, who was appointed by the shareholders meeting upon the recommendation of the supervisory board.

After 25 years, the codetermination system was required for all companies which have more than 2,000 employees through the Codetermination Act 1976. The Chairperson who had the casting vote, was appointed by shareholders' representatives and the Vice-Chairman was appointed by employees' representatives. The Chairman's casting vote increased the shareholders representational power, and this form becomes the 'quasi-parity codetermination,' rather than 'parity codetermination'. Later on, one-third of employees' codetermination in the supervisory board was prescribed through the Employees on the Supervisory Board Act of 2004, which ended the concept of parity supervisory codetermination.[39] Shareholders majority seats in the supervisory board is a step towards the UK shareholders' primacy approach. The German Supreme Court in Civil Matters held that the Codetermination Act was passed in the public interest, to serve the common weal of the community and the national economy.[40] Du Plessis argued that the so called 'Path

---

[36] Jill Solomon, *Corporate Governance and Accountability*, 2nd Ed. (Wiley, 2007) 205 - 206

[37] Simon Goulding, Lilian Miles, and Alexander Schall, 'Judicial Enforcement of Extra Legal Code in UK and German Company Law'2 ECFR 21 (2005) 20-62 at p. 41

[38] Jean J. Du Plessis, 'the Rise and fall of Supervisory Codetermination in Germany?' I.C.C.L.R. 2005, 16(2), 67-79

[39] Jean J. Du Plessis, (n.38) 69-70

[40] Jean J. Du Plessis, (n.38) 71

dependency'[41] and political consequences are the main obstacles for the abolishment of the traditional German-model.

On the other hand, Japan is a civil-law country, and has less flexibility in her procedural system. The traditional corporate governance model was the *Keiretsu*[42] and was popular and prevailed in the Japanese corporate market. The *Keiretsu*'s boards were large and composed entirely of executives. In companies' governance, the 'company community' had a key role; full-time core employees, members of the board and management, who shared their identity as 'company men,' were called the company community, except female employees who were treated as a temporary workforce. The company community ensured lifetime employment and seniority system for promotion and incentive purposes.[43] The 'employees' ownership'[44] called relationship preserving norms, and shareholders ownership is called end-game norms.[45] Corporations were usually monitored in three ways: First, in-house monitoring conducted by the 'company community'; second, monitoring by inside shareholders; last, monitoring by outside-shareholders through exit.[46] Therefore, it could be argued that the Japanese Model of Corporate Governance based on the stakeholder theory, rather than shareholder primacy theory.

Monitoring Through Company Auditors and Creditors

Japanese corporate law also provided the concept of statutory-auditors like the Italian model of corporate governance.[47] They were not board's members, but they could attend board meetings and express their opinions. Both boards of auditors and outside auditors monitored the illegal action of the directors. They prepared company reports regarding companies' financial matters, infringements of the commercial code, and articles of the company.

In Italy, partnerships with unlimited liability and limited liability companies are the main forms of business. Families, state, and block holders (i.e., coalition of different companies) are dominant shareholders of listed and unlisted companies.[48] The uniqueness of the Italian-modal is the tri-part governance system: board of directors, executive committee including

---

41 Revolutionary theory that express the idea; history matters-choices made in the past can affect the feasibility of choices made in future.

42 Keiretsu are networks of companies in Japan connected through cross-holding of shares and with interlocking directorships. Member companies including financial institutions tend to inter trade extensively.

43 ZenichiShishido, 'Japanese Corporate Governance: The Hidden Problems of Corporate Law and Their Solution' (2000) 25 Del. J. Corp. L. 189-233 202-204

44 The employees being human capital have a long term contractual relationship with corporations.

45 End-game consists of inside shareholders exercising their voice in the corporation and outsider shareholders have the option of exit by selling their shares.

46 ZenichiShishido, (n.43) 208

47 ZenichiShishido, (n.43) 206-207

48 Christine A. Mallin, *Corporate Governance*, Ed. 2nd (Oxford 2008) 167-180

Managing Director (MD) and board of statutory auditors.[49] The statutory audit board acts autonomously, and represents and protects the interests of the generality of the shareholders. The principal responsibility given to the board of auditors is to monitor directors' performance in the discharge of their duties, which is similar to British non-executive directors.[50] The internal auditing staff, internal control committee and external audit firm that appointed by the shareholders, are supposed to co-operate and share relevant information with the board of auditors.

POSSIBILITY OF RESPONSIBLE CORPORATE MONITORING IN EMERGING ECONOMIES LIKE PAKISTAN

Corporate governance has received wide attention of policy makers in the developed and developing countries during the last decade. The significant dimension of corporate governance issues in a developing country like Pakistan, are the underdeveloped nature of corporate culture, family dominated business group, regional instability due to war and terror, and ineffective regulatory mechanism. It is a fact that family dominated corporate ownership structures prevail in Pakistan, wherein the majority of companies or a large number of business groups are held and controlled by family networks. Minorities' interests neither find reasonable representation in the corporate decision-making process, nor the corporate frame work protects them from derivate-actions which are provided in the British Company Act 2006. The behavioral patterns of corporate governance, such as, the actual conduct of corporations in terms of performance, efficiency, growth, financial structure, treatment of shareholders, role of institutional shareholders and corporate social responsibility are not yet well established. Laws and regulations under which firms are operating, the functioning of the board of directors in relation to ownership structures, the responsibility of executive dispensation in determining and deciding firm performance, the relationships between labour policies and firm productivity, the role of multiple shareholders, and lack of transparent and accountable corporate and financial reporting frameworks, are some of the issues confronting the corporate sector in Pakistan.[51]

However, the Government of Pakistan established the Securities and Exchange Commission of Pakistan(SECP) in 1997, to lay down and improve the structure of good corporate governance, as well as build the regulatory framework for effective management of the corporate sector. The SECP in pursuance of its policy of regulation, has enacted and

[49] RaffaeleLener, 'The New Rules on Corporate Governance of Banks issued by the Bank of Italy and Milan Stock Exchange' J.I.B.L. R. 2008, 23 (7) 387-391

[50] Andrea Melis, 'On the Role of the Board of the Statutory Auditors in Italian Listed Companies' 2004 Corporate Governance 12 (1) 75 at pp. 77

[51] RasulBakhshRais, Regulatory Impact Assessment of SECP's Corporate Governance Code in Pakistan, CMER Working Paper no. 05-39 at (2007 & 2008) 1-25

enforced various laws and regulations including the Code of Corporate governance, to create and strengthen an "enabling business environment" for smooth and sustained functioning of corporate and economic development.

The shareholder primacy theory is attractive for investors, but it requires active corporate monitoring in which the institutional shareholders can play important role. However, free and fair functioning of institutional investors requires comprehensive review of their legal framework, because institutional shareholders (such as pension funds, insurance companies, investment companies and unit-trusts) in Pakistan, are working under the shadow of the federal government. Their functioning should be independent without bureaucratic interference, for healthy functioning of major shareholders. However, the stakeholder theory may also be applied, to provide job security to corporate employees through services laws, as well as to the general community through consumers' protection laws. The fiduciaries duties of the corporate directors and right of derivative actions for the protection of minority shareholders should also be incorporated in corporate law, to protect investors and to save them from managerial opportunism and agency issues.

Western institutional investors in contrast to major investors in the developing economies work independently in the best interests of their beneficiaries. For instance, in the UK, institutional investors have more than 87 percent equity ownership in their investee companies listed on the London Stock Exchange.[52] They have a significant role in the corporate governance of their investee companies being a steward of their companies. They are responsible for active involvement and monitor their companies while in the emerging economies, the major shareholders are absentee landlords in investee companies and that is detrimental to the minority shareholders and for corporate stability. However, the perfunctory monitoring behaviour of institutional investors is beneficial for corporate families, to keep complete control on their business firms, and to run them in their best political and economic interests. The ineffective monitoring of domestic institutions increases agency costs. The management exercises their powers and utilizes corporate resources without any fear of accountability.

With the existence of family domination in the corporate sector, political interference and ineffective monitoring of domestic institutions, creditors and professional auditors can play a responsible monitoring role. Their responsible monitoring can manage and mitigate agency problems, and provide corporate stability. The high quality of auditors' monitoring would not only enhance the confidence of domestic and foreign investors, but also ensure minority shareholders that their interest would be protected.[53] The relationship between auditor choice

---

[52] The UK, ONS Share Ownership Structure, <http://www.statistics.gov.uk/pdfdir/share0110.pdf> (8 September 2011)

[53] Joseph, P.H. Fan and T.J. Wong, "Do External Auditors Perform a Corporate Governance Role in Emerging Markets? Evidence from East Asia," Journal of Accounting Research, Vol. 43, No.1(March 2005): 35-72

and ownership structure is evident among firms frequently raising equity capital, wherein auditors play a governance role to mitigate agency problems and the issue of minority shareholders in emerging markets. The role of auditors would allow using these quantifiable measures to capture the quality of the corporate governance mechanisms used by a firm.

On the other hand, both the company's shareholders and creditors finance the company, but shareholders will often be more than merely finance providers in a company, because they have a role incorporated decision making and control of the board as monitors through their vote. However, creditors who are first and foremost providers of finance, have a limited role in the operations of the company, though their financial interests are clearly prejudiced, and they seek to exercise their contractual and proprietary protection. Creditors' role during insolvency proceedings is not enough to protect corporate stability and their own financial interests.[54] Family owned corporations exercise their political and bureaucratic influence in financial institutions to take overvalued heavy loans for their companies, and utilize this credit money for their personal benefits, and take the shield of corporate personality as a legal entity, in case of insolvency to protect them from personal liability.

Second, in concentrated financial markets, the directors cum shareholders such as family members, run the company to protect their own financial and political interests at the cost of the company. Managerial opportunism increases agency costs. Therefore, creditors as capital providers, should be in a position to play a significant role in corporate governance during solvency. Creditors may have a monitoring role, as a result of their contractual relationship with the company.[55] Finance is a life-blood for the corporate sector; therefore the relationship between shareholders and creditors should be understood in the dynamics of company financing decisions, in both the solvent and insolvent scenario.

Creditors should protect themselves against two dangers through possible monitoring: first, the borrower should deplete the assets, either by diminishing their value, or by substituting safe assets for more risky ones and second, should dilute the value of the creditor's debt by adding more liabilities, without correspondingly increasing the asset pool.[56] Unsecured creditors should be required to have extensive covenants which give them the ability to monitor the entire business of the borrowers and, in conjunction with that monitoring, to stop borrowers depleting the asset pool or increasing liabilities. Creditors' monitoring should be focused on the asset that is given as security. Responsible monitoring can be effective through creditors with a security interest over all the assets of the company.[57]

[54] Louise Gullifer and Jennifer, *Corporate Finance Law Principle and Policy,* (London: Hart Publishing, 2011) 80
[55] Gullifer and Jennifer, (n.54) 14
[56] Gullifer and Jennifer, (n.54)294
[57] Louise and Jennifer, (n.54)294-295

Needed Argus-Eyed Working and Performance by India's Public Sector Banks: Pre-Requisite of Basel-III Regulatory Norms

Rajiv Kumar Sinha, Surav Kumar[1] and Priyatam Kumar[2]
Agro-Economic Research Centre, Bihar
[1]RHRS, Bangalore
[2]Commerce College, Bhagalpur, Bihar

ABSTRACT

The article examines the preparedness of Indian banks for Basel III and action that may be taken for making Indian Banks more resilient and to reduce their ineptitude after BASEL III

Keywords: *Basel III, Indian Banks*

INTRODUCTION

Strong banking and financial systems are, no doubt, remarkable prerequisites for sustained economic growth of a country, or an economy. It is true that the world has today become integrated, and turned into a global financial market. A large number of depositors, investors and customers are closely tracking higher returns, and preferably flock to those financial institutions and banks, who offer competitive rates to savers. In the present milieu, when banks have to compete for retail deposits with other players, it is difficult to see how they can offer rates, which are out of sync with the market. As a matter of fact, in India, banking is not what it was in 1934 or 1949.

With the nationalization of major commercial banks in 1969 and 1980, the ownership and rich profile of banks in the country has undergone a sea change. A major share of the banking business in the country is handled by banks, where a majority of the shares (if not the sole shareholders), is held by the government. Further, 'capital adequacy' and 'income recognition norms' are well established, as per international standards (Basel I, II, III). The reference rates and open market operations are available with the regulator, as tools to regulate money supply. How efficiently the Indian financial system (IFS), particularly the Public Sector Banks (PSBs), could perform, or might be compelled to flunk over some of the provisions of Regulatory regime, which are likely to pose challenges before them-need to be thoroughly examined.

OBJECTIVES

In view of the earlier stated non-corresponding factors that the Indian banking sector is faced with, the article seeks to examine the following objectives:

(i) To develop an understanding about the BASEL provisions;
(ii) To examine the infallible doctrine of the CRR regulations and its possible amendment;
(iii) To examine the resilience of the Indian' banking system under BASEL III common requirements;
(iv) To understand the genesis and salient features of the BASEL III framework; and
(v) To suggest action points for making Indian banks more resilient and to reduce their ineptitude after BASEL III.

METHODOLOGY

The article is mainly based on secondary data, available information and reports of different regulatory bodies and the Reserve Bank of India (R.B.I)

ADDRESSING OBJECTIVES : RAPID LOOK BASEL – III: UNDESIRABLE HISS

The State Bank of India and its associates and subsidiaries will require about Rs.1 lakh crores of capital over the next five years (by the year 2017) to meet Basel-III norms (in addition to retained earnings). According to Mr. Diwakar Gupta, Managing Director and Chief Financial Officer of SBI, this was based on a 20 per cent growth rate and a return on equity of between 18 and 20 per cent. The estimate could vary, since growth rates during the last year (2011-12) as well as the current year are lower.

The RBI estimates that Indian banks would need about Rs. 5 lakh crores in the next five years (by the year 2017) to get ready for Basel-III norms, that will be effective from 2018. The norms, developed in the backdrop of the global crisis in 2008, impose higher capital prescriptions on banks to cater to various risks.

SBI received Rs. 7,900 crores infusion from the government in the last fiscal (2011-12). The State Bank of India would continue with its capital conservation strategy (routing SME, export credit through guarantee schemes, thereby reducing the credit risk on such assets, and also lowering capital requirements on loans). The measures had contributed to a 62 basis point rise in the Tier-I ratio of capital last fiscal (one basis point is one-hundredth of a percentage point). SBI had a capital adequacy ratio of 13.8 as of June -2012, with Tier-I ratio at 9.8 per cent. SBI was to improve the integrity around the data and around ratings better. The bank clawed back 91 basis points the last time. Hopefully, this year another 25-30 basis points will be gained based on the same parameters.

Asset quality is a problem for all banks, and therefore, the rating agencies are well within their rights to say that there is enough stress to warrant a ratings revision. But, another big item that they said affected the ratings was the inability of the State Bank to raise capital at will. Now, this has not changed since 1955. Why should this suddenly become an important factor, while reconsidering a rating? It is more a factor of perception than fact. The SBI should, of course, ask the rating agencies to review its performance which is quite strong. SBI was delivering the second largest corporate profit in the country, and was the largest tax payer. "That is something the rating agency should also look at."

CRR: Evinced Expostulation

According to Chairman, Pratip Choudhari, of the State Bank of India there is need for having a debate on doing away with the Cash Reserve Ratio (CRR), and the need to adjust rules in accordance with changing times.

"This (doing away with CRR) should not be the only view; there should be more discussion on this."

CRR is that slice of the deposits that banks are required to keep with the Reserve Bank of India. Currently, banks need to park Rs. 4.75 for every Rs. 100 deposit they collect. According to the SBI Chief, there are three reasons why the CRR should go:

First, CRR hurts the national economy; second, the funds parked with the RBI as CRR does not earn any interest for banks, and third, when insurance companies, NBFCs and mutual funds are not required to keep any CRR, it is the banks that are subjected to unfair treatment. Referring to the fact that the government amended the RBI Act in 2007, doing away with interest on CRR, the SBI Chairman opined that rules should change along with changing times. The laws cannot be rigid.... even the Constitution of the country has been amended more than 90 times. The SBI Chief's comment on phasing out CRR had sparked a controversy with the RBI Deputy Governor (K.C. Chakrabarty) making a strong statement that "If the SBI Chairman is not able to do business in this regulatory environment, he has to find out some other place. "

The SBI Chief observed that while some were saying that CRR could not be done away with, no one was giving the rationale why it could not be done.

CUT IN CRR : CENTRE'S FAVOUR

One of the important regulatory tools determining the working and performance, 'financial health' and activities of banks and other financial institutions/organizations – is CRR. In this context, ahead of the mid-quarter review of monetary policy, the Finance Ministry of India, on 12 June, 2012- made a case for lowering of the Cash Reserve Ratio (CRR); saying it would improve credit flow and spur economic growth. As per the Department of Financial Services Secretary (D.K. Mittal), on the sidelines of the meeting of the heads of PSU banks with the Finance Minister at New Delhi, – "CRR is an issue addressed by the regulator (the Reserve Bank of India), but as owner of banks, when we have to meet Basel-III requirements, we will welcome CRR cut."

CRR is that portion of deposits that banks are required to keep with the Central Bank. The RBI, in its mid-quarter review of monetary policy (on 18 June, 2012) – was widely expected to announce steps to boost sagging economic growth, which dipped to a nine –year low of 6.5 percent in 2011-12. In the opinion of the Department of Financial Services Secretary – "This (CRR cut) is a monetary policy issue, but you have to understand two aspects. CRR today is 4.75 percent, that is, the amount of money which is deposited by commercial banks with the RBI. I think banks have a cost, there is no money paid to them. '

BASEL- III NORMS : CRR CUT

There are Basel – III requirements, the DFSS observed, adding that, "There are deposits of Rs. 65 lakh crore, there is Rs. 3.20 lakh crore deposited with the RBI, which is interest free. If that much money is released in the banking system, credit flow would be available to that extent – is the second side. So, these are the two things, which have to be balanced. It is in the domain of the RBI to look at these issues. "But as owner of the banks, I would certainly like CRR to go down as early as possible" – the D.F.S.S. opined. In March, 2012, the RBI had cut the CRR by 0.75 percentage points to 4.75 percent, to infuse liquidity in the market. Besides, it had reduced the CRR by 0.50 percentage points to unlock primary liquidity in January, 2012 as well. Meanwhile, many banks, including the State Bank of India, also pitched for reducing CRR, so that their profitability could be improved. As per Ministry of Finance, Govt. of India's view – "Unless the interest rate is lower, there is difficulty in having higher growth rate. Today, higher interest rates are feeding into inflation."

In the light of this discussion, it may be considered as the need of the hour to encourage a national debate on 'efficacious CRR cut.'

BASEL – III FRUCTIFICATION OF IN BANKING ACTIVITIES

A strong and resilient banking system is considered as a prerequisite for economic growth and stability. However, due to the high degree of leverage and trust related responsibility, banking is a risky business and therefore, banks are subjected to stringent regulations. Moreover, in view of the increasingly globalised and integrated financial markets, it is necessary to create level playing fields, and eliminate instances of regulatory arbitrage through international convergence of regulatory standards. Framing banking regulations under the Basel framework has been a step in this direction. As the regulatory frameworks also evolve with market dynamics and emerging challenges, the Basel framework has also evolved from the initial Basel I standard, to the wider and comprehensive Basel II framework, and then, the current Basel-III reform measures emerged. Basel III have been developed especially as a response to challenges posed by the global financial crisis. The global crisis of 2008-09 had demonstrated the speed with which financial distress could be transmitted across the globe. This article attempts to analyze the genesis and salient features of the Basal III framework, as also its likely impact on banks in India. However, in order to understand the spirit and direction of regulatory structures, it is necessary to have a brief recapitulation of the Basel I and Basel II frameworks.

BASEL- I : COMMON CAPITAL REQUIREMENTS

The Basel Committee on Banking Supervision (BCBS) of the Bank for International Settlement (BIS) first introduced an international capital standard, called Basel I, thereby subjecting internationally active banks to common capital requirements. The major thrust of Basel I was on credit risk. However, the most important amendment to the Basel I capital accord was effected in 1996, with a view to incorporate market risk, to provide an explicit capital cushion for the price risks arising out of investment / trading activities of banks. These amendments were further revised by BCBS in November 2005, and were finally incorporated in the subsequent Basel II framework. In India, the Reserve Bank decided in April 1992 to introduce a risk asset ratio system for banks in India as a capital adequacy measure. Further, RBI issued guidelines to banks in June 2004 on the maintenance of capital charge for market risks on lines of 'Amendment to the capital accord to incorporate market risks' (1996).

However, the Basel I capital accord, while bringing uniformity and prescribing capital adequacy norms, did not adequately differentiate risk. Moreover, with the emergence of several credit risk mitigation techniques, such as : credit derivatives and securitization, banks used to circumvent capital requirements due to the absence of capital treatments in Basel I regarding these techniques.

BASEL - II : REVISED FRAMEWORK OF BASEL - I

Recognizing the limitations of the Basel I accord, which were also manifest during the Asian crisis of 1997-98, BCBS came out with a revised framework in June 2004. In July 2006, a comprehensive version of Basel II, including revisions to the market risk framework, was issued. Besides tweaking the credit and market risk framework, the Committee recognized operational risk also to be a major risk facing banks. Therefore, in addition to allocating capital to credit and market risk, the banks were required to capture the operational risk and allocate capital for the same. Basel II increased the scope, flexibility and risk sensitivity of capital charges by providing a menu of approaches for computation of capital charge for credit, market and operational risk in respect of banks of all sizes, and levels of sophistications. In compliance with the Basel II standards, it was decided that all commercial banks in India shall initially adopt Standardized Approach (SA) for credit risk, and Basic Indicator Approach (BIA) for operational risk, while continuing with the Standardized Duration Approach (SDA) for computing capital requirements for market risks. The foreign banks operating in India, as also Indian banks, having operational presence outside India, migrated to these approaches under Basel II with effect from 31 March, 2008. All other commercial banks moved over to these approaches by 31 March, 2009. The Internal Capital Adequacy Assessment Process (ICAAP) and Supervisory Review and Evaluation Process (SREP) was also put in place as a part of the pillar II process along with disclosure requirements under pillar III. Further, the Reserve Bank came out with a timeline for implementation of advanced approaches for computation of the regulatory capital under the Basel II framework in India in July 2009. The guidelines for the standardized approach (TSA)/Alternate Standardized Approach (ASA) for operational risk were issued in March 2010, and those for internal models approach (IMA) for market risk in April 2010. The amendments to the market risk framework issued by the BCBS in July 2009 were implemented in India by the Reserve Bank with effect from 31 March, 2010. Guidelines for advanced measurement approach (AMA) for operational risk were issued in April 2011, and guidelines for internal rating based (IRB) approach for credit risk are expected to be issued shortly.

CHECKING AND DEFLECTING COMPONENTS OF THE REGULATORY STRUCTURES

The global financial crisis exposed many weaknesses in the Basel II framework and as such, provided important lessons for strengthening banking regulations. First, the definition of regulatory capital overestimated the strength of the bank's Tier I capital's ability to absorb unexpected losses. Second, many risks, particularly those emanating from trading book exposures due to the growing proportion of illiquid investments were not adequately captured. The re-securitization exposures attracted the same capital charges as other securitization exposures, even though their risk profile was significantly higher. Third, the framework failed to limit disproportionate leverages and pro-cyclical effects. The buildup of excessive on and off balance sheet leverages by banks was one of the contributing factors for the severity and vast magnitude of the global financial crisis, which was accompanied by a gradual erosion in the level and quality of the capital base, and insufficient liquidity buffers. The Basel II framework primarily focused on having a capital cushion for credit, market and operational risks, while ignoring risks emanating from excessive leverages and illiquidity, which proved fatal for the global financial system, and necessitated reforms in the form of Basel III.

CITED EMERGENCE OF BASEL- III: REFORM MEASURES

Recognizing the weaknesses of the Basel II framework and drawing lessons from the crisis, the BCBS first revised the capital requirements for market risks and introduced specific requirements for re-securitizations in July 2009. Further, the consultative documents published in December 2009 formed the basis for the final Basel III standards published in December, 2010 as a part of the global initiatives to strengthen the financial regulatory system; endorsed by the Financial Stability Board (FSB) and the G-20 leaders. Primarily, these measures were intended towards tightening the definition of regulatory capital, strengthening the risk coverage of the capital framework, introducing a leverage ratio and liquidity standards, as also creation of capital buffers.

Basel III proposals are a set of reform measures, developed by the BCBS to strengthen the regulation, supervision and risk management of the banking sector. These include a number of fundamental reforms to the international regulatory framework, by introducing certain additional safeguards to the existing Basel II framework. Basel III is intended to strengthen micro prudential regulations, which will help raise the resilience of individual banking institutions in periods of stress. The reforms also have a macro prudential focus, addressing system wide risks that can build up across the banking sector, as well as the pro-cyclical amplification of these risks over time. Obviously, these micro and macro prudential approaches to supervision are interrelated, as greater resilience at the individual bank level reduces the risk of system wide shocks. The focus is on five core areas, viz. definition of capital, risk coverage, leverages, procyclicality and systemic risk and liquidity.

Revised Definition of Capital

The definition of regulatory capital has been revised to ensure that the banks hold more and higher quality of capital. The minimum level of Tier-I capital has been raised from 4 per cent to 6 percent of the risk weighted assets. Out of this, the common equity must be at last 4.5 per cent. The eligibility criteria for Tier-I capital have been tightened, so that only fully loss absorbing instruments may find place in Tier-I capital. Moreover, banks are required to publish a full reconciliation of all regulatory capital elements back to the balance sheet in the audited financial statements, along with a separate disclosure of all regulatory adjustments and the items not deducted from Tier-I common equity, as description of all limits and minima applied, and a description of the main features of capital instruments.

Enhanced Risk Coverage

Enhanced risk coverage is intended to raise capital requirements for the trading book and complex securitization exposures, a major source of losses for many internationally active banks. The enhanced treatment introduces a stressed value-at-risk (VaR) capital requirement, based on a continuous 12-month period of significant financial stress. In addition, the Committee has introduced higher capital requirements for securitizations in both the banking and the trading book. The reforms also raise the standards of the Pillar 2 supervisory review process, and strengthen Pillar 3 disclosures.

Leverage

As excessive leverage was one of the main problem areas during the global financial crisis, a leverage ratio consisting of Tier-I capital in the numerator and gross exposure in the denominator has been introduced, with a view to prevent banks from taking advantage of imperfections in the risk measurement methodologies primarily oriented towards credit, market and operational risks. In addition, additional safeguards are provided by it against model risk and measurement errors by supplementing the risk based measure with a simple, transparent, independent measure of risk.

Capital Buffers

The primary aim of the counter cyclical capital buffers is to use a buffer of capital to achieve the broader macro-prudential goal of protecting the banking sector from the ill-effects of the periods of excess aggregate credit growth, leading to the buildup of system-wide risk. Losses incurred in the banking sector could be extremely large, when a downturn is preceded by a period of excess credit growth. These losses can destabilize the banking sector and lead to a vicious circle, whereby problems in the financial system can contribute to a downturn in the real economy, that could again flow back to the banking system. The countercyclical buffer ensures that the banking sector capital requirements take account of the macro-financial environment, in which banks operate. It would be deployed by national jurisdictions, when excess aggregate credit growth is judged to be associated with a build-up of system-wide risk to ensure that the banking system has a buffer of capital to protect it against future potential losses. Each Basel Committee member would make decisions on the size of the countercyclical capital buffer between zero and 2.5 percent of risk weighted assets, depending on their judgment as to the extent of the buildup of system-wide risks. The buffer for internationally-active banks will be a weighted average of the buffers deployed across all the jurisdictions, to which it has credit exposures and, hence, the minimum capital requirements under Basel – II could go up from 8 percent to 10.05 percent.

Liquidity

BCBS has further strengthened the liquidity framework by developing two minimum standards for managing funding liquidity risk. These standards have been developed to achieve two separate but complementary objectives. The first objective is to promote short-term resilience of a bank's liquidity risk profile, by ensuring that it has sufficient high-quality liquid assets to survive a significant stress scenario lasting for at least a month. The Committee has developed the Liquidity Coverage Ratio (LCR) to achieve this objective. LCR is computed as a ratio of 'the stock of high quality liquid assets' to 'the total net cash outflows over the next 30 calendar days.' It is expected that LCR value should be greater than one. The second objective of promoting resilience over a longer time horizon has been achieved by creating additional incentives for banks to fund their activities with more stable sources of funding on an on-going basis. The Net Stable Funding Ratio (NSFR) has a time horizon of one year, and has been developed to provide a sustainable maturity structure of assets and liabilities. The NSFR is computed as a ratio of 'available amount of stable funding to 'the required amount of stable funding' and is expected to have a value greater than one. The LCR, including any revisions, is expected to be introduced on 1 January, 2015. The NSFR, including any revisions, is expected to move to become a minimum standard by 1 January, 2018.

Banks in India : Cogitating Impact

In the case of India, Basel III has stepped in before banks could have switched to advanced approaches under Basel II and, hence, they have to gear up for moving up the trajectory quite quickly. The Reserve Bank of India has expressed its commitment to internationally agreed phase-in period, beginning 1 January, 2013 for implementation of the reforms package under the Basel lll framework. Guidelines for implementation are under preparation, and steps are being taken to disseminate information on Basel III to help banks in the smooth implementation of the framework in India. In certain areas, such as minimum capital requirements and Tier-I capital, banks in India have already achieved the milestones now proposed under Basel III, as RBI from the very beginning had prescribed a higher level of 9 percent capital and at least 4.5 percent as minimum Tier-I capital. However, the requirement of minimum 4.5 per cent of risk weighted assets as common equity in Tier-I capital could pose problems in expanding the balance sheet, as a majority of Indian banks are in the public sector and, hence, are dependant on the government for capital infusions. On a positive note, the banks in India are not as highly leveraged compared to US counterparts, and exposure to re-securitizations and non-DVP transactions are non-existent. Certain other aspects of the Basel – III, such as phasing out of the innovative perpetual debt as a capital instrument, treatment of perpetual non-cumulative preference shares on a *pari-passu* basis with equity instruments, etc., are also not expected to have a major impact on Indian banks. Further, the calculation of the liquidity ratios and the leverage ratio would require clarity about inclusion and exclusion of specific balance sheet items, and there would also be a need for developing specific tools for generating desired information from the centralized data. On the disclosure front also, banks would have to put more information in the public domain, and would have to be conscious about its likely impact on the market discipline processes. However, in totality, the implementation of Basel III in India should not be a major issue, though the actual position will be known only after the guidelines are issued and implementation begins from 1 January, 2013.

Devised Action Points

(i) As per RBIs estimates, Indian banks will need about Rs 5 lakh crores by the year 2017 to get ready for Basel III norms. So, the Indian Financial System (IFS) has to be geared up, and we need to explore the possibility of generating such a heavy amount.

(ii) Actually BASEL III norms will be effective from 2018, and the norms have been developed in the backdrop of the global crisis (2008). So, ways and means can be explored by Indian banks and the government to generate funds (money) by that time.

(iii) Asset quality of banks needs to be strengthened. One of the possible measures to sanction secured loans may be honestly and minutely examining the projects, 'repayment capacity' and socio-economic profile of the loan seekers.

(iv) With the view to improve the investment climate in India, through which banks can ensure net returns on a long term basis, the number of small loans in the priority sectors may be enhanced and encouraged.

(v) 'Employment led recovery and structural reforms' need to be emphasized. In an agrarian economy like India, the possibility of increasing employment opportunities is largely concentrated in rural areas. So, public sector banks should generously provide assistance to rural enterprises, and entrepreneurs.

(vi) 'Risk Weighted Assets (RWAs)' of every bank need to be more perfectly and honestly measured. Otherwise, raising the minimum level of Tier-I capital from 4 percent to 6 percent will not be much helpful.

(vii) While leveraging, banks must be cautious and attentive to limit the risk of a ***destabilizing deleveraging process*** likely to take place, particularly during economic downturns.

(viii) PSBs should discern and make efforts to down right to enhance the stock of high quality liquid assets, so that even in case of ***larger total net cash outflows*** over the next 30 calender days, bank's short- term resilience risk profile is maintained.

(ix) Banks may chasten its trend and performance in regard to excess aggregate credit growth, and should comb more stable sources of funding on an ongoing basis, so that a 'longer time resilience for banks' is developed. But, it should avoid the raising of interest rates on credit given to weaker sections (viz; marginal and small farmers) of society.

(x) In the light of the R.B.I's commitment to internationally agreed phase- in period (beginning 1 January, 2013) for implementation of the reforms package under the Basel III framework, PSBs in India should start refining their functioning process and be discreet in their working, performance and behavior with customers.

(xi) Clear-cut and clicking guidelines should be prepared to be followed by *complexity free procedures.*

(xii) The shocks (if any) likely to arise before the banking sector from financial and economic stress – ought to overwhelmed/ and counteracted – by preferably adopting *the practice of lending small loans in large numbers* to expand and promote rural and agrarian economies. It will yield good returns for banks with sustainable demand of products from rural enterprises at affordable prices.

(xiii) As the banks in India are not as highly leveraged as their US counterparts, so *lesion of any division of banks* cannot be allowed by incurring expenditures in unproductive activities, assets or products.

(xiv) With a view to make 'the horizon of working and performance of Indian banking sector' resplendent, the practices of pretending in a few cases only by some of the financial institutions (not necessarily banks) – should be *done away with by adopting transparent and honest disclosure norms.*

(xv) The Reconciliation Statement of banks and other financial institutions – should urgently contain a separate disclosure of all regulatory adjustments and the items not deducted from Tier- I common equity.

(xvi) In every way, the matter and debate can be actively considered that *insurance companies, NBFCs and Mutual Funds (MFs) – should also be brought under the purview of CRR.*

(xvii) *Having obtained the erudite feedback/ opinions of all top ranking bankers, the Union Finance Ministry of India, noted 'Bank Economists' and 'Experts of Banking Issues' – decision may be taken to provide 1 or 2 percent exemption in mandatory retention of CRR of 4.75 percent to those banks, who have achieved the minimum required priority sector lending targets during the last two or three years.*

(xviii) In the light of the changing world and domestic socio-economic, *market demand related and financial scenario, the rules and provisions related to 'banking operational aspects' – may be changed/amended/ improved.*

REFERENCES

Chaudhary, Pratip "The Hindu Business Line", September 4, 2012, P-6.

Kumar, M.V.S. and Vageech, N.S. "SBI Group Requires Rs. 1 Lakh Crores To Meet Basel-III Norms", The Hindu Business Line", September 8, 2012, P-8.

Dr. Srivastava, Ashish "Basel-III-Towards More Resilient Banking Systems", "CAB CALLING", April-June, 2011, Vol.- 36, No.- 2, P. Nos.- 18-23.

Mittal, D.K. "Centre Pitches for Cut In CRR", "The Hindu (Kolkata)", June 13, 2012, P.- 10.

http://www.bis.org

International Convergence of Capital Measurement and Capital Standards (Basel I); http://bis.org/publ/bcbsc111.htm

Market Risk Amendment, 1996: http://www.bis.org/publ/bcbs24.htm

Amendment to the capital accord to incorporate market risks, November 2005; http://www.bis.org/ publ/bcbs119.htm

http://rbidocs.rbi.org.in/rdocs/Notification/PDFs/54581.pdf

Basel II: International Convergence of Capital Measurement and Capital Standards: A Revised Framework – Comprehensive Version, June 2006; http://www.bis.org/publ/bcbs128.htm

Enhancements to the Basel II framework, July 2009; http://www.bis.org/publ/bcbs157.htm; http://www.bis.org/publ/bcbs158.htm

Basel III: A global regulatory framework for more resilient banks and banking systems, December 2010; http://www.bis.org/publ/bcbs189.htm Basel III : international framework for liquidity risk measurement, standards and monitoring, December 2010; http://www.bis.org /publ/bcbs188.htm

Basel III : International framework for liquidity risk measurement, standards and monitoring, ibid.

Some Challenges of Corporate Governance on Performance: An Innovative Econometric Analysis for Sustainability of Firms

Pallavi Kapoori, R C Sharma[1], Deepak Kaul[2] and Nivedita Sharma[3]

Graduate School of Business, Indore

[1]Central University of Rajasthan, Ajmer

[2]CORE Business School , Indore

[3]Prestige Institute of Management, Dewas

ABSTRACT

As the emerging economy demands, Indian firms are switching from traditional business models to innovative approaches as a means to climb up the value chain. The focus has shifted to creating and delivering value for sustainability for a challenging competitive edge. Governance, transparency, predictability and accountability are key elements for establishing long-term domestic legitimacy of authorities. Corporate governance describes the processes, customs, policies, laws and institutions that direct organizations and corporations in the way they act, administer and control their operations. Efficient corporate governance provides an assurance that the management is acting in the best interests of the corporation, and contributing to business prosperity to the utmost. An analysis of these practices and the association of their adoption and effects on a firm's performances can form the basis for economic reforms in the context of the changing corporate environment. The present article discusses a few governance challenges being faced by Indian companies, and points out the norms which are instrumental in shaping firms' performance by empirically assessing the relative importance of the various norms, and finding out the best combination for improving a firm's performance. The study suggests that among the various corporate governance norms under the scope of the study, Presence of a Key Executive Director in the Audit Committee, an Optimum Representation of Non-Executive Directors on the Board, Inclusion of Directors' Remuneration in the Annual Report and Inclusion of Compliance Report in the Annual Report have been found to have an impact on performances of selected companies.

Keywords: *Corporate Governance, Audit Committee, Disclosure, Compliance Report, Certification, Non-Executive Directors*

INTRODUCTION

Corporate governance not only extends beyond good corporate performance and financial propriety, but fine corporate governance is an essential standard for sustainability and for establishing a striking investment environment which is needed by competitive companies, to gain a strong position to address , emerging challenges. In India also, corporate governance has been under scrutiny and is an issue that has gained widespread importance. Corporate governance is one of the key elements for improving microeconomic efficiency, and is an essential framework condition affecting the competitiveness of any organization. Better corporate governance, therefore, should manifest itself in enhanced corporate performance that can lead to higher economic growth.

Corporate governance has become a prominent research theme after the publication of the Cadbury Committee Report in the UK in the early 1990s. This is evident from the fact that the number of research papers published in peer-reviewed scholarly journals in the area of corporate governance have gone up from 641 in 1985-96 to 9717 in 1996-2006 (Balgobin, 2008). Annie and Kaczmarek (2012) recently conducted research which points to the importance of a careful selection process of directors by nomination committees. It underlines the role for active leadership on boards. A study by Renders and Gaeremynck (2012) examines the impact of principal-principal agency problems on the quality and effectiveness of corporate governance structures. Using the simultaneous equations model, they found that the conflict index affects the quality and effectiveness of corporate governance. In yet another study undertaken to compare two major sectors of the economy, the findings show that among the various corporate governance norms under the scope of the study, the Disclosure of Directors' Remuneration in the Annual Report has a major influence on the performance of an organization (Kapooria P, Sharma R C and Kaul D 2012). An empirical analysis of Indian companies revealed, that among the various corporate governance norms under the scope of the study, a key executive director in an audit committee has a major role for effective corporate performance. (Kapooria P, Sharma R C and Kaul D 2011). In a review by Khan H (2011), which is a collection of research articles on corporate governance, the significance of effective corporate governance is evident. Lishenga L (2011) found that outside members of boards are significantly more likely to respond to poor performance by dismissing the CEO. He also finds evidence suggesting that outside directors' act in the shareholders' interests in their decisions in the adoption of the poison pill provision.

Claessens et al (2012) have reviewed recent research on corporate governance, with special focus on emerging markets, and found that better corporate frameworks benefit firms through greater access to financing, lower costs of capital, better performance, and more favourable treatment of all stakeholders. As quoted by Claessens et al, numerous studies show these channels to operate at the level of firms, sectors and countries - with causality increasingly often clearly identified. He also quotes evidence which shows that voluntary and market corporate governance mechanisms have less effect when a country's governance system is weak. Importantly, how corporate governance regimes change over time, a and how this impacts firms are receiving more attention recently. As per Claessens et al, less evidence is available on the direct links between corporate governance and social and environmental performance. Claessens et al (2012) concludes by identifying issues requiring further study, including special corporate governance issues of banks, and family-owned and state-owned firms, and the nature and determinants of public and private enforcement.

Chatterjee S (2008) tried to understand the impact of corporate governance on an emerging economy like India. The article attempts to conceptually understand the meaning of corporate governance and examines how Indian companies have responded to the issue after the advent of the Sarbanes Oxley Act 2002 in the US, as well as in the aftermath of a slew of recommendations from committees initiated by the SEBI in India. Second, the article aims to analyse whether best practices of corporate governance in Indian companies are legislation driven, or go beyond the minimum threshold. The study developed a construct that compliance with corporate governance in letter and spirit alone can help profitable companies become good corporate citizens. Nayak et al (2008) examine the historically embedded and emerging characteristics of corporate governance in India, and demonstrate the complex linkages between institutions that play a role in shaping the culture and mindsets of Indian management. Theoretically, they argue that corporate governance is a mediating symbolic form that embeds institutional and social practices, as well as individual dispositions. Their aim was to demonstrate how issues of governance and institutions are better addressed at the practical and dispositional level rather than the national, industry or firm levels. Empirically, they draw on data on the lives, careers and networks of the board of directors of the top 100 companies in India, to demonstrate how national contexts are constituted by pre-existing social structures, norms and practices.

OBJECTIVE

An analysis of the adoption of best practices recommended by a governing apex body on the performance of Indian corporates can form the basis for economic reforms in the context of the changing corporate environment. Studying the impact of these best practices on companies across diverse sectors of the Indian economy would enable us to analyze the efficacy of the said practices. This study aims at exploring the impact of adoption of recommendations of Clause 49 of the Listing Agreement by SEBI pertaining to corporate governance, by select Indian corporates. The present study has taken into account certain practices and investigated their impact on firm performances.

HYPOTHESES

H_{11}:

An optimum representation of the non-executive directors on the board will lead to better performance of the firms **(NED)**

H_{12}:

Firms having established an audit committee should reflect higher performance than those who do not have such committees **(ACOM)**

H_{13}:

Representation of a key executive director in an audit committee will be associated with lower corporate performance **(KED)**

H_{14}:

Firms having established a remuneration committee should reflect higher performance than those who do not have such committees **(RCOM)**

H_{15}:

Disclosure of director remuneration in the annual reports has a positive impact on the performance **(DREM)**

H_{16}:

Certification of annual reports by CEO/ CFO has a positive impact on the performance **(CERT)**

H_{17}:

Inclusion of corporate governance compliance report in the annual report will be associated with higher corporate performance **(COMP)**

METHODOLOGY

Sample Selection

For the purpose of the present study, fifty companies, listed on the NSE, were selected, from across various sectors, on a random basis. These companies are necessarily those companies who have a paid up share capital of Rs 3 crores and above, or net worth of Rs 25 crores or more at any time in the history of the entity. A Panel study was aimed by analyzing 100 observations by obtaining the data of the fifty companies (50) selected over a period of two financial years (2 FY). An in-depth analysis of the annual reports of the selected companies was undertaken, wherein the financial data was obtained as well the statistics of the corporate governance norms practiced or otherwise was observed, in the stated duration by the selected companies.

Independent Variables

The independent variables (X) were captured from the Clause 49 Listing Agreement of SEBI pertaining to corporate governance. The scope was focused on a few norms namely representation of non-executive director on the board, composition of audit committee, presence and formulation of remuneration committee, disclosure of directors remuneration in annual report, CEO/ CFO certification of annual report, inclusion of corporate governance report in annual report and corporate governance compliance certificate. Since these variables are not quantifiable i.e., only their absence or presence can be observed, hence we have applied the *Dummy Variable Approach*. For the purpose of the study, the presence of each these variables is denoted by 1 and their absence by.

Dependent Variable

As the objective of the study is to establish a linkage between the selected corporate governance attributes and corporate performance, two financial ratios, namely P/E Ratio and Asset Turnover Ratio of these selected companies over a period of two financial years, as a measure of performance were observed. The average value of these ratios was used as the dependent variable (Y). On the basis of the selected corporate governance norms, efforts were made to examine the impact of these factors on the performance of the selected firms. For this, the dummy variable regression model has been used and an empirical study attempted. The study aims at analyzing the importance of the various corporate governance norms observed through multi- variant analysis, and ranking of a combination various norms and assessing the best combination derived by observing the mean performance.

MODELLING

A general panel model was written as:

$$Y_{it}=\alpha_1+\alpha_2 D_{2it}+\alpha_3 D_{3it}+\alpha_4 D_{4it}+\alpha_5 D_{5it}+\alpha_6 D_{6it}+\alpha_7 D_{7it}+\alpha_8 D_{8it}+U_{it} \quad \text{Eq (1)}$$

Where,
Y_{it} = Performance of ith firm in the ith year (PERF)
i = no of firms 1 to 50
t = no of year 1 and 2
α_1 = Intercept
α_2 to α_8 = Coefficients of dummy variables
D_{2it} to D_{8it} = Dummy variables
U_{it} = Stochastic error

Table 1: Variable Descriptive

Dummy variables are defined as follows:		
D_{2it}	1	if there is an optimum representation of non-executive directors & = 0,if otherwise (NED)
D_{3it}	1	if audit committee is present & = 0,if otherwise (ACOM)
D_{4it}	1	if there is a key executive director in audit committee & = 0,if otherwise (KED)
D_{5it}	1	if remuneration committee is present & = 0,if otherwise (RCOM)
D_{6it}	1	if directors' remuneration is included in annual report & = 0,if otherwise (DREM)
D_{7it}	1	if annual reports are certified by CEO/ CFO & = 0,if otherwise (CERT)
D_{8it}	1	if compliance report is included in the annual reports & = 0,if otherwise (COMP)

For an estimation of Equation No.1 that included all the seven dummy variables together, there were **128** combinations of mean performances, the equations for which can be written as

Equation for the mean performance with the presence of all the dummy variables:

$$E(Y_{it} \mid D_{2it}=1, D_{3it}=1, D_{4it}=1, D_{5it}=1, D_{6it}=1, D_{7it}=1, D8_{it}=1)$$
$$= \alpha_1 + \alpha_2 + \alpha_3 + \alpha_4 + \alpha_5 + \alpha_6 + \alpha_7 + \alpha_8$$

Equation for the mean performance with the absence of all the dummy variables:

$$E(Y_{it} \mid D_{2it}=0, D_{3it}=0, D_{4it}=0, D_{5it}=0, D_{6it}=0, D_{7it}=0, D8_{it}=0)$$
$$= \alpha_1$$

Similarly, equations for various combinations with presence and absence of dummy variables can be written.

EMPIRICAL ANALYSIS

Multi-variant analysis was attempted to assess the comparative importance of corporate governance norms. Substituting the values in the model, we get the following equation:

Table 2: The Equation

Y_{it} =	67.5 31	+11.085 D_{2it}	- 41.633D $_{3it}$	+44.62 $D4_{it}$	- 5.488D $_{5it}$	+5.271 D_{6it}	- 13.738D $_{7it}$	+13.769 D_{8it}
SE		-17.311	-29.147	-14.233	-10	-8.844	-9.028	-10.176
T		-0.64	-1.428	-3.135	-0.548	-0.596	-1.521	-1.353
Sig		-0.523	-0.156	-0.002	-0.584	-0.552	-0.131	-0.179

The result shows that the value of α_4 is significant at 5 precent level of significance. This means that only D_{4it} ie.KED (representation of a key executive director in the audit committee) has a major impact on the performance of the companies, and is a key determinant in affecting the performance of an organization. However, the managerial significance with positive/ negative signs and magnitudes of α's are also important with reference to the ranking of the performances. The statistical significance will however limit the combinations of the rankings up to certain groups.

The ranking technique was adopted to assess the best combination of corporate governance norms for best performance. To know the impact of various corporate governance norms, regression with an additive nature of dummy variables was applied. On the basis of itis model, various combinations of different corporate governance norms were framed, and certain conclusions drawn regarding the mean performance of companies adopting different combinations. The more the mean performance, the more effective the combination may be rated. Accordingly, a complete set of mean performances of seven corporate governance norms was estimated and the total number of 128 combinations were computed.

RESULTS AND DISCUSSIONS

Table 3: Mean Value and Ranks

The top ten mean values were selected and various combinations were ranked accordingly.

α_1	α2	α3	α4	α5	α5	α6	α7	MEAN	RANK
67.531	11.085	-41.633	44.626	-5.488	5.271	-13.738	13.769		
	D_{2it}	D_{3it}	D_{4it}	D_{5it}	D_{6it}	D_{7it}	D_{8it}	142.282	I
67.531	1	0	1	0	0	0	1	137.011	II
67.531	1	0	1	1	1	0	1	136.794	III
67.531	1	0	1	1	0	0	1	131.523	IV

67.531	0	0	1	0	1	0	1	131.197	V
67.531	1	0	1	0	1	1	1	128.544	VI
67.531	1	0	1	0	1	0	0	128.513	VII
67.531	0	0	1	0	0	0	1	125.926	VIII
67.531	0	0	1	1	1	0	1	125.709	IX
67.531	1	0	1	0	0	1	1	123.273	X

Equation for best mean performance with Rank I can be written as :

$$E\,(Y_{it} \mid D_{2it} = 1, D_{3it} = 0, D_{4it} = 1, D_{5it} = 0, D_{6it} = 1, D_{7it} = 0, D8_{it} = 1)$$
$$= 142.282$$

This clearly shows that the combination with the presence of a key executive director in audit committee, inclusion of directors' remuneration in annual report, inclusion of compliance report in the annual reports and an optimum representation of non-executive directors on board empirically suggests the best mean performance. This also suggests that the norms such as presence of an audit committee and remuneration committee and certification of annual reports by CEO/ CFO do not necessarily affect the performance of the firms. Likewise, equations for all the combinations can be written and conclusions can be derived accordingly.

Equation for the mean performance with the presence of all the norms:

$$E\,(Y_{it} \mid D_{2it} = 1, D_{3it} = 1, D_{4it} = 1, D_{5it} = 1, D_{6it} = 1, D_{7it} = 1, D8_{it} = 1)$$
$$= 81.423$$

Equation for the mean performance with the absence of all the norms:

$$E\,(Y_{it} \mid D_{2it} = 0, D_{3it} = 0, D_{4it} = 0, D_{5it} = 0, D_{6it} = 0, D_{7it} = 0, D8_{it} = 0)$$
$$= 67.531$$

CONCLUSION AND POLICY IMPLICATIONS

On the basis of the study, it may be concluded that the factors which have a vital impact on the performance of organizations are optimum representation of non-executive directors on board, presence of a key executive director in audit committee, inclusion of directors' remuneration in annual report and inclusion of compliance report in annual report. It may be suggested that these factors affect the performance of an organization to a great extent. The presence of these norms is of vital importance in shaping an organizations' productivity. Moreover, out of these norms, only the value of D_{4it} (i.e. KED presence of a key executive director in audit committee) has been found statistically significant. It shows that only this norm has statistical as well as managerial significance while others having an impact, have managerial significance in enhancing an organization's competitiveness leading to an elevated performance. Further analysis of the top ten best combinations, we derived that the norms whose presence doesn't affect the performance may be ignored while framing a set of desired combinations for best performance. The norms which have least significance are presence of an audit committee, presence of a remuneration committee and certification of annual reports by CEO/ CFO. Hence, based on our findings, certain policy implications may be suggested which may enhance the functioning of an organization leading to elevated performance. A key executive director has a strong hold on the functioning of any organization, and will be in a better position to initiate financial decisions in the interests of an organization. A right mix of executives and non-executive directors on board will add value to corporate functioning. Transparency with all the stakeholders pertaining to the benefits received by the directors of the company will instill great confidence in the minds of stakeholders leading to trust and enhanced image and competitiveness of an organization. A compliance report is extremely vital to infuse assurance in all the stakeholders and public at large. Thus, an organization should take utmost care to adhere to the norms so as to function effectively, and enhance performance by winning over the competitive edge and sustain the challenges with an innovative approach.

REFERENCE

Annie P and Kaczmarek S (2012), "Board Task-related Fault lines and Firm Performance: A Decade of Evidence" , Corporate Governance : An International Review, 20(4), pp.337-351.

Balgobin (2008), "Global Governance Practice: The Impact of Measures Taken to Restore Trust in Corporate Governance Practice Internationally" , Journal on Corporate Governance, 7(1), pp.7-8.

Cadbury A (1992), the Financial Aspects of Corporate Governance - A Report of the Committee on Corporate Governance, Gee and Co., London.

Chatterjee S (2008), "An Analysis of the Impact of Corporate Governance in India" , Special Conference on "Emerging India : Strategic Innovations in Flat World", hosted by ISB, Hyderabad.

Claessens, Stijn and Yurtoglu, B Burcin, "Corporate Governance in Emerging Markets: A Survey" (2012), Available at SSRN: http://ssrn.com/abstract=1988880 or http://dx.doi.org/10.2139/ssrn.1988880

Kapooria Pallavi, Sharma R C and Kaul Deepak (2012), "Impact of Corporate Governance on Firm Performance: A Comparative Analysis of IT and Finance Sector" Ch. 7, pp.53-57 in Ed. Rajendra Jain, Sanjay Dubey and Amitabh Joshi, "Developing Strategies for

Organizations in Global Economies: Prospects, Issues & Challenge" Excel Books, New Delhi. (ISBN No. 978-93-5062-002-1)

Kapooria Pallavi, Sharma R C and Kaul Deepak (2012), "Corporate Governance and Firm Performance : An Empirical Analysis of Finance & Pharmaceutical Sectors" , Management Research Journal "Prabandhan & Taqniki" , Vol.6 , pp. – 19 22. (ISSN No. 0974-8563)

Kapooria P, Sharma R C and Kaul D (2011), "Corporate Governance and Firm Performance : An Empirical Analysis with Dummy Variables " ,Management Research Journal "Prabandhan & Taqniki" ,Vol 5, pp.27- 31. (ISSN No: 0974-8563).

Khan H (2011)," A Literature Review of Corporate Governance", International Conference on E-business, Management and Economics IPEDR , 25, IACSIT Press, Singapore.

Lishenga L (2011), "Corporate Governance reaction to declining firm performance: Evidence from NSE", IJG, 1(1).

Nayak et al (2008), "Corporate Governance in India: A Practice Approach", Special Conference on "Emerging India : Strategic Innovations in Flat World", hosted by ISB, Hyderabad.

OECD (2004), Principles of Corporate Governance,www.oecd.org www.oecd. org/dataoecd /32/18/31557724.pdf.

Renders A and Gaeremynck A (2012), "Corporate Governance, Principal-Principal Agency , and Firm Value in European Listed Companies", Corporate Governance : An International Review, 20(2), pp.125-143.

http://www.sebi.gov.in

Corporate Governance and Information Asymmetry: Evidence from Iran

Shiva Hassan Pour
Islamic Azad University, Iran

ABSTRACT

Financial reports are important resources for economic decisions, but the information disclosure process causes information asymmetry for stockholders. Corporate governance improves the information disclosure process. The interest in this article is the relationship between corporate governance mechanisms and information asymmetry of companies listed on the Tehran Stock Exchange (TSE) between January 2008 to December 2011. We have used changes in market liquidity (price difference between stock selling and buying) at the time near to earnings declaration as representative of information asymmetry, and the non executive managers' board, the percentage ownership of institutional investors and internal auditing as representative of corporate governance mechanisms. Results show that the internal audit department and the non executive managers' board have a significant negative relationship with measures of information asymmetry. On the other hand, information asymmetry after earnings declaration is more, than before declaration.

Keywords: *Corporate Governance, Information Asymmetry, Market Liquidity*

INTRODUCTION

The agency theory and problems related to ownership separation cause opportunistic behaviour of (agent) managers for justifying their increasing wealth at the owners' expense (employer). Too much confidence in the numbers of the accounting department, create great motive for the managers to arrange profits in a way to optimize to them. The manager's motive may be a result of anxiety about job security. With regard to the information disclosure process, investors (the dealers) are facing an information asymmetry problem. This problem will appear at the time when one of the dealers have more information than others.[17]

Similar to earlier research works, cashable criteria (the stocks transaction price difference) has been used as an information asymmetry agent. The role of an information disclosure caretaker in corporate governance which encompasses control and procedures for confidence in corporate managements, lack of movement for personal benefits, and moving towards the path of maximizing stockholders benefits and corporate value.

EXPRESSING THE PROBLEM

The qualification of financial performance is a permanent matter between legislators and company accountants. Most of the scandals involve those companies which have violated accepted principles of accounting. The United States accounting bureau in a report said that 93 percent of 919 renewed financial cases during the years 1997 up to 2002 were because of income recognition before the appointed time.[9] The corporate governance mechanisms should show disclosed information by a company to its stockholders, and decrease the probability of not disclosing complete and sufficient information, and also decrease the uncovering of less valid information.[5] Studies show that very effective supervision of management by boards, the quality and the efficiency of disclosed information will increase.[9] Improvement in information disclosure by the company causes decrease of information asymmetry, and this decrease in information asymmetry will be accompanied with a less earning management.[15] In this article, different cases in the information field have been emphasized, and the effect of corporate governance quality on the information field in time of earning declarations is surveyed.

In the capital markets, the only way for investors to access information are declarations and notifications which are published by companies (like declaration of predicted earning of each portion). In this article, the value of the suggested price difference of stock transactions (around the earning declaration) is used as agents of information asymmetry[5] and institutional investors, and the existence of an internal audit department and the proportion of non executive managers to the managers on the board are used as components of corporate governance.[4]

INFORMATION ASYMMETRY AND CORPORATE GOVERNANCE

The managers' tendency for earnings management, and as a result, declaring incorrect information to stockholders, will cause damage to stockholders confidence, and thousands of stockholders will lose their property and may also run away from the exchange markets. This will ultimately have critical economic outcomes. Therefore, keeping the stockholders confidence protects the country's economic health. Corporate governance must provide methods by which financial suppliers will be assured that they earn suitable outcomes from their investments in corporations. Corporate governance with external organizational mechanisms, that mostly include rules and orders, and internal organizational mechanisms that mostly are voluntary, can lead to transparency, decrease the dilemmas of information asymmetry, increase stockholders confidence, and finally decrease earnings management. Financial statements provide information which cause a decrease in information asymmetry in the markets, and indicates that investors should completely apply this information to their investment decision making. [2] The market reaction to the earnings declaration can be the first pointer towards the existence of secret information. The existence of secret information, shows an information asymmetry in the market field. Cai, Lui and Qian in their research have (2008) shown that market liquidity increases with decreasing information asymmetry.[4] Cash ability, means of changing the properties to cashable money without any losses and expenses. The suggestion transaction price difference of proportional stock are including the cashable criteria, as the agent of information asymmetry.[7] The difference of highest buying suggestion price and the lowest selling suggestion price, is called the transaction suggestion price difference. The transaction occurs when the highest buying suggestion price is equal to the lowest selling suggestion price.

Corporate governance has a variety of mechanisms to reward corporate managers who are making decisions to maximize the value of the corporation for the owners.[7] It seems that the role of internal audit is one of the most important key factors of corporate governance mechanisms and will increase day by day. According to the internal audit charter, authorized by the corporate managers board of Tehran Security and Exchange Committee (SEC), May 2008, the internal audit organization is doing its duty under the supervision of the managers board.[8] From the agency theory point of view, the presence of non executive managers (non administrative), independent in corporate managers board and their supervision performance as independent individuals, will be a great help in decreasing the existing benefit contrasted between the stockholders and corporate managers. Some portion of corporations' ownership is in the authority of low rank stockholders. This group is totally satisfied with the public information (public financial statements). Another part of ownership is in the authority of the fundamental stockholders, who get internal valuable information about future outlooks and commercial strategies, due to their direct relationship with the corporation.[4] On the basis of draft regulations of corporation origins guide, the fundamental stockholder is the one who can independently appoint at least one member on the managers board.[6]

Research studies show that better corporate governance mechanisms increases the quality and quantity of the disclosed information. In accordance with market sub structural research, market cashability, will increase in case of decreasing information asymmetry. On the basis of these findings, increasing the information asymmetry around the season earning notifications, is less for those corporations which have more powerful corporate governance. Cai et al (2008) showed that corporations with strong corporation governance have less information asymmetry around the earnings declaration.[4]

Reviewing the Research Literature

Lee and partners (1993) found that the market depth and suggesting price difference of stock transaction around the earnings declaration will decrease.[16] Meanwhile Lee and Krinsky (1996) expressed that asymmetry information in the primary capital market increases.[10] Walker (1995) showed there is a reverse relationship between disclosure quality and the rate of suggesting stock transactions price difference. As a result, it is expected that increasing the level of information disclosure along with a suitable strategic principle of the corporation, will decrease the suggesting price difference (information asymmetry agent).[18] Marrakchi (2001) expressed that validity and earning acceptability increases with managers board quality. This finding suggests that corporate governance quality should be less related to asymmetry information around the reported earnings.[12] Cai at el (2008) studied the information asymmetry effect on three fundamental mechanisms of corporate governance (supervision intensity of management board, market discipline and payment sensitivity for master management performance). They found that corporations with information asymmetry are more likely to be those with least management board supervision, more market discipline and having higher management performance.[4] They show that the average of suggesting price difference of stock exchange effectively around the earnings declaration is less for those corporations which are more dependent and have an active management board. The average of market depth decrease is effectively less for those corporations which have more collateral stock proportion with corporation managers and chiefs.[4] Ben Ali (2009) showed that American fundamental investors in France decrease the agency expenses, and request for useful and better disclosures and as a result, are able to decrease the information asymmetry.[9]

In Iran, Vatanparast (2005), while calculating the suggesting price difference found that the information asymmetry before earning declaration is more than after.[16] Maryam Esmaeli (2006) found that the percent of non executive and percent of manager board members has caused an increase in the earning quality and therefore promotes disclosure.[13] Rasanian (2006) while surveying the relationship between risk criteria and the suggesting price difference of a transaction, found that risk criteria (some financial proportions) will measure 68 percent of suggesting price difference of a stock exchange.[2] Azad (2008) showed, following the increase of information asymmetry between investors, demand to apply conservatism in financial reporting will increase, and thus the conservatism beneficiary is one of the qualitative specifications of financial statements that will be qualified.[1]

Research Assumptions

1. There is a negative relationship between internal audit in a corporation and stock exchange price difference.

2. There is a negative relationship between fundamental investors' ownership proportion and stock exchange suggesting price difference.
3. There is a negative relationship between the percent of members of the non executive management board and stock exchange suggesting price difference.

RESEARCH METHOD

This is an applied research study where descriptive statistics and correlations have been used. Non-parametric tests have been done for determining the relationship between variables.

Control Variables

1. *The corporation size:* as a natural logarithm of the corporate earnings is calculated at the end of the second or third month of the year under investigation.
2. *The stock price:* is calculated as the price average of daily transactions.
3. *The stock volume:* natural logarithm (ln) of the transaction volume in the earnings day declaration.

Independent variables

1. The percent of corporation stock that is kept by fundamental investment institutes to the total published stocks and stockholders
2. Percent of non executive members of the managers board to the total members of managers board
3. The internal audit department: in case of the existence of internal audit department (+1) and case of non existence of internal audit department (0) will be put

Dependent variables

The difference of the suggestion transaction price using the best buying suggestion price (BP) and the best selling suggestion price (AP), average price difference of transaction will be gained. Whenever the difference reaches zero, information asymmetry is less.

%SPREAD=(AP-BP)/((AP+BP)/2)

STATISTICAL COMMUNITY, SAMPLE AND DATA COLLECTION

The statistical community of current research is formed from the accepted corporations in Tehran SEC that are within the following conditions:

1. Should not be a part of mediator industries, investments, and insurance corporations.
2. Should be accepted in Tehran SEC before the year 2008.

3. To increase comparison capability, their financial period should be lasting till the end of March 19.
4. Should not have any losing condition during the years of 2008 up to 2011.
5. Should not have any activity change or financial period change during the years 2008 up to 2011.
6. The predicted earnings of each corporate portion, ending and third quarter should be declared.

The group of corporations belonging to SEC are selected first in the surveying years, and have tried to publish the predicted earnings of each portion at the end of the third quarter, and second the related information to the suggesting price difference of stock transactions is present. Current research data has been formed from 240 yearly observations relating to four years (2008 up to 2011) including information and data of 124 corporations. Each of the observations is as the "corporation year" and from the 240 observations, about 57 observations relate to the year 2008, 78 observations to the year of 2009, 63 observations to the year of 2010 and 42 observations are related to the year of 2011. The related data with best suggesting buying price, best suggesting selling price, earnings declarations have been extracted from Tehran SEC, and the data related to non executive managers from the decision summary reports of the normal social assembly published by Tehran SEC, and also yearly activity reports of the managers board to the assembly. Even though corporation do not publish the information of the internal audit department, they were gathered using the corporations information bank (existing in an internet base of Tehran SEC) and directly collected from sample corporations (personal visits and telephone calls).

ANALYSIS OF DATA

The fit condition for a regression model is the normal distribution of variables. Therefore, before doing any task, the assumption of being normal should be tested. The survey results on the base of Kolmogorov- Smirnov, is explained in Table (1). With regard to non justifiable fundamental indexes of the parametric test, and non parametric test has been used. So for studying the relationships, Pearson and Yooman Vitni correlation test for the internal audit and Spearman correlation and Kandalles tau_b were used for the non executive manager portion, managers board and percent of fundamental investors ownership. The calculation of each one of these research variables, except the internal audit has been performed on the basis of their related formulas, and has become the variables amounts. In order to describe these variables, the central tendency and dispersion indexes have been used. In order to do the descriptive and perceptive analysis, the statistical software package SPSS and Excel were used.

Table 1: The Result of Normal Test Related to Variables Distribution with Proportional Scale (One-sample Kolmogorov- Smirnov test)

		Mail Investors	Percent of non executive managers	The suggestion price difference before declaration	The suggestion price difference after declaration
N		240	240	240	240
Normal Parameters	Mean	65.299	0.628	5.757	7.654
	Std. Deviation	22.466	0.195	19.841	15.996
Most Extreme	Absolute	0.140	0.229	0.208	0.185
Differences	Positive	0. 0959	0.178	0.197	0.185
	Negative	-0.140	-0.299	-0.208	-0.177
Kolmogorov- Smirnov Z		2.153	3.596	3.107	2.806
Asymp. Sig. (2-Taild)		0.000	0.000	0.000	0.000

a: test distribution is normal
b: calculated from data

Research Result

Table 2: The Result of First Assumption Test(Chi-square tests)

	value	df	Asymp. Sig. (2-Taild)	Exact sig. (1sided)	Exact sig. (1sided)
Pearson chi-square	0.315^{b}	1	0.566		
Continuity correction	0.170	1	0.680		
Likelihood ratio	0.315	1	0.566		
Fishers exact test				0.653	0.345
Linear-by-linear					
Association	0.313	1	0.567		
N of valid cases	240				

a: computed only for a 2×2 table
b: 0 cells (0%) have expected count less than 5. The minimum expected count is 29.87

With regard to the matter that the calculated statistic of Pearson chi-square is less than the critical amount, and on the other hand, the significant level is larger than 0.05 , as a result, the test sample function is not related in the capital part. Therefore, this assumption of zero has not failed, and it cannot be accepted that there is a significant relationship between the existence of internal audit in the corporation, and the suggesting price difference. This result also with Fishers exact test is not significant.

Table 3: The Second Assumption Test Results (Correlations)

			Fundamental investors	The suggestion price difference
Kandalles tau_b	Fundamental investors	Correlation coefficient	1.000	-0.074
		Sig. (1-tailed)		0.039
		N	240	240
	The suggestion price difference	Correlation coefficient	-0.074	1.000
		Sig. (1-tailed)	0.039	
		N	240	240
Spearman rho	Fundamental investors	Correlation coefficient	1.000	-0.120
		Sig. (1-tailed)		0.037
		N	240	240
	The suggestion price difference	Correlation coefficient	-0.120	1.000
		Sig. (1-tailed)	0.037	
		N	240	240

*correlation is significant at the 0.05 level (1-tailed)

Table 4: The Result of Third assumption Test (Correlations)

			Percent of non executive managers	The suggestion price difference
Kandalles tau_b	Percent of non executive managers	Correlation coefficient	1.000	0.004
		Sig. (1-tailed)		0.456
		n	240	240
	The suggestion price difference	Correlation coefficient	0.004	1.000
		Sig. (1-tailed)	0.456	
		n	240	240
Spearman rho	Percent of non executive managers	Correlation coefficient	1.000	0.003
		Sig. (1-tailed)		0.497
		n	240	240
	The suggestion price difference	Correlation coefficient	0.003	1.000
		Sig. (1-tailed)	0.497	
		n	240	240

*correlation is significant at the 0.05 level (1-tailed)

About the second assumption, the level of calculated error is less than 0.05 and the gained index is also negative, therefore the zero assumption at the level of 95 percent confidence failed and research assumptions have been qualified. As a result, between the fundamental investors and suggesting price difference there is orderly a negative relationship.

About the third assumption, the level of the calculated error is more than 0.05, therefore this zero assumption has not failed and has qualified as the research assumption. As a result, there is no significant relationship between the portion of non executive managers and suggesting price difference and the research assumption has failed.

CONCLUSION

The results of the research do not support the significant relationship between the existence of internal audit and the suggesting price difference variables. But, the results support the significant relationship between two variables of fundamental investors' ownership percent and the suggesting price difference reversely. This result is equal with the findings of Ben Ali (2009). Also, the results have not supported the existence of any significant relationship between the portion of non executive managers of the management board, and the suggesting price difference variables. The average of the suggesting price difference row in the period of ten days after earnings declaration is more than the average of ten days before earnings declaration, similar to the findings of Lee et all (1993). The results express this reality that governance mechanisms in this research, because of non appropriate application in Iran, does not have the necessary utility to decrease the information asymmetry, and it should survey other mechanisms of corporate governance with regard to the market environment and company's specifications to decrease information asymmetry.

THE LIMITATIONS OF RESEARCH

1. In the research process, other factors like changes of government rules, managers' substitution, or internal controlling systems weakness may have some effects on the declared earning have not been controlled.
2. In this research, those managers that did not have an executive position in the company were expressed as non executive managers, and it is assumed that they are independent from the companies, but this may not be the case.

REFERENCES

Abdullah Azad , Rezazadeh Javad. 'The Relationship Between Information Asymmetry and Conservatism in Financial Reporting". Audit and Accounting Survey Journal 2008

Ahmadpoor Ahmad, Rezarian Amir. "The Relationship Between Risk Criteria and Stock Transactions Suggesting Price Difference in Tehran SEC". Audit and Accounting Survey Journal 2007

Ben Ali Chira. "Disclosure Quality and Corporate Governance in a Coxxxntext of Minority Expropriation". 2009, Available at Ssrn:Http://Ssrn.Com/Abstract

Cai Jie. Lui Yixin, Qian Yiming. "Information Asymmetry and Corporate Governance". 2008. Available at: Http://Ssrn.Com

Carcello Joseph V., Hollingsworth Carl W., Klein April. "Audit Committee Financial Expertise, Competing Corporate, Governance Mechanism, and Earning Management". 2006

Corporate Strategic Procedural Principles in Accepted Corporations in Tehran SEC (Draft), Suggested by Supervision Assistance on Stock Exchange and Publishers, Research Management Information Base, Progress and Islamic Studies of Tehran SEC 2006

Denis Diane K., Mcconnell John J. "International Corporate Governance". ECGI-Finance Working Paper 2003

Internal Audit Charter, Tehran SEC. May 2008

Karamanou Irene, Vafeas Nikos. "The Association Between Corporate Boards, Audit Committees, and Management Earning Forcasts". Journal of Accounting Research 2005

Krinsky I., Lee J. "Earning Announcements and Components of the Bidask Spread". Journal of Finanace 1996

Lee C.M., Macklow B. "Spreads, Depths and the Impact of Earning Information: an Intraday Analysis". Review of Finanacial Studies 1993

Marrakchi Chtourou, Sonda Bedard, Jean And Courteau. "Corporation Governance and Earning Management". 2001, Available at Ssrn:Http://Ssrn.Com/Abstract

Mashayekh Shahnaz, Esmaily Maryam. "Survey of the Relationship Between Earning Quality and Some Strategic Principles in Accepted Corporations in Tehran SEC". Audit and Accounting Survey Journal 2008

Moradzadehfard Mehdi, Nazemi Mehdi, Gholami Reza, Farzani Hojatolla. "Survey of The Relationship Between Stock Fundamental Possession and Earning Management in Accepted Corporations in Tehran SEC".Audit and Accounting Survey Journal 2009

Noravesh Iraj, Hosseini Seyed Ali. "Survey of the Relationship Between Disclosure Quality (Reliability and Being on Time) and Earning Management". Audit and Accounting Survey Journal 2009

Qaemi Mohammad Hossein, Vatanparast Mohammadreza. "Survey of Accounting Information Role in Decreasing the Information Asymmetry in Tehran SEC". Audit and Accounting Survey Journal 2006

Scott W.R.T. "Financial Accounting Theory", Second Edition(Canada: Prentice-Hall), 2003

Walker M. "Dosclosure Policy, Information Asymmetry and Liquidity in Equity Markets". Contemprory Accounting Research 1995

Global Corporate Governance – Evolving Guidelines for Multinational Enterprises

Roopinder Oberoi
Kirori Mal College, Delhi

ABSTRACT

The twenty first century global enterprises vary substantially from their predecessors. Any attempt to understand global corporate governance needs to be contextualized with the changing nature and patterns of business. The notion of authority over responsibility of enterprises was traditionally defined in terms of nations, or domicile, and worked as the key operating principles for establishing accountability. This characterisation has changed due to the sweep of globalisation and liberalization. As enterprises expand their operations into virtually all parts of the world, the need is to evolve a coherent approach to corporate governance.

The global corporate governance aims at developing an extensive paradigm which will meet the key goals of transparency, independent oversight and accountability. Amongst all these developments weaving together, the 'best interest of the corporation' and the 'best interest of all stakeholders' provide conflicting answers. At present, calibrating that commitment to achieve maximum value seems like a daunting task. The fundamental question is - what is the prospect of the global convergence of standards of corporate governance and their effective implementation, especially for multinational enterprises which have high stakes in global markets. Currently despite many international initiatives and corporate codes, the enforcement mechanisms are insufficient and weak for ensuring compliance. The article looks at some international initiatives by global agencies to redefine the codes of governance to smoothly facilitate global economic integration.

Keywords: *Globalisation, Corporate, Governance, Multinational Companies, Convergences, Divergence*

TOWARDS GLOBAL GOVERNANCE

In the 21st century, it seems that all clashes between political ideologies of communism and capitalism, cultures, economic systems and religions have been overshadowed by the triumph of one overarching belief in the system of global capitalism. The 'end of ideology' debate following the collapse of the communist bloc, has led to 'near consensus' about the merits of a liberal setup with market mechanisms as a tool to establish economic stability. Contemporary globalisation is distinguished by an unique spatio-temporal and organisational features, creating a world in which the extensive reach of global relations and networks is matched by their high intensity, high velocity and high impact propensity across many facets of social life, from the economic to the environmental. In fact, it is now said, business can go where diplomats cannot. David Held accepts the amorphous nature of the term 'globalisation' which has become the cliché of our times: a 'big idea which encompasses everything from a global financial market to the Internet, but which delivers little substantive insight into the contemporary human condition' (Held 1999,: 1). Globalization implies both deep integration and interconnectedness; networks of relationships between a large number of heterogeneous organizations. 'The spatial reach and density of global and transnational interconnectedness weave complex webs and networks of relations between communities, states, international institutions, non-governmental organizations, and multinational corporations which make up the global order' (Held, et al. 1999, :27). Key hallmarks of the modern economy, therefore are the continuing expansion and increasing significance of global integration led by multinational enterprises. Globalization also conveys the emergence of a sort of post-sovereign governance. Daniel Bell suggests that nation states are becoming too small for big problems in life, and too big for the small problems, leaving them with trappings and ceremony of authority, but with very little actual power. The rise of supra-territoriality has promoted moves towards multilayered governance, where regulatory competences are more dispersed across manifold sub-state, state, or supra-state arrangements and agencies i.e. 'complex multilateralism'. (Bell 1976: 35-37)

The term global governance can be seen as "a heuristic device to capture and describe the confusing and seemingly ever-accelerating transformation of the international system."(Weiss 2001: 796.) At issue is whether the thickening institutional density, expanding jurisdiction, intensifying transnational politics and deepening impact of supra-state regulation denotes a qualitative-structural shift in how global affairs and trans-boundary issues are governed. Rosenau sums up his understanding of global governance in his often quoted definition stating that "global governance is conceived to include systems of rule at all levels of human activity—from the family to the international organization—in which the pursuit of goals through the exercise of control has transnational repercussions." (J. Rosenau1995:13). This definition has four constitutive elements: systems of rule, levels of human activity, the pursuit of goals, and transnational repercussions. For Rosenau and many others, these developments represent the evolving infrastructure of a fragile system of global governance- a new complex multilateralism (ibid: 34). Just how far this system embodies a radical break with traditional modes of regulating the world order, or whether indeed it is displacing or supplementing them, remains the source of continuing disagreement. (Cox 1997; Gill 2000; Keohane and Nye 2000).

The Commission on Global Governance (United Nations) defines global governance as "the sum of the many ways individuals and institutions, public and private, manage their common affairs. It is a continuing process through which conflicting or diverse interests may accommodate, and cooperative action may be taken. It includes formal institutions and regimes empowered to enforce compliance, as well as informal arrangements that people and institutions either have agreed to or perceive to be in their interest. [...] At the global level, governance has been viewed primarily as intergovernmental relationships, but it must now be understood as also involving non-governmental organizations, citizen's movements, multinational corporations, and the global capital market. Interacting with these are global mass media of dramatically enlarged influence." Several observations regarding the institutional architecture of global governance can be briefly summed as – It is *multilayered, polyarchic structurally complex.* Growing literature indicates the formulation and implementation of global policy occurring within an expanding array of political networks: trans-governmental, tri-sectoral (public, corporate and NGOs) and transnational.

REGULATING CORPORATES IN THE AGE OF GLOBALIZATION

A globalised economy also produces global externalities and enhances global inequities. In recent years, we have witnessed a dramatic growth of campaigns against multinational corporations. Organisations like Nike, The Gap and McDonald's have come under the spotlight due to pressure groups accusing these companies of violating human rights, labour regulations, causing environmental hazards, and employing children. Incidents like the explosion at Union Carbide in Bhopal, India in 1984, the oil spillage at Prince William Sound, Alaska, USA, 2001, corporate scandals like Polly Peck, 1992, WorldCom 2002 remain fresh and indelible in our minds.

At the same time, the demise of corporations like Enron and the unethical practices that these cases highlighted, have raised public concerns regarding the activities of the modern corporations. Protests and mass demonstrations have been organised to coincide with meetings of key international institutions from Seattle to Washington, asking for more concerns towards people and the environment. At the broader level, the issue is regarding the scale and economic power and influence which these corporations are able to wield without any accountability.

Naomi Klein's (2000) *No Logo* in fact maps out the processes through which large corporate brands are colonizing peoples lives. Traditional cultural and political spaces, she claims are being removed and replaced by neatly packed branded equivalents. Brands sell to individuals a lifestyle. As she suggests 'Nike, Microsoft and Starbucks have sought to become the chief communicators of all that is good and cherished in our culture.' Similarly,

McDonald's has become a byword for globalisation, uniformity, predictability, calculation and control. The predatory instinct of corporations destroys the culture and indigenous way of living, besides causing harm to *others* – workers, consumers, communities and environment. (Klein 1999: 56-65) Corporations have an inbuilt compulsion to externalize their costs – every cost they can unload onto someone else is a benefit to themselves, a direct route to profit, thus making these institutions needing regulation and control referred to as corporate governance.

Corporations always seem to have more complexity and vitality than can be constrained by definitions or laws. They are about the aspirations and assumptions of people and not simply 'a nexus of contracts.' While in law, a corporation is considered to be a fictional 'person,' at its core each corporation is a structure, developed over time to respond to the needs for more complexity. The enduring appeal of corporations stems from their pervasive element, and the wide range of purposes they serve. On the other hand, corporations are termed as notoriously complex adaptive systems, designed to be so vital and robust that it is like an 'externalizing machine,' set up to do whatever it can to hang on to its earning and push its costs off its balance sheet.

The perennial question today is - Can business do well by doing good? Traditionalists believed in the inherent conflict between the two, as in policy terms we want corporations to behave consistently with the public good, and in economic terms we want them to externalize their costs onto the community. How to reconcile this contradiction evades answers?

Carl Kaysen has outlined various alternatives to limit and control corporate power. He says "broadly there are three alternative possibilities. The first is limitation of business power through promoting more competitive markets; second is broader control of business power by agencies external to business; third the institutionalization within the firm of responsibility for exercise of power." (Edward S.Mason 1956: 103).

Corporate governance systems reflect public policy choices. Some countries have rigorous prohibitions on insider trading, vigorous markets for control, strong protection of minority shareholders (rules on accounting, corporate boards, securities), and effective rules for product-market competition and antitrust. These countries have diffuse patterns of share ownership and managerial supervision through boards elected by their shareholders. Other countries encourage block-holding by allowing pyramid leveraging and cross-shareholding, restricting markets for control, limiting competition, and offering weak protection to minority shareholders.

If the 20th century was viewed as the age of management, the early 21st century is focused on governance. Both terms address control of corporations, but governance has always required an examination of underlying purpose and legitimacy. Two sets of laws govern the constituent groups of the corporation One are the laws imposed by legislatures and other agreements' between private players like employees, customers, suppliers, investors and community. The key is finding the right system of checks and balances. Some scholars have proposed an 'ethical contract.' It assumes any executive legitimacy can only be sustained by interaction of these relationships with other stakeholders. Together they underpin the 'corporate contract.'

Gourvevitch and Shinn in their book '*Political Power and Corporate Control*' define global politics of corporate governance as " the authority structure of a firm - such as who has claim to the cash flow of the firm, who has a say in its strategy and its allocation of resources ....It creates temptations for cheating and the rewards for honesty, inside the firm and more generally in the body politic ....influences social mobility, stability and fluidity... It is no wonder then, that corporate governance provokes conflict. Anything so important will be fought over... like other decisions about authority, corporate governance structures are fundamentally the result of political decisions." (Gourvevitch and Shinn 2003:34-46).

The Power of Multinational Corporations

Although modern multinational firms date from the late nineteenth century, the term multinational corporation did not appear until 1960. From the beginning, the multinational corporation was defined in terms of 'jurisdiction and potential jurisdictional conflict.' In a seminal series of lectures two years before the publication of '*Sovereignty at Bay*, ' Charles Kindleberger (1969:207) argued that the 'nation-state is just about through as an economic unit.' George Ball (1967) predicted increased conflicts between the MNE, a 'modern concept evolved to meet the requirements of the modern age' and the nation-state which is 'a very old-fashioned idea and badly adapted to serve the needs of our present complex world.' Global corporations are demanding '... the right to transcend the nation-state, and in the process, to transform it' (Barnet and Muller 1974:16). Networks are replacing hierarchies. Non-territorial networks are developing into a transnational 'civil' society, linking a variety of economic, social and political actors electronically. MNEs represent nodes of private authority in the international system; and markets are migrating to cyberspace. All these changes make the boundaries of the firms unfixable. It forces one to abandon the static concept of corporations.

Multinational enterprises account for a sizable portion of the world output and trade. Furthermore, their sales and assets have been growing faster than the world gross domestic product, world exports, and world gross fixed capital formations (UNCTAD, 1997). In Robert Gilpin's words, (1975) '... national economies [are] now enmeshed in a web of interdependence from which they cannot escape.' Another argument supporting economically integrated regimes is, that it contributes to political stability in the globe with democratic liberal economies less likely to engage in wars. The hegemony of economies increasingly dominates the lexicon of policy formation (Monk 2007: 23-39).

A networked world economy entails a complex web of transactions, rather than a series of dyadic or triadic cooperative arrangements between firms. Many alliances are not equity based, but rather constellations of companies, or parts of companies tied together -- often on a project basis. Mytelka and Delapierre (1999) argue that new, global, knowledge-based networked oligopolies are emerging in industries. Again, the impact of these new forms of organizations is to disengage the market from the state (and from state control), and to increase dependence of the state on the MNE for technology and technological development. Diebert (1997: ix) has characterized the post-modern world order as "a place inhabited by de-territorialized communities, fragmented identities, transnational corporations, and cyber spatial flows of finance." A clash between corporate interests and national interests is to be expected, and the assumption is that when it occurs, the former will dominate the latter.

The intense phase of financial capital with multinational enterprises deepening their investments in various countries has its inevitable costs, especially when there is no binding regulation adequately making multinational enterprises comply with minimum regulations, human rights, labour, and environmental standards. The argument proceeds from the starting point that markets need to be embedded in a range of non-market institutions, in order to work well. Regulatory regimes and institutions perform several functions critical to markets' performance: they create, regulate, stabilize, and legitimize markets. The second point is that there is no simple or unique mapping between these functions, and the form that the institutional infrastructure can take. American style capitalism differs greatly from Japanese-style capitalism; there is tremendous variety in labour-market and welfare-state institutions, even within Europe; and low-income countries often require heterodox institutional arrangements to embark on development. The third point is, that institutional diversity of this kind is a significant impediment to full economic integration.

Indeed, now that formal restrictions on trade and investments have mostly disappeared, regulatory and jurisdictional discontinuities created by heterogeneous national institutions constitute the most important barriers to international commerce. "Deep integration" would require removing these transaction costs through institutional harmonization—an agenda on which international institutions and world organizations have embarked.

Corporate Governance Convergence - Is it Possible?

There are good reasons for institutional diversity, and why national institutions are resistant to convergence. For one thing, societies differ in their history, values and norms that shape their institutional choices. For e.g. Europeans correspondingly favour extensive redistribution and social protection schemes and Americans, for their part, tend to focus on equality of opportunity, liberty and tolerate much larger amounts of disparity. 'Asian values' make the nature of business different in Asia, as compared to western countries.

There is a second, subtler reason for the absence of convergence in institutional arrangements. Different elements of a society's institutional configuration tend to be mutually reinforcing. Consider, for example, the manner in which Japanese society provides its citizens with social protection. Unlike Europe, the Japanese government does not maintain an expensive welfare state financed by transfers from taxpayers. Instead, social insurance has been provided in the post-war period through a combination of elements unique to "Japanese-style" capitalism: lifetime employment in large enterprises, protection of agriculture and small-scale services, government-organized cartels, and regulation of product markets. All of these, have in turn, repercussions for other parts of the institutional landscape.

The last major category of reasons for institutional diversity has to do with the special needs of developing nations. Maintaining economic growth in this century requires institutional innovations that depart significantly from the American or Western ideals of "best practice." Consider China again, the most spectacular case of success in the developing world in the last quarter century. A western trained economist advocated a complete overhaul of the socialist economic regime: private property rights in land, corporatization of state enterprises, deregulation and price liberalization, currency unification, tax reforms, reduction of import tariffs and elimination of quantitative restrictions on imports. Instead, the Chinese leadership devised highly effective institutional arrangements like Township and Village Enterprises, Special Economic Zones, and Two-Tier Pricing, among many other innovations, enabling the Chinese government to stimulate incentives for production and investments without a wholesale restructuring of the existing legal, social, and political regime. (Dani Rodrik 1995: 145)

The experience of China represents not an exception; transitions to high growth in many emerging economies are typically sparked by a relatively narrow range of reforms that mix orthodoxy with domestic institutional innovations, and not by comprehensive transformations that mimic the west.

India since the early 1980s is another significant example of this strategy. It has followed an unique pattern of reforms, even when it ventured on the path of liberalization in the 1990s. In the age of global inter-linkages, international corporations rely on sovereign countries political systems for permission to operate, and political regimes rely on corporations for investments. Foreign investment contributes significantly to the economy in terms of generating wealth and jobs. So there exists a symbiotic relationship between countries and corporations pursuing expansion and investments abroad.

EVOLVING A COMMON FRAMEWORK FOR GLOBAL CORPORATE GOVERNANCE

Within these nuances of particularity of institutional arrangements of different countries, there is much being debated about the gamut of political regimes to control multinational corporations. There appears asymmetry between the enforceability of laws and functioning of multinational corporations. There is also marked asymmetry in the scope of operations, and objectives between the nation-state and the MNE, between 'the global strategies of MNEs designed to advance corporate profitability and growth, and the strategies of governments intended to promote the economic and social welfare of their citizens'(Dunning 1991: 65).

Recognizing this complexity, many nations are concerned for devising standards and guidelines of international governance. It is difficult, if not impossible, to disentangle the complex transnational production networks of the MNE which would allow a state to exert a significant degree of control over the system.

The ability and incentives for institutional investors to transcend the rules and limitations of their domicile economies is evident, from the creation of international associations dedicated to sharing information and developing global policies on investments and shareholder rights and responsibilities. In fact, the development of a framework for common guidelines started with the adoption in 1948 of the Universal Declaration of Human Rights, thereafter, instruments have been adopted including the ILO Declaration on Fundamental Principles and Rights at Work, the Rio Declaration on Environment and Development and Agenda 21 and the Copenhagen Declaration for Social Development. The most significant among them is the International Corporate Governance Network (ICGN) established in 1995. Its primary functions were a) to provide an investors –led network for the exchange of views and information about corporate governance issues internationally b) to examine corporate governance principles and practices c) to develop and encourage adherence to corporate governance standards and d) to promote good corporate governance. The Global Corporate Governance Forum actively contributes to the efforts of the international community to promote the private sector as an engine of growth, reduce the vulnerability of developing and transition economies against financial crisis, and provide incentives for corporations to invest and perform efficiently in a socially responsible manner. It fosters cooperation with various corporations and plays the coordinating role among donors, founders and other institutions. It is an attempt to establish a delicate balance of incentivizing the wealth creation capability of corporations, without incurring unacceptable costs to the various affected constituencies. Governance Metrics International (GMI) is an independent research and rating agency founded in 2001, to provide institutional investors an objective way of assessing corporate governance risk, as well as governance leaders in their portfolios. GMI starts the rating process by developing a governance profile, incorporating hundreds of variables per company plus analysts' insights. It also reviews regulatory actions, legal proceedings and other sources, to determine whether company conduct is consistent with its stated policies.

The OECD has also been contributing to the international policy framework. Recent developments include the adoption of the Convention on Combating Bribery of Foreign Public Officials in International Business Transactions and of the OECD Principles of Corporate Governance, the OECD Guidelines for Consumer Protection in the Context of

Electronic Commerce, and OECD Guidelines on Transfer Pricing for Multinational Enterprises and Tax Administrations. The Report on the Observance of Standards and Codes (ROSC) also identifies weaknesses that can cause financial vulnerabilities. As part of the Reports on the Observance of Standards and Codes (ROSC) initiative, the World Bank has established a program to assist its member countries in strengthening their corporate governance frameworks.

The implementation procedures for the OECD Guidelines are focussed on activities within individual adhering countries, and their effectiveness depends on the 33 "National Contact Points." The National Contact Point (NCP) gathers information on national experiences with the Guidelines, handles enquiries, discusses matters related to the Guidelines, and assists in solving problems that may arise in this connection.

At present, despite all global efforts there remain gaps in terms of enforceable codes and regulations bringing various MNCs under a common umbrella. As Leipziger (2003: 19) suggests 'there is no single code or standard, no panacea that will lead to corporate responsibility. Each company is different, with its own challenges, corporate culture, unique set of stakeholders and management systems. Corporate responsibility is a journey for which there is no single map but hundreds of guides. Codes and standards are maps that can be combined in new ways for different journeys.'

CONCLUDING OBSERVATIONS

There has been a dramatic increase in the power of multinational corporations relative to national governments and civil society. But there has simultaneously been a marked loss of accountability and democratic control, resulting from the shift of power from national governments to the market and international institutions. Deregulation and neo-liberalism have extended the scope and power of the market to envelop all aspects of social, cultural and political life. It is a force for homogenization: the "McDonaldization" of the world. With globalisation, labour and capital are redirected more easily than ever before in history, and there remains a risk of 'race to the bottom' that reflects collective concerns of all.

On the global scale, conflicts occur as corporate interests and political interests try to control one another. Corporations rely on sovereign countries for permission to operate, and for protection from liability and competition. Political regimes rely on multinational enterprises for flow of capital, job creation and contributions to the economy.

We know that there are global differences in economic, cultural and legal systems affecting management and investors. Besides till date, most of the focus and energy in the field of global corporate governance has been on the 'supply side' of corporate governance i.e. what managers and directors must do. But, it is equally important to make sure that the 'demand side' is set up with the authority, ability and incentives aligned to enable effective oversight and market response. Extending the gamut of responsibility of global economic players in terms of the impact on indigenous people and climate has to be brought within the discourse in the international arena.

The incentives to converge for global corporate governance are indeed high. International corporate activity will achieve the goal of sustainable wealth maximization, if it is compatible with the long-term policy of protection of all stakeholders – investors, suppliers, home and host country, customers and the community at large. None of the problems thrown-up by globalization… can be effectively tackled without accountable and representative institutions for global governance. The present controversy surrounding globalization, reminds us of the work of Karl Polanyi, particularly in *The Great Transformation* (1957). Polanyi believed that the historical evidence indicates that self-regulating markets are not sustainable; that markets must be embedded in the social and political order to survive. In a postmodern world system, however, the appropriate social and political order in which markets are to be re-embedded is, as of now, problematic.

To conclude, we can say that the world wide process of politically managing globalization is still in its nascent stages. Obstacles to global governance still exist, including power imbalances and national and international problems with democracy and legitimization; the almost lack of an ethical-normative consensus ("global ethos") is still interfering with the creation of a strong system of global governance. . . . At this point in time, global governance is still more of a vision than a description of the actual state of the international system. (Bundestag 2002: 67)

In the words of Paul Wapner, global governance is "one of the most perennial and daunting challenges in world history": Ever since the Stoics imagined a single world, organized by a set of common principles, thinkers and practitioners have worked to conceptualise and bring into reality mechanisms to coordinate the diverse activities of a complex, multifarious world. For some, this project meant establishing a world government to legislate common laws and policies. For others, it meant simply building institutions of common understanding and practices supported by sovereign entities below the level of world government.(Paul Wapner 1999: 82)

REFERENCES

Alberto Alesina, Rafael di Tella, and Robert MacCulloch, (2001) ' Inequality and Happiness: Are Europeans and Americans Different?' National Bureau of Economic Research Working Paper, 8198, Cambridge, MA, April.

Albrow, Martin. (1997), 'The Global Age', Stanford, Stanford University Press.

Barnet, Richard J. and Ronald E. Muller. (1974). 'Global Reach: The Power of the Multinational Corporations', New York: Simon and Schuster.

Boli J (1999) 'Conclusion: world authority structures and legitimisation', in Boli and G.M. Thomas(ed) Constructing World Culture: International Nongovernmental Organisations since 1975, Stanford University Press.

Claire A. Cutler, Virginia Haufler, and Tony Porter, (1999) (ED), 'Private Authority and International Affairs' Albany: SUNY Press

Colin Mayer,(2002) 'Corporate Cultures and Governance: Ownership, Control, and Governance of European and US Corporations,' Said Business School, University of Oxford, Oxford.

Cox, R W (e d) (1997) 'The new realism: Perspectives on multilateralism and world order', London, Macmillan.

Deutscher Bundestag, (2002) Study Commission, (2002) 'Globalization of the World Economy: Challenges and Answers,' Short Version of the Final Report, Berlin: German Bundestag, 14th legislative period.

Dicken, Peter. (1994). 'The Roepke Lecture in Economic Geography- Global Local Tensions: Firms and States in the Global Space-Economy', Economic Geography, 70.

Doris A. Fuchs, (2002) 'Globalization and Global Governance: Discourses on Political Order at the Turn of the Century,' in Doris Fuchs and Friedrich Kratochwil, eds., Transformative Change and Global Order: Reflections on Theory and Practice, Münster: LIT Verlag.

Dunning, John H. (1991). 'Governments and Multinational Enterprise: From Confrontation to Co-operation?' Millennium, 20.

Gilpin, Robert. (1975). 'U.S. Power and the Multinational Corporation' New York: Basic Books.

Held D and McGrew, and Perraton (1999), 'Global Transformation: Politics, Economics and Culture', Polity Press. Cambridge.

Kaysen Carl, (1979) 'The corporation; How much power?' In Edward S.Mason(Ed), The corporation in Modern Society Harvard University Press, Cambridge.

Kenichi Ohmae, (1995) 'The End of the Nation State: The Rise of Regional Economies', Harper Collins. London

Kindleberger, Charles P. (1969). 'American Business Abroad: Six Lectures on Direct Investment' Yale University Press. New Haven.

Klaus Dingwerth and Philipp Pattberg (2006) 'Global Governance as a Perspective on World Politic Global Governance', 12.

Klein, N, (2000) *No Logo*, London, Flamingo

Lilienthal, David. (1960). 'The Multinational Corporation' in Melvin, Ashen and G.L. Bach, (ED), Management and Corporations, (1985). McGraw-Hill. New York.

Masahiko Aoki, (1997) 'Unintended Fit: Organizational Evolution and Government Design of Institutions in Japan,' in M. Aoki et al, eds., The Role of Government in East Asian Economic Development: Comparative Institutional Analysis, Clarendon Press, Oxford.

Monks AG Robert& Minnow Neil (2008) 'Corporate Governance' John Wiley & Spns ltd

Mytelka, Lynn K.and Michel Delapierre. (1999) 'Strategic Partnerships, Knowledge-Based Network Oligopolies, and the State' in Cutler, A. Claire, Haufler, and Porter, (ED) Private authority and international affairs. Albany, State University of New York Press, N.Y

Paul Hirst, (2000) 'Democracy and Governance,' in Jon Pierre, ed., Debating Governance Oxford University Press, Oxford:

Paul Wapner, (1997) 'Governance in Global Civil Society,' in Oran R. Young, ed., Global Governance: Drawing Insights from Environmental Experience: MIT Press. Cambridge

Philip G. Cerny (Autumn 1995), 'Globalisation and the Changing Logic of Collective Action', International Organization, 49(4)

Polanyi, Karl. (1957). 'The Great Transformation', Beacon Press. Boston

R. A. W. Rhodes, (1996) 'The New Governance: Governing Without Government,' Political Studies 44, no. 4

R. N. Haas and R. E. Litan, "Globalisation and Its Discontents: Navigating the Dangers of a Tangled World", Foreign Affairs 77(3)

Richard Freeman, (2000) 'Single Peaked vs. Diversified Capitalism: The Relation between Economic Institutions and Outcomes,' National Bureau of Economic Research Working Paper 7556, Cambridge, MA, February 2000.

Rodrik, D (1997) 'Has globalisation gone too far?' California Management Review, 39(3) Califonia.

Rosenau J.N (1999) 'Toward an ontology for global governance' in M. Hewson and T.J Sinclair(ED) Approaches to Global Governance Theory, Albany: State University of New York Press.

Rosenau, J.N (1990) 'Turbulence in World Politics', Princeton: Princeton University Press.

Rosenau, J.N (2002) 'Globalization and Governance: Sustainability between Fragmentation and Integration,' paper prepared for the conference "Governance and Sustainability: New Challenges for the State, Business and Civil Society," Berlin.

Rosenau, J.N (1995) 'Governance in the Twenty-first Century,' Global Governance 1, no. 1: 13.

Smouts, M C. (2001) International cooperation: from coexistence to world governance' in M.C Smouts(ed) The New International Relations, Hurst. London.

Stamford, John and Susan Strange. (1991) 'Rival States, Rival Firms: Competition for World Market Shares' Cambridge: Cambridge University Press. Cambridge.

Susan Strange, (1996) 'The Retreat of the State: The Diffusion of Power in The World Economy', Cambridge University Press, Cambridge

Tarun Khanna, Joe Kogan, and Krishna Palepu, (2001) 'Globalization and Corporate Governance Convergence? A Cross-Country Analysis,' Harvard Business School, NewYork.

Thomas G. Weiss, (2000) 'Governance, Good Governance and Global Governance: Conceptual and Actual Challenges,' Third World Quarterly 21, no. 5.

Ulrich Brand, (2003) 'After Fordism: Global governance as the new hegemonic discourse in international politics', Zeitschrift für Internationale Beziehungen 10, No. 1.

UNCTAD (1999) World Investment Report: 1999. United Nations, New York and Geneva

UNCTAD (2000) World Investment Report: 2000. United Nations, New York and Geneva

Vernon, Raymond. (1998). In the Hurricane's Eye: The Troubled Prospects of Multinational Enterprises. Cambridge: Harvard University Press, N.Y

Yingyi Qian, 'How Reform Worked in China,' in Dani Rodrik, ed., In Search of Prosperity: Analytic Narratives on Economic Growth, Princeton University Press, Princeton, NJ.

Is The Institution of Independent Directors Irrelevant? A Critical Inquiry Into why the Institution has Failed to Lead to Better Corporate Governance

Satheesh Kumar T.N
DC School of Management and Technology, Kerala

ABSTRACT

One of the strong pillars of modern corporate governance laws and regulations anywhere in the world, is the institution called Independent Directors (IDs). A majority of the board-structure related reforms in corporate governance revolve around this very institution. A number of corporate governance experts and watchers have written on the subject and some of them provide evidence for the lack of any improvement in corporate performance, and also in the governance practices and processes. This article, from a conceptual framework, tries to look into the arguments and/or reasons as to why independent directors, supposed to be the backbone of the new age governance practices and processes, have failed to make any impact, leading to a general feeling that they are irrelevant, and hence the laws or regulations making them mandatory on boards may be abolished, and what needs to be done to resurrect the respectability that was expected from this institution.

Keywords: *Independent Directors , Corporate Performance , Conflicts of Interests , Real Independence*

INTRODUCTION

In the aftermath of the corporate debacles like Enron, WorldCom, Global Crossing etc in the early 2000s, the pressure to improve corporate governance increased dramatically in the west. The pressure was felt across the world, considering that the world economy was globalizing at a faster pace. Indian law makers and regulators also took measured steps to improve the governance of Indian corporates. The Securities Exchange Board of India (SEBI), the capital market regulator has been very proactive in moving ahead with a number of regulatory measures, which they incorporated into the listing agreement of the companies with the stock exchanges in the form of Clause 49 of the listing agreement. The said Clause 49 evolved from the corporate governance guidelines that are in force in the US and the UK, and also based on a number of recommendations/guidelines evolved by various committees constituted by it in India, and also drawing from suggestions from bodies like the CII. Clause 49 was implemented in phases starting 2002, and SEBI made it mandatory for all listed companies to meet the requirements latest by 31 December, 2005. It was made applicable to even listed public sector undertakings (PSUs. As is common with other regulations/guidelines, Clause 49 also insists a lot on changes in the board and governance structure. One of the strong pillars of the modern corporate governance laws and regulations anywhere in the world, is the institution called Independent Directors (IDs). A majority of the board-structure related reforms in corporate governance revolve around this very institution. Having been in legitimate existence for more than a decade, at least in developed nations like the US and the UK, and almost seven years in India, a number of studies have already been conducted to ascertain the contribution and relevance of IDs in corporate performance and governance practices. A number of corporate governance experts and watchers have written on the subject, and some of them provide evidence for the lack of any improvement in corporate performance, and also in the governance practices and processes. This article, from a conceptual framework, tries to look into the arguments and/or reasons as to why independent directors, supposed to be the backbone of new age governance practices and processes, have failed to make any impact, leading to a general feeling that they are irrelevant, and hence may be abolished, and what needs to be done to resurrect the respectability that was expected from this institution. While examples from across the globe might be referred to in the process, the study basically concerns with examples and practices followed in the Indian context.

PREAMBLE

Serious concerns have been raised by eminent authors and experts regarding the very relevance of the institution of independent directors (IDs) or their effectiveness on boards. While some focus on the role of IDs in improving corporate performance, some go further to explain their irrelevance even from the point of view of corporate governance practices, while some others are even seriously concerned about the very commitment of the IDs. Professor Donald C.Clarke, of George Washington University (*Economic Times*, 21 July, 2012) questioned the very relevance of independent directors, on the ground that there exists no empirical evidence of better performance of companies and consequent better shareholder value due to their presence. Mr.Prithvi Haldea, Chairman of Prime Database, writing on the myth of independent directorship (*Economic Times*, 27 July, 2012) felt that the only role of IDs was to protect the interests of the minority shareholders, and that since nothing much has been achieved on that front, and that better corporate governance can be achieved through simple laws which companies fear, the very institution of IDs needs to be abolished.

Mr.R.S.Sharma, former Chairman of ONGC made an observation recently that there may be board members who do not even read the agenda of a meeting, forcing ONGC to take a decision on the performance evaluation of the IDs (*Economic Times*,29 August,2012).While the institution of IDs has not proved its effectiveness on the corporate performance front, or the governance front in the short period of less than a decade , doing away with the institution merely on these two grounds will be akin to the proverbial throwing of the baby with the bathwater. To reach such conclusions without making a thorough analysis of why they have failed to be effective, in contributing to the causes of better corporate performance or better corporate governance might be a little too hasty. A majority of the studies today to ascertain the relevance of IDs is skewed from the point of view of assuming that the IDs are really independent. The apparent findings have to be correlated with studies on whether the so called IDs are really independent, and whether they have been acting or conducting themselves as 'real' independent directors during their tenures in various companies. It is not that easy to conduct such studies, as boardroom proceedings and processes happen behind closed doors, and it may be very difficult to get hold of the minutes of board meetings narrating the participation of IDs in the meeting processes, and that the Chairman of board/meeting has the freedom to change the minutes if he feels that they are detrimental to the company. This article makes an attempt to identify and analyze the very reasons why the institution of IDs don't work as expected by the regulators, or other interested stakeholders and make a few suggestions to make them relevant.

Analysis of Why the ID Institution Has Not Been Working Up to the Expectations

Having narrated the various concerns and allegations about the ineffectiveness of the institution of IDs, let us now try to analyze the various reasons that lead to situations rendering them ineffective. There are many reasons; they act independently and together to defeat the very purpose of having independent directors on corporate boards.

The flawed assumption about why corporate governance is required. Most people think or assume that governance is required because the company has chosen to raise money from the public.That is not necessarily the primary reason; the primary reason for the requirement of a governance mechanism is that the company, by virtue of its incorporation, is a separate entity, distinct from promoters/owners. Promoters, by and large, have a tendency to treat companies as their private properties, and will find it difficult to appreciate it as a separate entity which has an existence of its own, delineated from them.Whether it is Azim Premji with more that 80 percent stake in Wipro, or Mr.Sudhir Reddy with only 11.18 percent in IVRCL, one has to keep this in mind(annual reports of Wipro and IVRCL for 2011-12).The very concept of inducting IDs on to the boards of corporate entities must have been borne out of the premise(or fact), that the promoter will find it extremely difficult to draw a line dileneating his interest and the company's interests.Some of the world's best known companies like General Electric(GE) continue to be run well, eventhough the promoter lineage doesn't exist now, precisely because of this concept.

*The IDs not exercising the power vested with them.*Blaming the institution of IDs as useless, irrelevant and ineffective is rather easy, but how to make it work is difficult and more important.Two instances of governance failure in the recent past can be cited in support of this.One involves Satyam Computer Services Ltd., the watershed corporate governance case from India. After the confession of Mr.Ramalinga Raju of fraud and declaring that the balance sheet of the company was unreliable, why did some of the more prominent IDs resign and let the government supersede the board as a whole?The board, with 50 percent IDs, should, instead have sacked the Chairman and working directors and have taken control of the affairs of the company.Thereafter, if they thought they could not set things right, they could have approached the government for help, rather than the government superceding the board.They were only party to many of the decisions because of their lack of information.Now that they were given information by the CMD himself, presumably because there were no escape routes, they should have acted decisively based on the information.

Another instance from the recent past was with respect to Everonn Education. Dr.J.J.Irani, the independent Chairman chose to resign from the position after the company's CEO Mr.Kishore was arrested by the CBI for allegedly bribing an income-tax official, who had detected undisclosed income of Rs. 116 crores. The bribe was paid presumably for helping the company reducing the taxable amount by Rs.60 crores from Rs.116 crores. Dr. Irani had a very long association with the Tata group, and an immaculate reputation and also headed a former government committee to recommend amendments to company law provisions on corporate governance. One would have appreciated Dr.Irani's resignation had it happened at the time of the raid, provided that he came to know that the company and its CEO were indulging in fraudulent or unethical practices, if his intention was to protect his reputation. Resigning after the arrest of the CEO only led to a weakening of the very institution of IDs.Instead, he should have taken control of the situation as an independent Chairman of the board, and with the support of the other IDs on the board, sacking all the executive directors(or at least suspending them till enquiries about their involvement in the issue were completed).

When IDs resigned from the Satyam board after the scam broke out, and when Dr.Irani resigned from Everonn after the Everonn fraud became public and the promoter arrested, the institution of IDs was weakened rather than strengthened. Had Dr. Irani asserted as an independent Chairman, investors would have gained a lot of confidence. He would not have hastily and meakly resigned, had he acknowledged the importance of governance(because corporation is an entity separate from promoters) and appreciated the role of IDs in the governance process.Many of the critics of the institution of IDs, felt and continue to feel that it was time to write an obituary on the instutution of IDs.The best practice, it seems , has been one of resigning (a case of isomorphism), rather than exerting influence using power and expertise of the IDs.A director resignation will help only if that is good for the organization (the corporate entity), at least from the point of view of bringing attention to an incorrigible board or management.

The recent controversy at Jindal Steel & Power, to authorise the Chairman & Managing Director "to revise, from time to time, remuneration of wholetime directors of the company, by whatever designation they are called, by way of annual increments or otherwise" (Annual Report, 2011-12, JSPL) once again proved the failure of IDs to exert influence. The company stated that it does not have a remuneration committee. Permitting the head of management to write the cheque for him and his colleagues on management, is like the teacher permitting students to evaluate their own answer papers. The company has eminent and knowledgeable personalities as IDs on the board. Here, even the conventional allegation that the IDs were maintaining a stoic silence, presumably because of the high remuneration they were paid by the company, is not applicable as IDs are paid a pittance. It is sincerely felt that these are the instances where the IDs should have taken a strong stand, or even resigned to strengthen the institution of IDs.

Company Performance & It's Relationship to Presence of IDs Prof.Clarke, in his article, citing various studies, asserts that there is no relationship between the presence of IDs and corporate performance.At the outset, one must first appreciate that corporate performance and corporate governance are two distinct things.Satyam, till Mr.Raju made the confession the other way, was supposed to have been performing well.Any company would appear to be performing well (whether it has IDs or not), till it is proved that it has not been.In the case of Satyam, had the IDs taken more serious interest about their roles, the problems would not have prolonged for nearly ten years, as claimed by the promoters. In fact, timely action by IDs would have in fact nullified what was perceived to be good performance of Satyam over the years.That they did not act at the right time in the right manner, only created this wrong perception. But, such action by them would have led to better governance for the distinct entity whose very existence would otherwise have been in jeopardy, had the problems continued for some more time. It is felt that the very presence of IDs should at times result in a not-so-wonderful performance, because they do not permit the sometimes erratic ways of management to show better performances.The board as a whole, and IDs in particular in companies, where promoters are actively involved in management has a unique responsibility to mitigate the short cuts or risks taken on by management, in its anxiety to show better performance.

IDs & Commitment of Time Right now, there are a handful of IDs who sit across as many boards as the law permits.Earlier there was actually no limit set by law about the number of directorships by an individual.While the exact number of directorships by a person can take on is debatable, multiple directorships can set a severe limit on the time that an individual can devote to a company.Please remember that many of the IDs (at least some who are in heavy demand) are CEOs or Chairman of some companies, and have to necessarily devote considerable time for managing the affairs of the company where they work full time.For example, Deepak S.Parekh, while he was Executive Chairman of HDFC, was an independent director on 12 publicly listed companies, and also was on the board of a number of private and/or unlisted companies(Kumar,2010). Mr.Parekh also used to be a member of the audit committee in most of the boards where he was a member, thus putting his responsibilities in those companies even higher. It is very difficult to comprehend that he can show excellent commitment to all his independent directorships, while being hands on at his company. Such multiple directorships actually put lots of pressure on director time, can lead to lack of attendance, or at least dilution of their expected duties, leading to a denigration of the very institution of IDs.To cite an interesting example,Kumar Mangalam Birla was an independent director on the board of Maruti, and was also a member of the investor grievance committee between 2003 and 2006. But, he did not attend even a single board or committee meeting, or any annual general meetings during his tenure(Annual Reports of Maruti Suzuki India Ltd. for the years 2003,2004, 2005 and 2006). The law in force today permits upto 15 directorships.But this number might be too big for somebody who has executive responsibilities at his company.While the law may be lenient on the number of directorships, it is the ID who has to set a limit by himself to show commitment to the company by devoting quality time to a limited number of companies,thereby strengthening the very institution of IDs.

Estimates by Carter and Lorsch(2004) put the time to be devoted by any Non-Executive Director (NED)for a company from about 80 hours(for a stable and satisfactory company situation and industry complexity, where the board simply plays a watchdog role) to 320 hours (for a challenging company situation and industry complexity, where the board plays the role of a pilot).Hence, any NED/ID will have to devote about 10 to 40 days to each company depending on the nature and complexity of the companies.

IDs and Conflicts Of Interests Yet another factor that weakens the institution of IDs is the acceptance of IDships by individuals who are beset with conflicts of interests.While promoters wouldn't mind having IDs who may have conflicts of interests, it is the responsibility of the IDs to resist the temptation of becoming IDs in such companies. Again, the law might have set certain limits regarding the permissible level of pecuniary conflicts of interests, which should not be taken as an excuse by the prospective IDs.There are any number of examples that can be cited.M.L.Bhakta is the lead independent director on the board of RIL. He is a senior partner of Kanga & Company who are the Solicitors for the company. How can he be considered independent, when his firm has pecuniary interests with the company?During the last five years Kanga & Company was paid Rs.86.09 lakhs, Rs.152 lakhs, Rs. 42 lakhs, Rs.64 lakhs and Rs.57 lakhs respectively, in addition to total remunerations of Rs.23.6 lakhs,Rs.23.4 lakhs, Rs.24 lakhs,Rs.23.8 lakhs and Rs.23.20 lakhs respectively(Annual Reports of RIL for the years 2007-08, 2008-09, 2009-10, 2010-11 and 2011-12).Same is true of R.K.Kulkarni, ID and member of the audit committee at Mahindra & Mahindra.Kulkarni is a senior partner at Khaitan & Company, the solicitors for the company.During the last five years Khaitan & Company was paid Rs.121.13 lakhs,Rs.85.63 lakhs, Rs.112.77lakhs,Rs.340.61 lakhs and 153.6 lakhs respectively, in addition to remunerations of Rs.9.8 lakhs, Rs.9.7 lakhs, Rs.10.1 lakhs, Rs.17.6 lakhs and Rs.17.6 lakhs paid to Mr.Kulkarni by way of commission and sitting fees(Annual Reports of Mahindra & Mahindra for the years 2007-08, 2008-09, 2009-10, 2010-11 and 2011-12).One interesting observation from the 2011-12 Annual Report is that footnotes state that both the commission and sitting fees shown against Mr.Kulkarni have been paid to M/S.Khaitan & Company.

IDs and Real Independence Prof.Clarke asserts that the IDs have been effective and add value only when they had stock positions in the companies.But what kind of value addition are we talking about?If the value addition was in terms of better financial performance of the firm, then it needs a thorough relook.This was discussed earlier.But whether IDs add value to the enterprise as a separate entity is extremely difficult to assess, by the very fact that their real independence has always been a question mark ever since the institution of IDs was compulsorily co-opted for board governance.The analysis of their contribution and/or value addition makes sense only if they are really independent.It is the considered opinion that IDs shall be independent in every sense of the term, including stock ownership. Even the SEBI permitted that 2 percent is enough to make a director not independent in the real sense.While such a director may be meeting all the requirements of independence, he is still not independent of ownership- ownership of the separate entity he is supposed to oversee and govern. To cite an example, take the shareholding of the IDs of Mahindra & Mahindra Ltd.Nadir Godrej holds 3,04,284 shares whose value as on 8 October, 2012 was Rs.26.34 crores.The ertswhile Promoter-Chairman of the company, Mr.Keshub Mahindra, held only 4,02,296 shares.The holding of other IDs are:D.S.Parekh 1,12,180(Rs.9.71cr),M.M.Murugappan,N.Vaghul,Dr.A.S.Ganguly 1,00,000 each(Rs.8.66 cr),R.K.Kulkarni 82,576(Rs.7.14 cr).Can these IDs with such holdings and consequent financial stake be called really independent?According to Carter and Lorsch, "The more shares a director owns, the more he has a personal interest to worry about- in effect, the more danger he is in of losing some aspects of his independence."(Carter and Lorsch, 2004).

Another serious concern are the long tenures served by the IDs. A large number of IDs have been with their respective companies for long periods.Mr.M.L.Bhakta, has been with RIL since 1977.Nusli Wadia has been on the boards of Tata Steel,Tata Chemicals and Tata Motors for 33 years,31 years and 14 years respectively. Some experts feel that such long tenures will lead to a situation where they are likely to act more as insiders.Patty Stonecifer,CEO of Bill & Melinda Gates Foundation and an Amazon board member, has observed that "if directors serve too long, it becomes very difficult for them to discharge their watchdog function.After many years on the board, they can become so associated with the management("co-opted" as someone else put it), that they are the ones who need to be watched!" (Bowen 2004). Carter and Lorcsh (2004) felt that "long service helps a director to understand the company better, but emotional attachment means she can't be truly independent."Such emotional attachments will ensure that the questioning culture is absent in the board room.

Companies like Bajaj Auto and Tata Motors were among the companies which failed the test of real independence.The Annual Report of 2007-08 was special, in that it was the first annual report of Bajaj Auto after the much talked about demerger.All the directors of the pre-demerger Bajaj Auto retained their seats on the board in the post-demerger Bajaj Auto but D.S.Mehta, who was whole-time director for many years including 2006-07, suddenly got transformed into a non-executive, independent director. There is no explanation in the Annual Report as to how this change happened. (Annual Report of Bajaj Auto Ltd. For 2006-07 and 2007-08).

According to Clause 49 of the listing agreement, which deals with corporate governance regulations for companies, an independent director is one who "has not been an executive of the company in the immediately preceding three financial years" along with other criteria for independence. It is true that SEBI (Clause 49) does not mention about such possible corporate transformations, and the consequent changes in the board structures. Having served the company for many years as a whole-time director, there may be no question about the value that Mr.D.S.Mehta could add to the board. But, if that is so, the company should have retained him as an ordinary non-executive director.

In Tata Motors(TELCO till 2002-03), J.K.Sethna who was designated as non-executive, promoter director in the company's 2002-03 annual report, got transformed to non-executive, independent director in the 2003-04 annual report(Tata Motors). He was also a member on the boards of Tata Sons (the apex Tata company) and four other Tata companies at the time. He continued to be designated as non-executive independent director till his retirement in 2006.

CEOs/Whole Time Directors(WTDs) Not Restrained by Their Boards on Outside Membership No company except for Infosys, among major companies, have put any limit on outside directorships by their CEOs/WTDs, according to published details available.Infosys puts a restriction on the number of outside directorships to two, making it very clear that these directors have to commit large chunks of time to their own companies.Even while they may be hot independent director candidates,this restriction enables the directors to devote whatever additional/sparable time they have, for at the most to two companies, where they can be commit sufficient time.

Time Period Too Short to Make a Verdict on the Efficacy of IDs The naysayers of the institution of IDs must also be conscious of the fact that the institution has been in existence for only about a decade in the developed world, and about seven years in India for all listed companies.This is too short a period for a dramatic change in the behaviour of promoters, management, shareholders, boards and also IDs. Many of the good concepts in management, and even in governance, took many years to sink in and make an impact on the way companies are managed or governed. Considering that many of those directors had no specific designations for their board positions, and have been there since their formation, might find it difficult to change their behaviours in the board room suddenly.For example,M.L.Bhakta, lead ID at RIL, was on the board alongside Dhirubhai back in 1977 when the company went public(Reliance Textile Industries Ltd. Annual Report for1977).Today, to assume that he has to change his board behaviour, despite being designated lead ID, may be a difficult proposition. Even during the split between the Ambani brothers, the IDs of RIL maintained a more or less stoic silence.

Suggestions for Strengthening the Institution of IDs and Making Them Relevant The following are the suggestions for improving the effectiveness of the IDs on boards and to resurrect their relevance. While some might advocate a more stringent regulatory framework, the same is not favoured here as IDs and companies will try to find loopholes in the laws, and/or regulations, or ways and means to circumvent them.The suggestions listed as follows put the onus on IDs and the boards themselves.

IDs must exercise their power to see that the interests of the company as a separate entity are protected. IDs should exercise whatever power they are vested with by laws and regulations, and also by conventions, to ensure that the interests of the corporate entity are protected. While boards should function collegially, the IDs should raise questions on the promoters' or management's intentions in the interests of the entity.With shareholder activism yet to take roots, the onus on questioning the management rests with the IDs. It is gratifying to note that at least two instances have recently been reported where IDs took a firm stand against some of the policies of the management.The IDs at Coal India Ltd., raised serious questions on the management's decision in respect of supply agreements for imported coal at subsidized prices with power companies (*Indian Express*, 11 October, 2012).The final outcome on this is awaited, but at least apparently the IDs at Coal India took a decisive step in the right direction.

The second instance is with respect to DLF where the IDs have stated that the controversial transactions between the company and Mr.Robert Vadra, son-in-law of Mrs.Sonia Gandhi, the UPA Chief, were not discussed by the board and that the allegations, if established, shall be investigated(*Economic Times*, 8 October, 2012).Such instances representing courageous behavior of IDs, while commendable, they are rare far in between, and according to Bowen(2004), "In the corporate world in particular, courage and the will to act are often the attributes in scarcest supply."

IDs shall be really independent -When an individual is approached with an offer by a company to become an ID, he/she must accept it only if he is really independent. One should thoroughly scrutinize independence from all angles well beyond the requirements of law.Law may overlook or even be silent on many aspects relating to independence.If the intention of the ID is to strengthen the institution of IDs, he shall not entertain any compromise with respect to his independence, in terms of conflicts of interest,relationship of any sort with the management, or other directors, situations leading to cross directorships, situation arising from restructuring of the company etc.

While Bajaj Auto might be complying with all the SEBI regulations in force today, was it "right" from an ethical point of view? While conformance is a must, conformance exploiting the loopholes in laws and regulations will not be respected by any.

According to pension fund CALPERS "Independence is the cornerstone of accountability" and hence "A substantial majority of the board consists of directors who are independent" and "independence also requires a lack of conflict between the director's personal, financial or professional interests, and the interests of the shareowners" (*http//www.calpers.ca.gov*).

Restrict directorships to a manageable few - As we had seen earlier, a large number of directors across a vast majority of big companies are the same. And a number of them have their own companies to take care as CEO or Chairman.This definitely puts a lot of pressure on them and may find difficult to spend quality time on the companies where they serve.While it is better for the directors themselves to put such restrictions, the companies where they work full time, shall also take some steps in this direction, by restricting the number of directorships their full time members can take on.Considering the responsibility that IDs are entrusted with today,each director is expected to devote a decent chunk of time for a company. In the US, the average number of outside boards for a sitting CEO used to be two, it is now less than one and about 25 percent of active CEOs of S&P companies don't serve on outside boards, according to Bowen(2004).While the percentage of active CEOs becoming IDs in the US was 48 percent in 2001, it has come down to 29 percent in 2006(Bowe 2004).

CONCLUSION

There have been and are a number of concerns raised from various quarters that the institution of independent directors are not relevant based on their performance so far.The article tried to analyse the reasons for such concerns with examples from practice.It is felt that once the reasons are addressed, the relevance of the institution can be re-established. A few suggestions aimed at making the institution of IDs not only relevant but also stronger, have also been made.

REFERENCES

Annual Report of Bajaj Aulo Ltd. for 2006-07

Annual Report of Bajaj Aulo Ltd. for 2007-08

Annual reports of IVRCL for 2011-12

Annual Report,2011-12,JSPL

Annual Reports of Mahindra & Mahindra for the years 2007-08,

Annual Reports of Mahindra & Mahindra for the years 2008-09

Annual Reports of Mahindra & Mahindra for the years 2009-10

Annual Reports of Mahindra & Mahindra for the years 2010-11

Annual Reports of Mahindra & Mahindra for the years 2011-12

Annual Report of Maruti Suzuki India Ltd. for 2003

Annual Report of Maruti Suzuki India Ltd. for 2004

Annual Report of Maruti Suzuki India Ltd. for 2004

Annual Report of Maruti Suzuki India Ltd. for 2006

Annual Reports of RIL for 2007-08

Annual Reports of RIL for 2008-09

Annual Reports of RIL for 2009-10

Annual Reports of RIL for 2010-11

Annual Reports of RIL for 2011-12

Annual Report of Tata Motors(TELCO) for 2002-03

Annual Report of Tata Motors for 2003-04

Annual reports of Wipro for 2011-12

Bowen, William G.,2008, *The Board Book:An Insider's Guide For Directors and Trustees,*Norton,New York

Carter, Colin B. and Jay W. Lorsch(2004),*Back To The Drawing Board,*HBS Press,Boston

Clarke, Donald C.,*Economic Times*, "How To Be A Good Independent Director: Irrelevance of Independent Directors", July 21,2012

Economic Times, "DLF Iindependent directors in the dark over Vadra Deals",October 8, 2012

Haldea,Prithvi, *Economic Times,* "Independent Director: Where Is He?",July 27,2012

http//www.calpers.ca.gov

Indian Express, " Why subsidize private firms on important coal: Coal India Directors",September 17,2012

Kumar, Satheesh, 2010, *Corporate Governance*, OUP,New Delhi

"ONGC to scrutinise performance of independent directors", *Economic Times*,29 August,2012

A Study on The Code of Governance Practices of Smes in Emerging Economies

Amit Majumder, Sajal Kr. Maiti[1] and Sudipti Banerjea[2]
Goenka College of Commerce & Business Administration, Kolkata
[1]Hooghly Mohsin College, Hooghly
[2]University of Calcutta, Kolkata

ABSTRACT

The present article attempts to make a comparative analysis among major governance codes of six emerging economies in different continents of the world-UAE, Hong Kong, Colombia, India, Morocco and Lebanon, based on eight different significant parameters of corporate governance.

Keywords: *Codes of Good Governance, SMEs, Emerging Economies, Board of Directors, Succession Policy*

INTRODUCTION

The term *corporate governance* is not only a buzzword in management literature, but also a much-discussed concept, influencing in a big way different categories of stakeholders who are directly/indirectly associated with the corporate world. Everybody, in all types of organisations expects good governance in his/her organisation. However, the word *governance* has a latin root, i.e., *gubernare*, which denotes 'to steer.' *Corporate governance* may, therefore, be interpreted as guidance of a corporate organisation's affairs. Although the subject has been mooted since 1600, with a Royal Charter being granted to the East India Company, which was to be governed by a Court of Directors, there is certainly a significant increase in interest over the past few decades, with several countries issuing new governance reports/codes, and several countries issuing codes of best practices. The term *corporate governance* conveys how a corporate organisation is directed and controlled, the basis being a set of missions and values. It is a term, implying greater transparency of the management system in corporate entities. In common parlance, it is a responsibility-based relationship among various categories of participants in the corporate functioning, in determining the direction and performance of such an entity. However, in its broadest sense, *corporate governance* is all about the stewardship responsibility of the corporate board of directors, to guide the journey towards achievement of the goals, formulate appropriate strategies, and foster timely implementation of such strategies, thereby, facilitating the accomplishment of the missions. This understanding was vindicated by a survey conducted by an internationally-acclaimed management consultancy organisation, which revealed that more than two-thirds of Foreign Institutional Investors (FIIs) were putting *corporate governance* high on their agenda, at the time of investing money in any concern (*McKinsey Co.*, 2000) In fact, for survival and growth, adherence to the *corporate governance* mechanism has now become a pre-requisite, with special reference to companies in emerging economies. As developing countries begin to compete in the global markets, and translate their growth into more mature, sustainable economies, they must put in place rules and principles that stabilize markets and support entrepreneurial innovation. Corporate governance has become a major issue in development, since it relates directly to the establishment of long-term productivity and sustained growth. The future of emerging markets depends on improving governance within and around corporations.

The issue of what constitutes a small or medium enterprise is a major concern in SME literature. Different authors, policymakers and regulators around the globe in most cases, have given different definitions for SMEs architecture, based on the magnitude of the capital asset used in the business (Ló pez and Aybar, 2000), degree of employment (Van der Wijst, 1989; Jordan, 1998; Michaelas, 1999), turnover level of the firm, legal status assigned to the firm, ownership structure, value of fixed assets used (Weston and Copeland, 1998) and production methods used by the firm. In February 1996, however, the European Commission adopted the definitions for SMEs as firms with less than 250 employees; less than Euro 40 million turnover and less than Euro 27 million total assets (Mira, 2002). This fact suggests that there is no general consensus over what a small business is. It is however, generally admitted, that most definitions of SMEs are centred around size, or on the number of employees. In the Indian context, as per the Micro Small and Medium Enterprise Development Act, 2006, the definition of MSME is as follows.

Small and Medium Enterprises (SMEs) are engines of growth, especially in emerging economies and play an important role in creating economic growth. SMEs contribute to economic development by creating employment for the rural and urban population, providing flexibility and innovation through entrepreneurship, and increase international trade by diversifying economic activity. In developing economies, characterized by an abundance of labour and dearth of capital, the SMEs took the conclusive form of labour-intensive business practices. For example, in the Philippines, SMEs are responsible for 99 percent of total manufacturing establishments, and 45 per cent of employment, while in Thailand, SMEs are contributing 90 percent of manufacturing establishments and 65 per cent of employment. Likewise, in Bangladesh, the SMEs had contributed to 50 percent of industrial GDP and accountable for providing 82 per cent of the country's total industrial sector employment and in Pakistan, SMEs contribution in GDP is 30 percent. Moreover, SMEs constitute more than 98 per cent of all business establishments and account for 63 per cent of the value-added segment in Nepal. In India, SMEs' contribution to GDP is 30 percent. (Mahmood, 2007). Moreover, in both developing and developed countries, there exists a lot of instances of the successful saga of the transformation of the so-called 'Lilliput' to a corporate 'Giant' like Microsoft and Apple in the USA, Lenovo in China and Infosys in India.

Table 1: Definition of MSME

Manufacturing Enterprises – Investment in Plant Machinery		
Description	*INR*	*USD($)*
Micro Enterprises	upto Rs. 25Lakhs	upto $ 62,500
Small Enterprises	above Rs. 25 Lakhs upto Rs. 5 Crores	above $ 62,500 upto $ 1.25 million
Medium Enterprises	above Rs. 5 Crores upto Rs. 10 Crores	above $ 1.25 million upto $ 2.5 million

Service Enterprises – Investment in Equipments		
Description	*INR*	*USD($)*
Micro Enterprises	upto Rs. 10Lakhs	upto $ 25,000
Small Enterprises	above Rs. 10 Lakhs upto Rs. 2 Crores	above $ 25,000 upto $ 0.5 million
Medium Enterprises	above Rs. 2 Crores upto Rs. 5 Crores	above $ 0.5 million upto $ 1.5 million

The Need for Adherence to Good Governance Code in SMEs

However, the issue of corporate governance is not exactly common in the small business setting. Generally, this concept of implementing an effective controlling mechanism to ensure the fact that the business is in the path to protect 'the best interests of all' stakeholders, belongs to the domain of large business houses. Moreover, the genesis of debate on corporate governance stems from the 'agency theory' problem, which generally falls in the domain of corporate management and control of large corporations, where the divorce between ownership and control is a common and somewhat indispensable phenomenon, for ensuring sustainable development and a competitive edge. However, the occurrence of the agency problem in SMEs is less likely to occur, since management and ownership of these businesses generally rests in the same person, i.e., to the entrepreneur or his nearest relatives. Yet, there exist a number of key factors which are responsible for substantiating the fact that behind adherence to good governance norms in business DNAs of the SMEs

Drivers for growth: SMEs which are aspiring to follow a higher growth trajectory, had no other option but to follow the principles of good governance as proposed by the regulatory body, or various national and international committees, or codes. As entrepreneurial firms need access to resources for growth, they could gain this through the appointment of outside non-executive directors who are prepared to share their networks, ideas and access to resources (McGuire, 2002; Abor and Biekpe, 2007; Gao and Zhang, 2009; Sampson-Akpuru, 2009; Chen Shenglan, 2010, Yang and Yu, 2011). Gill (2011) by observing 91 Canadian manufacturing firms listed on the Toronto Stock Exchange (TSX) for a period of three years, found that firm growth is positively associated with CEO duality, firm size, and return on assets, and negatively associated with the board size. Gill, Mand and Mathur (2012) by examining the relationship between corporate governance and the growth of small business service firms in Punjab, India found that that the growth of small business service firms in India is positively associated with CEO tenure, CEO duality, number of board meetings, and total assets, and negatively associated with the board size.

Catalyst behind better performance: Adherence to good governance norms may provide insights for effective business operations, good strategy and best practices, through the presence of external board members. It was observed that the strategy of listed corporations and corporate performances were positively associated (McGahan, Porter, 1997), as well as a positive influence of the external board members on strategy formulation of these companies was also observed (Pettigrew, McNulty, 1995). Moreover, in a survey on the influence on the various corporate governance parameters like ownership structures on financial performance of Chinese SMEs of the Shenzhen exchange, a positive association was also observed (Zuo Zhi-gang, 2010). In another study on the impact of 50 Tunisian SMEs ownership structures on financial performance, a positive association was revealed (Hamad and Karoui, 2011).

Assisting better decision making: The existence of independent directors on boards is instrumental in eliminating information asymmetry in the board, managing the risk profile of the SMEs in a better way and inculcating new, and innovative ideas leading to better decision making by the SMEs for achieving a sustainable competitive advantage (Gabrielsson and Huse, 2005). Moreover, outside directors brought valuable expertise, experiences and access to valuable resources, by making their business and personal networks available to small firms (Borch and Huse, 1993).

Impetus for better corporate management and business improvement: Adherence to good governance practices by any entity in a true spirit, will lead towards greater transparency, discipline, fairness and accountability in the overall activities of that organization. Moreover, adherence to good governance norms helps SMEs to survive in an increasingly competitive environment through mergers, acquisitions, partnerships, and risk reduction through asset diversification.

Counter agency problems of the future: When entrepreneurial firms grow, the need to introduce professional management practices arises, as the SME-owners need professional managers to coordinate and develop businesses further, leading to the same agency problems that the big firms used to face. To counter this situation, the SMEs should adhere to the principle of good governance norms in a true spirit. Moreover, alignment of the executive directors' remuneration with corporate performance, introduction of an effective audit committee, along with proper accounting controls and internal audit may also be followed.

Beneficial for firms aspiring for an IPO issue: The growing number of entrepreneurial firms aspiring for public offerings for financing their capital requirements have to follow good governance norms, and to disclose about it as per the requirements of regulatory bodies, or stock exchange authorities (for example, in Indian context, SEBI had proposed Clause 52 for listing in the SME Exchange). Adherence to good governance norms by these entities at an early stage, will be very helpful for them to move towards listing in later stages.

Ease in obtaining external financing: Adherence to good governance norms will improve SMEs' prospects of obtaining funding from banks, investors and venture capitalists, since it will lead towards greater transparency, independence in judgement, higher disclosures and better risk management processes. The same thought had been shared by the Deputy Governor of the RBI at the *Economic Times Thought Leadership Conclave, 2012* that instilling the good governance framework by SMEs in India has been instrumental in ushering the path of higher growth trajectories.

Stakeholders' value creation: Using a stakeholder approach, a firm is not just responsible to its shareholders but also to its constituency of stakeholders like contractual partners, employees, suppliers; social stakeholders like members of community; and the environment. This approach emphasises long-term performance-enhancing contributions by stakeholders, and also views corporations as socially responsible institutions. Thus, an appraisal of a firm will not only include financial performance but also employment, market share and growth in trading relations with suppliers and purchasers. Since corporate governance can protect the interest of stakeholders, it is suggested that it should be introduced in SMEs.

Higher employee retention and loyalty-----Adherence to good governance norms will lead towards independent and unbiased norms for evaluating the performance of employees, and equitable compensation packages, leading towards higher employee retention, better employee morality, increased employee loyalty and lower employee turnover.

CODE OF GOOD GOVERNANCE FOR SMEs IN A FEW EMERGING ECONOMIES

Among the various solutions proposed for countering the 'agency theory' problem, the most formidable and well-accepted instrument across the world is nothing, but adherence to corporate governance norms for the best practices of the companies (Aguilera and Cuervo-Cazurra, 2004). The code of good governance, is basically a set of recommendations, or guidelines prescribed for companies to usher in the path of greater transparency, increased accountability, ensuring independence and better disclosure practices. The codes should play a more pro-active role, rather than a re-active one, for ensuring the spirit of good governance that should prevail in the organization. But, unfortunately the regulatory bodies in various nations, come across with a brand new prescription for good governance, when one or two big corporate scams are being unearthed (like BCCI, Enron, WorldCom, Adelphia, Tyco, Satyam etc.). However, the first such serious attempts towards drafting codes for good practices for business houses can be linked to the high profile Cadbury Code of the UK in 1992, which later spread all over the world and by 2005, 95 countries had issued a total of 144 codes (Zattoni and Cuomo, 2008). However, the code for good governance prescribed around the world is generally restricted towards the large listed companies' domain. But, as the far as the issue of governance of SMEs is concerned, a few separate and unique codes of good governance have been prescribed around the world, despite the fact of the growing importance of SMEs in the respective economies, in terms of its share of GDP, employment, mobility of funds etc. However, recognising the fact of sustainability in a fiercely competitive market, and ushering the path of growth and stability, different emerging economies in South-East Asia (like Hong Kong), Middle East and North Africa (MENA) (like Algeria, Egypt, Tunisia, Saudi Arabia, Oman, Jordan, Qatar, Lebanon, Morocco etc.) and Latin America (like Colombia), have developed unique governance codes and guidelines for the SMEs operating in their regions. In the Indian context, SEBI had introduced a voluntary guideline for governance of SMEs in the form of Clause 52 of the Listing Agreement for SMEs aspiring for public issues through the SME Exchanges in bourses. In this article, a comparative analysis of various corporate governance codes/ guidelines of SMEs have been made, based on various issues of good governance.

In this article, a comparative study on the code of corporate governance for SMEs in six emerging economies is discussed, based on eight pertinent issues of good governance.

(a) *The Corporate Governance Code for Small and Medium Enterprises (SMEs), 2011* proposed by the Department of Economic Development, Dubai, UAE in conjunction with Hawkamah, The Institute of Corporate Governance, Dubai, UAE,

(b) *Guidelines on Corporate Governance for SMEs in Hong Kong (2nd Edition)*, 2009 published by The Hong Kong Institute of Directors Limited,

(c) *Framework Code of Good Corporate Governance for Small and Medium-size Enterprises, 2000* proposed by the Specialized Management Network – "Colombia Compite" Network, Ministry of Commerce, Industry and Tourism, Colombia,

(d) *Clause 52 of Model Equity Listing Agreement, 2010* proposed by the Securities Exchange Board of India (SEBI) for SME Exchange, India,

(e) *Moroccan Code of Good Corporate Governance Practices for SMEs, 2008* proposed by the National Commission on Corporate Governance, Morocco,

(f) *The Lebanese Code of Corporate Governance, 2006* proposed by the Lebanese Transparency Association, Lebanon.

Issue 1: Protection of Owners or Partners or Shareholders Rights

The genesis of the debate on adherence to good corporate governance practices may be linked to the age-old 'agency theory' problem, where it was supposed that professional managers are more eager towards achievement of their personal targets, rather than protecting their principal's interests i.e. the owners interests. In order to ensure that the enterprises are managed in the best interests of their owners, protection of their rights and maximization of owner's interests, the code of good governance for SMEs of various emerging economies had addressed issues in multifaceted capacities.

Issue 2: Succession Planning Process

The succession planning is particularly crucial for growing SMEs and family businesses. Absence of proper succession planning represents a risk to the business, both in terms of business continuity and survival. A succession plan allows the company to develop and facilitate change of leadership in a progressive, planned and non-disruptive manner, assuring shareholders, employees, customers and other stakeholders on the longevity of the company, preserving its reputation and brand value.

Table 2: Protection of Owners or Partners or Shareholders Rights

Dubai Code	*Hong Kong Code*	*Colombian Code*	*Cl. 52, India*	*Moroccan Code*	*Lebanese Code*
Partners' and shareholders' rights and obligations should be clearly set out and delegation of authority should be formalized in writing defining the role of the management and specifying matters reserved for shareholders and the board of directors. All shareholders should be treated equitably and companies should establish clear lines of communication with their shareholders.	Once a company has several shareholders it becomes necessary to consider their rights, and it may be important to demonstrate that the company offers attractive investment possibilities. If there are comparatively few shareholders it may be appropriate for each of them to be a member of the board, or for the directors to be people who are personally known to the shareholders and who enjoy their confidence.	Partners/shareholders in SMEs are to be protected under the company's rules of corporate governance, which should ensure that their rights are duly respected and that their interests are duly protected. They should have a say in the appointment and dismissal of administrators and evaluate their performance.	Shareholders right to be protected by the organization in the form of allowing them voting in AGM, appointment and re-appointment of directors, grievance redressal through Investors' Grievance Committee. Moreover, the financial information of the company to be communicated to the employee on time.	The enterprise must protect the rights of shareholders and partners, and facilitate the exercise thereof (through distant voting, postal vote). It must also ensure the equitable treatment ('one share one vote' principle) of all shareholders and partners, including minority and non-resident shareholders and partners.	Shareholders enjoy the equal right to vote at assemblies, the right to dividends, to transfer their shares, the preferential right to subscribe to capital increases, right to vote on major transactions. A List of Shareholder's Rights to be made available to all Shareholders. Shares should necessarily be physically issued and remitted to the relevant Shareholder within thirty days of the date of the Assembly verified their legal issuance.

Table 3: Succession Planning Process

Dubai Code	*Hong Kong Code*	*Colombian Code*	*Cl. 52, India*	*Moroccan Code*	*Lebanese Code*
A company's strategic planning should encompass succession issues – addressing both managerial succession and ownership succession. Succession planning should be aligned with the company's business objectives and potential exit strategies of SME owners. Moreover, companies should have a rigorous succession planning methodology in place providing for both planned and emergency scenarios.	A succession plan that will provide for the continuance of the business should be developed if the entrepreneur being unable to continue. In family business, careful planning for succession to be developed to find second generation family members who are sufficiently able and well trained, and at the same time willing and sufficiently patient to take over the leadership of the family company at a time that is suitable to the founder.	In case of family businesses, in order to ensure the firm's continuity, the Board of Directors should advocate the adoption of a Family Business Protocol or Agreement including a succession plan and encourage family members involved in the business to undergo professional training.	No such provision.	Governing body is responsible to prepare succession plan for the key executives including governing body members itself. It should ensure that the succession plans for its members are adequate, and ascertains that the selection or reappointment of executive and non executive members guarantee a balance of skills and experience.	Family businesses should have a written succession plan describing the process of succession. The selection process is a board decision.

ISSUE 3: COMPOSITION OF BOARD OF DIRECTORS

The culture and practice of good governance stems from a well-structured, effective and independent board of directors-the apex body of any form of corporate structure. Every good governance code and law around the world, has carefully addressed the issue of the composition of the board, where the essence of independence, and effectiveness can be maintained, not in mere words but in a true spirit. The Corporate Governance Codes for SMEs in emerging nations have aptly addressed these issues, by referring to the number of outside directors to be included in the board, for promoting fairness and independence of opinion in the decision making process of the board.

Table 4: Composition of Board of Directors

Dubai Code	*Hong Kong Code*	*Colombian Code*	*Cl. 52, India*	*Moroccan Code*	*Lebanese Code*
Smaller companies may wish to set up an "advisory" board with no formal decision making powers but which offers its expertise and networks to guide and support the business with outside directors. Two to three people is a sufficient size for an advisory	For smaller companies Boards of advisers can be appointed by those. who control enterprises and asked to provide advice on selected matters. For growing SMEs going for public issue the Articles of Association will normally establish the maximum size of the board and may lay down some basic rules about its	The members of the Board of Directors and the chief executive officer are company administrators, who are to act in good faith, with the loyalty and due diligence of good businessmen. They are to act in the company's best interests, bearing in mind the interests of its partners/shareholders . The Board of Directors should have an odd number of members ranging from a minimum of three (3) up to a maximum of nine (9), according to the needs of the firm in question. The Board of Directors should include at least one outside and/or independent director.	The Board of directors of the Issuer shall have an optimum combination of executive and non-executive directors with not less than fifty percent of the board of directors comprising of nonexecutive directors. Where the Chairman of the Board is a non-executive director, at least one-third of the Board should comprise of	The governing body is in charge of the strategic orientation and effective surveillance of the management of the enterprise. It is accountable to majority and minority shareholders and partners, and must be motivated by a genuine "affection societatis" in its respect for the other enterprise stakeholders (its employees, its customers, its creditors, the Administration	The Board of Directors is entrusted with the duty of ensuring the proper managemen t of the Company in the best interest of the Company and all shareholder s in accordance with applicable laws and regulations. At least [20]% of the board members should be non-executive

board for a small business. When creating a board, the owner(s) must decide whether to appoint "inside" or "outside" directors. The appropriate number of members is determined by the size of the company, but a good practice for SMEs would be between five and ten members. Many businesses keep the number odd so they can hold votes without ties.	composition and its operations. While the shareholders formally elect the directors, the members of the board are in a far better position to know which of them are performing well, what type of person would contribute most when a vacancy occurs, and who would best fit the specification of the ideal candidate.		independent directors and in case he is an executive director, at least half of the Board should comprise of independent directors.	, etc.). In a joint stock company the governing body is the Board of Directors (in a monist structure), or the Supervisory Board or Management Board depending on the case (in a dual structure). For the other forms of companies, the governing body is the management board.	members who do not hold any management or executive position in the Company. Every group of shareholders representing {10%} of the Company's share capital should be entitled to be represented by a board member of their choice.

ISSUE 4: INDEPENDENCE IN BOARD

In order to promote the independence of the board, to promote unbiased opinions in the decision making process, and to inculcate the culture of value sharing, the codes for good governance for SMEs in various emerging nations promoted the issue of a inclusion of a substantive number of independent outside directors on boards, as well as in various board committees.

Table 5: Independence in Board

Dubai Code	*Hong Kong Code*	*Colombian Code*	*Cl. 52, India*	*Moroccan Code*	*Lebanese Code*
As companies evolve, they may find it useful to appoint "outside" or independent nonexecutive directors to their boards. Independent directors give minority investors assurance that the interests of all shareholders, rather than the interests of a particular group, are being protected and represented at the board level. They also bring fresh views and more objective thinking into	A majority of members of the board of SMEs should be independent of management, of any substantial shareholder, and of any other interest or relationship which could materially interfere with the director's ability to act in the best interests of the company as a whole. The chairman of the board should be an independent director and not the CEO or a controlling shareholder. The independent non-	The Board of Directors should include at least one outside and/or independent director. The independent members must have mutually complementary, interdisciplinary skills and attributes as well as experience in business. They may not simultaneously sit on more than five Boards.	Where the Chairman of the Board is a non-executive director, at least one-third of the Board should comprise of independent directors and in case he is an executive director, at least half of the Board should comprise of independent directors. Provided that where the non-executive Chairman is a promoter of the Issuer or is related to any promoter or person occupying managemen	The governing body should be independent both of enterprise management and of its shareholders and partners, and in particular of the shareholders or partners of reference. The independence of the governing body is determined principally by its composition and structure. The non executive or outside members are full members who must take an objective view of the enterprise and contribute to enriching reflection and decision-making, in particular thanks to their assiduousness,	The board of directors should have a minimum of 20% unrelated or independent directors to ensure professionalism on board.

the board room.	executive directors (INED) should be at least three.		t positions at the Board level or at one level below the Board, at least one-half of the Board of the Issuer shall consist of independent directors.	professionalism, and independence.	

ISSUE 5: SEPARATION OF THE ROLE OF CHAIRMAN AND CEO

The code for good governance around the world has addressed the issue of the duality of the role of the Chairman and CEO for promoting an independent and multifaceted opinion, and discouraging the spirit of concentration of the entire supreme decision making power in a single hand. Adhering to this new concept in the corporate governance literature, the codes for SMEs in a few emerging nations, had taken the stance of separating the role of the Chairman and CEO of enterprises.

Table 6: Separation of Role of the Chairman and CEO

Dubai Code	*Hong Kong Code*	*Colombian Code*	*Cl. 52, India*	*Moroccan Code*	*Lebanese Code*
For the board oversight over management to be truly effective, the roles of the chairman and the chief executive should be separated. In smaller companies, such a separation may not always be possible or	The chairman of the board is an independent director and not the CEO or a controlling shareholder.	No such provision.	No such provision	The separation of powers between the key executives like Chairman, Chief Executive, manager, co-manager, etc. should be made.	Under current applicable Lebanese law, it is not possible to separate between the functions of chairman and general manager. Until such separation becomes legally feasible, it was advised that the board of directors appoint a deputy general manager who reports to the board. As soon as it becomes possible

feasible.					under applicable law, it was further advised that the Company should separate between the functions of chairman and general manager so as the same person is not entitled to hold both functions.

ISSUE 6: AUDIT COMMITTEE: COMPOSITION AND ROLE

The onus for promoting good corporate governance and audit, as well as prevention of corporate fraud, primarily rests on an efficient and well structured audit committee. The codes of good governance for SMEs of emerging nations aptly addressed this issue, by providing guidelines for the composition of the committee, its charter, frequency of meetings as well as roles and responsibilities towards internal and external auditing mechanisms.

Table 7: Audit Committee: Composition and Role

Dubai Code	*Hong Kong Code*	*Colombian Code*	*Cl. 52, India*	*Moroccan Code*	*Lebanese Code*
No such provision.	If the board is sufficiently large it may be desirable to establish an Audit Committee (AC) with written charters. For listed SMEs it is required to establish an AC comprising NEDs only and a minimum of three members. AC	It is recommended that the Board of Directors should form committees to advise it on specific matters such as auditing, corporate governance, hiring and compensation with exclusively, wherever possible, independent Board members. They	A qualified and independent AC shall be set up with minimum three directors as members. Two-thirds of the members of audit committee shall be independent directors with Chairman as an independent director. All members of audit committee shall be financially literate and at	The AC must be made up of governing body members, majority of non executive or outside members with solid knowledge of the accounting and financial details of the enterprise's activity, and who are capable of assessing the risks to which the enterprise is exposed. The AC ensures the	An AC may be formed whose mission shall be to prepare and/or review the Company's financial records and accounts; and to ensure compliance with appropriate financial accounting and reporting

	should review all financial statements, company's accounting policies, company's system of internal control review and evaluate the results of the external and internal audits. The Committee shall hold at least three regular meetings per year.	may also include outside experts in their specific sphere of work.	least one member shall have accounting or related financial management expertise. The audit committee should meet at least four times in a year and not more than four months shall elapse between two meetings. AC should recommend to the Board, the appointment, re-appointment and, if required, the replacement or removal of the statutory auditor and the fixation of audit fees. AC should review the adequacy of internal audit function and risk management process.	integrity of financial information, and the relevance and consistency of the accounting methods used in closing the accounts. AC shall meet as necessary and at least twice a year. The AC recommends to governing body on the selection, appointment, renewal, and compensation of the external auditors.	standards. AC must produce quarterly financial reports and a detailed annual report, which shall be submitted to the Board for its review and for inclusion in the Company's annual report.

ISSUE 7: INTERNAL CONTROL FRAMEWORK AND THE RISK MANAGEMENT PROCESS

Implementation of a good governance mechanism hinges on an effective internal control framework to a large extent. In order to ensure an effective internal control process, and proper risk management mechanisms to thwart various operational and strategic risk postures, the code of good governance for SMEs in various emerging nations have addressed this pertinent issue of ensuring good governance mechanisms inside the corporate management process. A few codes were also proposed for construction of a separate risk management committee, or for bestowing the responsibility of the risk management process on the audit committee of the enterprise.

Table 8: Internal Control Framework and Risk Management Process:

Dubai Code	*Hong Kong Code*	*Colombian Code*	*Cl. 52, India*	*Moroccan Code*	*Lebanese Code*
Companies should establish a formal process for identifying significant business risks and the management should adopt formal control mechanisms. More developed companies should set up a specialized board-level committee to monitor the overall control environment of the company. Moreover, companies should consider establishing an internal audit function to ensure	A simple analysis of the risks facing the company and basic policies for managing them will assist the entrepreneur to avoid disaster. A formal process of identifying, evaluating and management of risk should be in place. The board should ensure proper internal control framework for risk management process. AC should be formed to strengthen the systems of internal control and risk	Board of directors should devise effective risk management plan.	The Issuer of SMEs shall lay down procedures to inform Board members about the risk assessment and minimization procedures. These procedures shall be periodically reviewed to ensure that executive management controls risk through means of a properly defined framework. CEO and CFO should accept responsibility for establishing and maintaining internal controls for financial reporting and evaluate the effectiveness of internal	Governing body should ensure existence of adequate internal control and risk management systems. The AC must monitor the efficient functioning and internal control systems of the enterprise and risk management process. In its management report, the enterprise shall inform shareholders or partners of its internal control and risk management policy. A report on internal control must be submitted	The Board should establish an efficient system for internal audit with the internal audit function being managed by a [full time] senior level manager reporting directly to the Board for establishment and monitoring of systems for evaluating and controlling risk management.

effective risk management.	management process.		control systems in connivance with AC.	to the governing body.	

ISSUE 8: STAKEHOLDERS RELATIONSHIP

As per the 'stakeholder theory' of corporate governance, the objective of the company should be to protect and maximize the interests of all parties who are directly or indirectly affected by the activities of the concern. In order to ensure that the SMEs are following the right path of optimizing the value of stakeholders, the codes of good governance for SMEs in different emerging nations have proposed various guidelines, such as formulation of stakeholders policy, disclosure of information, and even formation of a separate board committee for maintaining relations with the stakeholders of enterprises.

Table 9: Stakeholders Relationship

Dubai Code	*Hong Kong Code*	*Colombian Code*	*Cl. 52, India*	*Moroccan Code*	*Lebanese Code*
SMEs should formulate policies outlining their values and objectives in relation to areas such as customer satisfaction, product safety, employee relations, health and safety, the environment and the community in which the company operates. Moreover, targets	All SMEs by their activities must earn the respect, or at least the tolerance, of their stakeholders – customers, creditors, employees, suppliers, and the communities within which they operate. Moreover, companies should recognize the rights of stakeholders as established by law and encourage active co	Companies are to establish mechanisms designed to expeditiously, economically and skilfully settle disputes stemming from company relations with administrators and interest groups or stakeholders. To this end, they are to establish direct negotiation programs, mediation mechanisms and specialized arbitration procedures tailored to their	No such provision.	The enterprise must provide information on stakeholders that is likely to affect its performance like the relationship between the management of the enterprise and employees and, in particular, the human resource policy and any other significant relationship with other stakeholders (employees, customers, creditors, Administration, etc.). Where appropriate, the	A Stakeholder Relations Committee may be formed whose mission shall be to develop and monitor the Company's relationship to various stakeholders, including employees, customers, clients, suppliers, business partners and any other interested parties impacted by

relating to the management of stakeholder relations should be set and progress against the targets be monitored and measured.	operation between corporations and stakeholders in creating wealth, jobs, and the sustainability of financially sound enterprises.	specific needs and characteristics.		firm will report the scores of social, societal, and environmental rating agencies, and any changes which may have occurred during the financial year. The enterprise must respect the rights of stakeholders and take every possible step to treat them equitably and establish mutually profitable relationships with them. Companies should adopt principles of corporate responsibility.	the Company's activities or products. The Committee is charged with ensuring that the interests of stakeholders are considered by the Board when it makes decisions that impact various stakeholders. The Committee must produce a detailed annual report, which shall be submitted to the Board for its review and for inclusion in the Company's annual report.

CONCLUSION

The code for good governance for Small and Medium Enterprises (SMEs) are neither readily available around the globe (like major listed organizations), nor of proper interest has been shown by both government and the private sectors in general, to devise pertinent and effective guidelines for good practices, addressing the specialized characteristics and contexts of SMEs. However, a few noteworthy endeavours have been undertaken by various emerging nations (like the UAE, Hong Kong, Colombia, Morocco, Lebanon etc.) to devise a specialized code for good governance for SMEs. It is observed that there exist underlying commonalities within these codes of good governance for SMEs, with respect to various issues. Based on a few significant parameters of good governance, like protection of owners/partners/shareholders rights, succession policy, composition of the board of directors, promoting independence of the board, separation of the Chairman and Managing Director's role, audit committee composition and role, internal control framework and risk management process, as well as maintenance of stakeholders relationship, it appears that all the six codes have addressed these pertinent issues in an assertive way in a majority. However, issues like separation of the role of the Chairman and CEO, formation of relevant board committees, like remuneration committee, investor grievance committee, nomination committee, risk management committee etc., holding separate meetings of independent directors, in the absence of executive directors, and existence of an effective whistle blowing mechanism, are still to be addressed in these codes of good governance for SMEs. However, SMEs should consider the issue of operational costs for implementing various internationally recognised best practices for ensuring good governance for all the stakeholders. The techniques of cost-benefit analysis, and feasibility study may be very useful, along with adherence to various regulatory provisions, before implementing measures of good governance in SMEs.

REFERENCES

Abor, J. and Biekpe N. (2007). Corporate governance, ownership structure and performance of SMEs in Ghana: Implications for financing opportunities," *Corporate Governance,* 7(3),288 - 300.

Aguilera, R.V. and Cuervo-Cazurra, A. (2004). Codes of good governance worldwide: what's the trigger?. *Organization Studies*, 25: 417-446.

Borch, O. J. and Huse, M. (1993). Informal strategic networks and boards of directors, *Entrepreneurship: Theory and Practice*, 18(1): 23-36.

Gao, L. and Zhang, J. (2009). Corporate governance, earnings management, and firm growth ,*Economic Theory and Business Management*, 12, 53-59.

Gabrielsson, J. And Huse, M. (2005). Outside directors in SME boards: a call for theoretical reflections, *Corporate Board: role, duties composition,* 1(1), 28-37.

Gill, A. (2011). The impact of board size and CEO duality on the potential growth of

Canadian manufacturing firms, *International Accounting Conference (IAC)* held on 24 – 25 November 2011 in Universitas Negeri Surabaya, Indonesia.

Gill, A.S., Mand, H.S. and Mathur, N. (2012). Corporate governance and the growth of small business service firms in India, *International Research Journal of Finance and Economics,* 96 (2012), [http://www.internationalresearchjournaloffinanceandeconomics.com], (last accessed on 13th September, 2012).

Hamad, S.B. and Karoui, A. (2011). The SMEs governance mechanisms practices and financial performance: case of Tunisian industrial SMEs, *International Journal of Business and Management,* 6(7), 216-225

Jordan, J., Lowe, J. and Taylor, P. (1998), Strategy and financial policy in UK small firms, *Journal of Business Finance and Accounting*, 25(1), 1-27.

Liang, T.W. and Meng, T.T. (2010). Applying corporate governance codes to entrepreneurial firms, *Singapore Accountant*, February, 28-31.

Lo´pez, G.J. and Aybar, A.C. (2000). An empirical approach to the financial behaviour of small and medium sized companies, *Small Business Economics*, 14, 55-63.

McGahan, A. M. and Porter, M.E. (1997). How much does industry matter really? *Strategic Management Journal*, 18 (Summer Special Issue), 15-30.

McGuire, J. (2000). Corporate governance and growth potential: an empirical analysis, *Corporate Governance: An International Review*, 8, 32–42.

McKinsey & Company (2000), *Investor Opinion Survey on Corporate Governance*, [http://www.oecd.org/dataoecd/56/7/1922101.pdf] (last accessed on 15th September,2012)

Michaelas, N., Chittenden, F. and Poutziouris, P. (1999). Financial policy and capital structure choice in UK SMEs: empirical evidence from company panel data, *Small Business Economics,*12, 113-130.

Mira, F.S. (2002). On capital structure in the small and medium enterprises: the Spanish case, working paper series, Instituto de Estudios Europeos – Universidad San Pablo CEU, Madrid.

Mohammed Bin Rashid Establishment for SME Development (Dubai SME), (2011). *The Corporate Governance Code for Small and Medium Enterprises (SMEs): Building the foundations for growth and sustainability,* (English Version), UAE.

National Commission on Corporate Governance. (2008). *Moroccan Code of Good Corporate Governance Practices for SMEs,* Ministere Des Affaires Economiques et Generales, Morocco.

Network Colombia Compite. (2000). *Framework Code of Good Corporate Governance for Small and Medium-size Enterprises,* (English Version), Ministry of Commerce, Industry and Tourism, Colombia.

Pettigrew, A. and McNulty, T. (1991). Power and influence in and around the boardroom, *Human Relations*, 48(8), 845-873.

Sampson-Akpuru, M. (2009). Is CEO/chair duality associated with greater likelihood of an international acquisition?, *Michigan Journal of Business,* 2(1), pp. 81-97.

Securities Exchange Board of India (SEBI). (2010). *Clause 52 of Model Equity Listing Agreement.* India.

Shenglan, C. (2010). Board governance and corporate growth: an empirical research of SMEs, *International Conference on the Development of Small and Medium-sized Enterprises, Enterprise Grows in Sustaining Efficiency and Effectiveness*, ISBN: 978-0-9807687-4-9, 280-285.

Storey, D.J. (1985). Small Firms in Regional Economic Development, Cambridge University Press, Cambridge.

The Hong Kong Institute of Directors Limited. (2009). *Guidelines on Corporate Governance for SMEs in Hong Kong (2nd Edition),* ISBN: 978-988-97441-8-2.

The Lebanese Transparency Association. (2006). *The Lebanese Code of Corporate Governance,* ISBN: 9953-470-73-1.

Van der Wijst, D. (1989), Financial Structure in Small Business: Theory, Tests and Applications, Lecture Notes in Economics and Mathematical Systems series, No. 320, Springer-Verlag, Berlin.

Weston, J.F. and Copeland, T.E. (1998). Managerial Finance, CBS College Publishing, New York, NY.

Yang, Y. and Yu, W.Y. (2011). Effect of board governance on corporate growth-based on empirical data of Chinese A-share top 500 listed companies, *Journal of Xidian University(Social Science Edition)*, 2011(3). Retrieved July 1, 2012 from http://en.cnki.com.cn/Article_en/CJFDTOTAL-XADZ201103003.htm, last accessed on 13th September, 2012.

Zattoni, A. and Cuomo, F. (2008). Why adopt codes of good governance? a comparison of institutional and efficiency perspectives, *Corporate Governance: An International Review,* 16: 1-15

Zuo Zhi-gang. (2010). SMEs governance and financial performance: Chinese evidence, *International Conference on Engineering and Business Management (EBM 2010)*, ISBN:978-1-935068-05-1, 758-761.

Author Index